RMAN

REET
RFACE
ILWAY
NCHISES
OF
YORK
ITY

HE
491
V55
287s

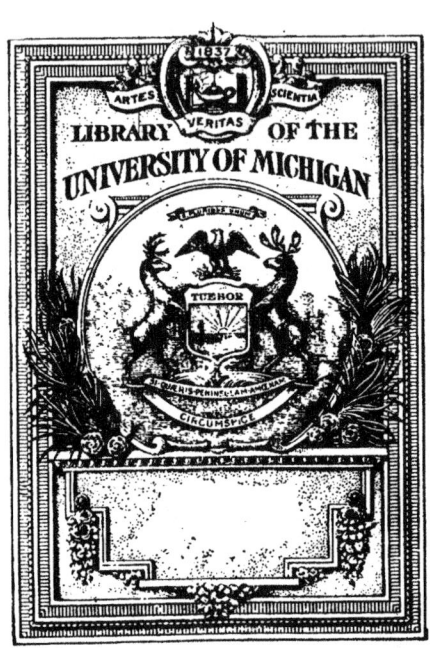

HE
4491
.N55
C287a

THE STREET SURFACE RAILWAY FRANCHISES OF NEW YORK CITY

BY

HARRY JAMES CARMAN, A. M.
Instructor in History, Columbia University

SUBMITTED IN PARTIAL FULFILMENT OF THE REQUIREMENTS
FOR THE DEGREE OF DOCTOR OF PHILOSOPHY
IN THE
FACULTY OF POLITICAL SCIENCE
COLUMBIA UNIVERSITY

NEW YORK
1919

THE STREET SURFACE RAILWAY FRANCHISES OF NEW YORK CITY

BY

HARRY JAMES CARMAN, A. M.
Instructor in History, Columbia University

SUBMITTED IN PARTIAL FULFILMENT OF THE REQUIREMENTS
FOR THE DEGREE OF DOCTOR OF PHILOSOPHY
IN THE
FACULTY OF POLITICAL SCIENCE
COLUMBIA UNIVERSITY

NEW YORK
1919

CONTENTS

CHAPTER I
THE FIRST STREET RAILWAY FRANCHISES

	PAGE
FOREWORD	9
Introduction	11
1. The New York and Harlem Railroad Grants	17
2. The Grants to the Hudson River Railroad Company	33

CHAPTER II
HISTORY OF RAILWAYS INCORPORATED BETWEEN 1850 AND 1860

1. The Sixth and Eighth Avenue Railroad Companies	39
2. The Second Avenue Railroad Company	54
3. The Third Avenue Railway Company	59
4. The Ninth Avenue Railroad Company	72

CHAPTER III
THE FIGHT FOR BROADWAY, 1852 to 1884 78

CHAPTER IV
HISTORY OF RAILWAYS INCORPORATED BETWEEN 1860 AND 1875

1. The Central Park, North and East River Railroad Company	108
2. The Forty-second Street and Grand Street Ferry Railroad Company	112
3. The Dry Dock, East Broadway and Battery Railroad Company	114
4. The Broadway and Seventh Avenue Railroad Company	119
5. The Bleecker Street and Fulton Ferry Railroad Company	121
6. The Twenty-third Street Railway Company	130
7. The Avenue C Railroad Company	132
8. The Houston, West Street and Pavonia Ferry Railroad Company	133
9. The One Hundred and Twenty-fifth Street Railroad Company	135
10. The Central Crosstown Railroad Company of New York	137
11. The Christopher and Tenth Street Railroad Company	139
12. The South Ferry Railway Company	141

CHAPTER V

HISTORY OF RAILWAYS INCORPORATED BETWEEN 1875 AND 1884

1. The Forty-second Street, Manhattanville and St. Nicholas Avenue Railway Company 148

CHAPTER VI

THE GENERAL LAW OF 1884 AND THE BROADWAY GRANT 154

CHAPTER VII

HISTORY OF RAILWAYS INCORPORATED BETWEEN 1884 AND 1897

1. The Chambers Street and Grand Street Ferry Railroad Company 173
2. The Thirty-fourth Street Railroad Company 176
3. The Thirty-fourth Street Ferry and Eleventh Avenue Railroad Company 177
4. The Cable Plan 179
5. The Cantor Act 183
6. The Twenty-eighth and Twenty-ninth Street Railroad Company 185
7. The North and East River Railroad Company and the Fulton Street Railroad Company 189
8. The Metropolitan Crosstown Railway Company 195
9. Lexington Avenue and Pavonia Ferry Railroad Company .. 198
10. Columbus and Ninth Avenue Railroad Company. 201

CHAPTER VIII

THE ERA OF CONSOLIDATION. 204

CHAPTER IX

FRANCHISE GRANTS UNDER THE CHARTER OF GREATER NEW YORK. 221

CHAPTER X

GENERAL CONCLUSIONS. 235

BIBLIOGRAPHY 249

FOREWORD

IN recent years there has been considerable agitation for municipal ownership of the street surface railways of New York city. In this monograph an attempt has been made to trace the franchise history of the street surface railways of Manhattan Island and to point out in connection therewith some of the difficulties which will be met in any program for municipalization. According to statistics published in 1913 by the Public Service Commission of the First District of the State of New York, seven hundred and twenty-six railway companies have been organized to operate routes — steam, surface, elevated, and subway — within the present limits of Greater New York. Over four hundred and fifty of these are now extinct, about two hundred of the remainder have lost their identity by merger, mortgage foreclosure, or change of name, and of the others, many are operating under lease or agreement. The following investigation is limited to the surface railways of Manhattan and to those companies whose lines were consolidated in forming the present street railway systems. No attempt has been made in this thesis to give a detailed account of the financial history of the street surface railways, although it has been found necessary to make frequent reference to this exceedingly interesting phase of the life of the street railway corporations.

The author desires to express his sincere gratitude to Professor Howard Lee McBain, under whose direction the work has been done and who, aside from reading the manuscript and suggesting valuable revisions, has performed the trying task of reading proof. The author is also deeply indebted to Professor Dixon Ryan Fox, who read the manuscript and gave much helpful criticism. Among others who rendered valuable assistance in this study the author desires to make special mention of Dr. Charles A. Beard, of the Bureau of Municipal Research, who suggested the topic, Professor Thomas Reed Powell, Dr. Delos F. Wilcox, former Chief of the Bureau of Franchises of the Public Service Commission for the First District of New York, Mr. R. R. Monroe, Franchise Assistant to the Public Service Commission for the First District of New York, and, lastly, my wife for her faithful assistance and constant encouragement.

HARRY JAMES CARMAN.

COLUMBIA UNIVERSITY, MARCH, 1919.

CHAPTER I

THE FIRST STREET RAILWAY FRANCHISES

FEW commercial capitals have grown with such marvelous rapidity as New York city, yet the American Metropolis in 1830 extended but little above Fourteenth street.[1] It is true that Manhattan Island, as early as 1811, had been surveyed and mapped out into streets, squares and lots as far north as One Hundred and Fifth-fifth street;[2] the commissioners appointed by Mayor Dewitt Clinton to make the survey seem to have anticipated this rapid growth, although at that time their optimism was ridiculed by an incredulous public.[3]

By 1830 some thirty thousand houses, clustered together in the southern end of the island, sheltered the greater portion of a total population of two hundred and two thousand, five hundred and eighty-nine.[4] At that time the select

[1] Burr, David H., *Map of the City and County of New York with Adjacent Country in 1832*; King, Moses, *Handbook of New York City* (Boston, 1832), p. 39; Watson, John F., *Annals and Occurrences of New York City and State in the Olden Time* (Philadelphia, 1846), p. 143; Janvier, Thomas A., *In Old New York* (N. Y., 1894), p. 58.

[2] Jenkins, Stephen, *The Greatest Street in the World, The Story of Old Broadway* (N. Y., 1911), p. 175; Richmond, J. F., *New York and Its Institutions, 1609-1871* (N. Y., 1871), p. 106; see also Burr's *Map of the City, 1832, op. cit.*; Janvier, Thomas A., *op. cit.*, pp. 56-62.

[3] Jenkins, Stephen, *op. cit.*, p. 175; *Laws of the State of New York, 1807*, ch. 95; Ruggles, Edward, *A Picture of New York in 1846* (N. Y., 1846), p. 18. The Commissioners were Simeon Dewitt, Gouverneur Morris and John Rutherford, with John Randall, Jr., as Surveyor. The work was finished and the plan submitted in 1821. Jenkins, Stephen, *op. cit.*; Ruggles, Edward, *op. cit.*; Janvier, Thomas A., *op. cit.*

[4] Lamb, Martha J., *History of the City of New York: Its Origin, Rise and Progress* (N. Y., 1877-1896), vol. ii, p. 721; Leonard, John W.,

PLATE I

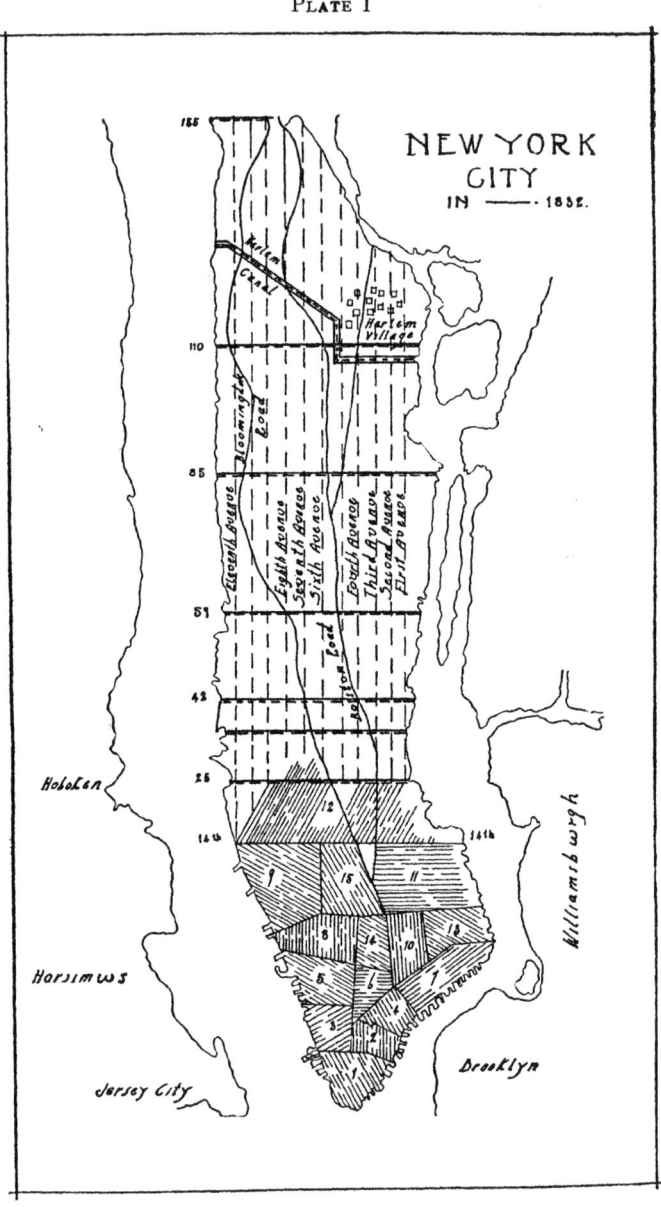

residential section of the city surrounded the academic block on which Kings College was first built—Barclay and Murray streets, Church street and College Place. Warren street was the upper limit of ultra-fashionable society, although a number of palatial residences were to be found as far north as Chambers street.[1] Lots above Fourteenth street sold for twenty-five dollars each; even upper Bleecker street still had its pastures where the small boys picked berries which they exchanged for taffy and cakes at Peter Cooper's grocery which stood in the triangle at the junction of Third and Fourth avenues.[2] In 1833 Washington Square, which prior to 1827 had been the " Potters Field," was considered " quite a long distance from the city." [3] The present site of Gramercy Park was a swamp in 1830,[4] and it was not until 1847 that the dreary underbrush region at the fork of the Boston and Bloomingdale roads was cleared and beautified to become the well-known Madison Square. As late as 1852 a little story-and-a-half

History of the City of New York, 1609-1909 (N. Y., 1909), p. 337; Richmond, J. F., *New York and Its Institutions, 1609-1871*, p. 103; Watson, John F., *Annals and Occurrences of New York City and State in the Olden Time*, p. 143; Williams, Edwin, *New York as It Is in 1833* (N. Y., 1833), p. 12. New York City in 1832 had fifteen wards, only one of which was above Fourteenth Street (see accompanying map). The assessed valuation of all property, real and personal, was $115,000,000. Watson, John F., *op. cit.*, p. 143; Holley, O. L., *A Description of New York in 1847* (N. Y., 1847), p. 12.

[1] Wilson, J. G., *Memorial History of the City of New York* (N. Y., 1893), vol. iii, p. 359. Two houses built of marble on Chambers street about this period were " considered foolish extravagances because too high uptown." Wilson, J. G., *op. cit.*, p. 359.

[2] King, Charles, *Progress of the City of New York During the Last Fifty Years* (N. Y., 1852), p. 59; King, Moses, *Handbook of New York City*, p. 40; Wilson, Rufus R., *New York Old and New, Its Story, Streets and Landmarks* (Philadelphia, 1909), vol. ii, p. 172.

[3] *Ibid.*; Comstock, Sarah, *Old Roads from the Heart of New York* (N. Y., 1915), p. 365; Janvier, Thomas A., *In Old New York*, pp. 69, 120.

[4] King, Charles, *op. cit.*, p. 62; Wilson, Rufus R., *op. cit.*, p. 257.

cottage stood on the plot where later the magnificent Fifth Avenue Hotel was built.[1] The famous Greenwich village was a suburb of the city proper, while in the vicinity of West Twenty-third street the roofs of Chelsea village could be seen over the tree-tops. The present Broadway was a winding country highway, along either side of which alternated rugged, craggy pastures and level meadow lands. In 1845 Bloomingdale, a village of four hundred people, was perched on the present Morningside Heights; one mile further north was Manhattanville, a flourishing town of five hundred people.[2] If one journeyed up the old Boston Post Road [3] he would pass through Yorkville, a suburban village connected with the city by a stage line.[4] Several miles farther to the north the road gradually turned to the east through Harlem, a thriving town near the Harlem river.[5] Here and there along this stretch of country road between the city and the northern village were the famous road-houses, renowned for their hospitality in the thirties and forties.[6]

[1] King, Moses, *op. cit.*, p. 40; Wilson, Rufus R., *op. cit.*, pp. 241-243. This hotel was recently torn down to make way for a modern office building.

[2] Ruggles, Edward, *A Picture of New York in 1846*, pp. 19-22; King Moses, *A Handbook of New York City*, p. 40; Wilson, J. G., *Memorial History of the City of New York*, vol. iii, p. 375; Hemstreet, Charles, *When Old New York Was Young* (N. Y., 1902), pp. 161-162, 333-345; Wilson, Rufus R., *New York: Old and New, Its Story, Streets and Landmarks*, vol. ii, pp. 199-245; Janvier, Thomas A., *In Old New York*, see ch. ii entitled "Greenwich Village."

[3] This road started at the foot of Broadway, opposite Bowling Green, and at Madison Square it divided, one part going to Bloomingdale; Wilson, Rufus R., *op. cit.*, p. 250; Comstock, Sarah, *Old Roads From the Heart of New York*, p. 305.

[4] Wilson, J. G., *op. cit.*, p. 375; Bayles, W. H., *Old Taverns of New York* (N. Y., 1915), p. 462. Stages were first introduced in 1830, the first line running between Bowling Green and Bleecker street.

[5] Ruggles, Edward, *op. cit.*, pp. 22-23; Wilson, J. G., *op. cit.*, p. 375.

[6] Bayles, W. H., *op. cit.*, pp. 462-463. Among them were Cato Alexan-

But New York city was bound to grow. By nature the city was peculiarly well fitted to play an important rôle in the economic development of America. With its sheltered deep-water harbor it could boast of the finest port on the Atlantic coast. Moreover the city commanded the entrance to the gateway of the West — the Hudson and Mohawk valleys. In addition to its superb location, three important factors contributed largely to the growth of the city. These were (1) the growth of commerce; (2) the growth of immigration; and (3) the development of manufactures, which had a decided influence by the middle of the nineteenth century.

Commercially New York city has had a phenomenal growth.[1] The invention and perfection of the steam-boat

der's at about Fifty-fifth street, at that time four miles north of the city; the Hazzard House at Eighty-fourth street; and Bradshaw's at the corner of Third avenue and One Hundred Twenty-fifth street.

[1] GROWTH OF COMMERCE OF THE UNITED STATES AND AT THE PORT OF NEW YORK. TOTAL EXPORTS AND IMPORTS FOR SPECIFIED YEARS

Year.	Total Exports and Imports for United States.	Total Exports and Imports at the Port of New York.	Per cent. of Total for United States Entered at Port of New York.
1790	$43,205,156	$2,505,465	5.7 per cent.
1800	163,224,548	14,045,079	8.6 "
1810	152,157,970	17,242,330	11.3 "
1820	144,141,669	13,163,244	9.1 "
1830	144,726,428	55,322,053	36.8 "
1840	239,227,465	94,704,830	39.5 "
1850	230,037,038	163,836,313	71.2 "
1860	687,192,176	311,358,064	45.3 "
1870	828,730,176	477,663,559	57.6 "
1880	1,503,593,404	852,497,243	56.6 "
1890	1,647,139,093	865,478,484	52.7 "
1900	2,244,424,266	1,056,071,753	47.0 "
1910	3,427,415,895	1,624,493,354	47.4 "

The foregoing table was compiled by Pratt, E. E., *Industrial Causes of Congestion of Population in New York City* (N. Y., 1911), p. 37, Table 10.

marked a new era of transportation in the world's history, and particularly did it influence the growth of New York city, which was to develop her trade and manufactures largely with the aid of steam transportation. Another important agency which facilitated commerce and communication was the opening of the great artificial waterway through central New York. By 1825 the Erie Canal had been completed, and it gave extraordinary impetus to the development of New York city in furnishing a direct water communication between the seaboard and the Great Lakes region. There is little doubt that this canal entirely changed the direction of the internal commerce and made the city of New York the greatest commercial center of the Western Hemisphere.[1]

New York city early became the western terminus of ocean travel between Europe and America; hither every year came the immigrant until by 1830 immigration had so increased as to dwarf all migratory movements of modern history.[2] Great streams of foreigners poured into New

[1] Pratt, E. E., *Industrial Causes of Congestion of Population in New York City*, p. 38; Leonard, John W., *History of the City of New York, 1609-1909*, p. 329; Lamb, Martha J., *History of the City of New York: Its Origin, Rise and Progress*, pp. 665-666; Roosevelt, Theodore, *New York* (N. Y., 1895), p. 177; Wilson, J. G., *Memorial History of the City of New York*, p. 346; Wilson, Rufus R., *New York: Old and New, Its Story, Streets and Landmarks*, vol. i, p. 325.

[2] Wilson, Rufus R., *op. cit.*, p. 325; Byrne, Stephen, *Irish Immigration* (N. Y., 1873), p. 18; Lamb, Martha J., *op. cit.*, p. 741; Roosevelt, Theodore, *op. cit.*, p. 183; Holley, O. L., *A Description of New York in 1847*, p. 12; Leonard, John W., *op. cit.*, p. 346. The population and wealth of New York reflect its growth:

Year	Population	Wealth
1825	166,086	$101,160,046
1830	202,589	125,288,518
1835	270,089	218,723,703
1840	312,785	252,843,163

See Holley, O. L., *op. cit.*; Butler, W. A., *New York City, Its Growth, Misgovernment and Needs* (pamphlet), pp. 22-23; Richmond, J. F., *New York and Its Institutions, 1609-1871*, p. 103.

York city, and owing to the lack of any effective system for distributing these newcomers to inland centers, where their services were needed and where they would have had greater opportunity for development, they settled on lower Manhattan, thus swelling the city's population.[1] Expansion was inevitable, and it was accelerated locally by the introduction of a new means of transportation — the street railway.[2]

1. THE NEW YORK AND HARLEM RAILROAD GRANTS

The first street-railway franchise in New York city, and, incidentally, the earliest street-railway franchise in the United States,[3] was obtained by the New York and Harlem Railroad Company. This company, chartered by a special act[4] of the New York legislature, passed April 25, 1831, was permitted to lay a single or double track railroad " from any point on the north bounds of Twenty-third street to any point on the Harlem river between the east bounds of the Third avenue and the west bounds of the Eighth avenue," for the transportation of persons and property " by the power and force of steam, of animals, or of any mechanical or other power, or of any combination of them which the said company may choose to employ." [5] The franchise was to continue for thirty years, with the further provision that, unless the road was commenced within two years and completed within four years, the cor-

[1] Pratt, E. E., *Industrial Causes of Congestion of Population in New York City*, pp. 38-39.

[2] For the effect of street railways on the distribution of population see Wilcox, Delos F., *Municipal Franchises* (N. Y., 1911), vol. ii, p. 6 *et seq.*

[3] Wilcox, Delos F., *Municipal Franchises*, vol. ii, p. 101; Leonard, John W., *History of the City of New York, 1609-1909* (N. Y., 1909), p. 337.

[4] New York State had no general railroad law at this time.

[5] *Laws of the State of New York, 1831*, ch. 263.

poration " shall thenceforth forever cease, and this act shall be null and void."[1] The act prohibited the company from taking any lands " without the consent of the owner or owners thereof, exceeding forty feet in width from east to west, and . . . in case of their locating the route of the said railroad in or along any public street or avenue now laid out on the map or plan of the city of New York, [they were to] leave sufficient space in the said street or avenue on each side of the said railroad for a public highway for carriages and for a sidewalk for foot-passengers."[2]

By section sixteen of the same act, the right of the company to construct any part of its line on thoroughfares within the limits of the city were made subject to the consent of the city authorities.

Nothing in this act shall be deemed to authorize the said corporation to construct or use their single or double railroad or way across or along any of the streets or avenues as designated on the map of the City of New York, whether such streets or avenues shall have been opened or not, without the consent of the Mayor, Aldermen, and Commonalty of said city, who are hereby authorized to grant permission to the said corporation to construct their said railroad or way across or along said streets or avenues, or prohibit them from constructing the same; and, after the same shall be constructed, to regulate the time and manner of using the same, or any part thereof; and nothing in this act contained shall prevent the Legislature from granting to any other corporation or persons the right of constructing a railroad or roads parallel with the one herein mentioned, or any part of it, on any lands, street, road or avenue, not occupied by the railroad or way hereby authorized, or the right of crossing or intersecting the same at any point or points, without making compensation for injuries sustained thereby.[3]

[1] *Laws of the State of New York, 1831*; ch. 263.
[2] *Ibid.* [3] *Ibid.*

The act specifically prohibited any person who was at the time a member of either branch of the common council from acting as a commissioner or director of the company.

PLATE II

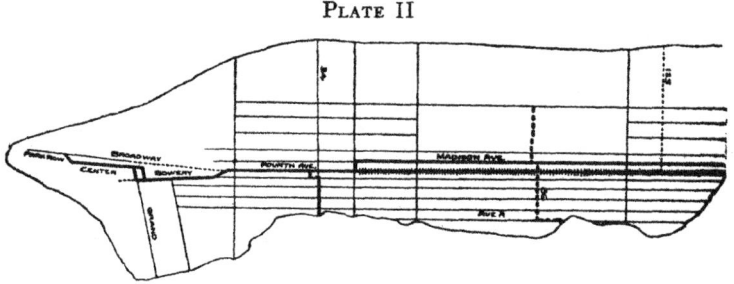

NEW YORK AND HARLEM RAILROAD COMPANY

- - - - - trackage rights obtained on tracks of other companies
. . . . . franchise routes neither constructed nor operated by this company

By an amendatory act passed April 6, 1832, the company was authorized, with the consent of the city authorities, to extend its line along Fourth avenue to Fourteenth street and through such other streets of the city as the local authorities " may from time to time permit, subject to such prudential rules as are prescribed by this act " and by the common council.[1] This act also provided that no carriage or vehicle should be drawn or propelled " by any other than horse-power through any street of said city south of Fourteenth street "; moreover, " every carriage or vehicle drawn or propelled on the said railroad shall be provided with suitable safeguards projecting in a descending direction to near the surface of the rails in front of each forward wheel, in such manner as to insure the greatest safety against accidents." A speed limit of five miles an hour was provided for all cars operating south of Fourteenth street.[2]

[1] *Laws of the State of New York, 1832*; ch. 93.
[2] *Ibid.*

Prior to the passage of the amendatory act of 1832, the New York and Harlem Company had selected a route and had been duly authorized by the city authorities, by an ordinance approved December 22, 1831, and accepted January 9, 1832, to lay a single or double railroad on Fourth avenue from Twenty-third street to the Harlem river. Permission was also given to build a branch through One Hundred and Twenty-fifth street from Fourth avenue to the Hudson river.[1] Among other things, the ordinance under section three expressly reserved to the city the right to regulate the motive power and the speed of the cars. The grant, although made for a thirty-year period, was rendered terminable under certain conditions, for section two provided that if at any time it should appear to the mayor, aldermen and commonalty that the railway, or any part of it, constituted an obstruction or impediment to the future regulation of the city, or the ordinary use of any street or avenue, the company should, upon receiving notification from the city authorities, take proper means to remedy the abuse to the satisfaction of the officials and the people of the city. If the company failed to find such remedy, they were then required, within one month from the date of the aforesaid notification, to remove the railway and replace the street in proper condition. Should the company decline or neglect to obey the city's demand, the authorities were empowered to remove the railway or obstruction and, at the expense of the railroad company, to repair the streets or avenues. The franchise also provided that the company should make its " railroad path, from time to time, conform to what may hereafter be the regulation of the avenue and road through which such railroad passes." If the com-

[1] Valentine, David T., *A Compilation of Existing Ferry Leases and Railroad Grants made by the City of New York and the Legislature of the State for the Use of the Streets of New York City* (N. Y., 1866), p. 197.

pany failed to complete the line within the time limit set by its charter, or if the railroad should be discontinued at any future time, or not be kept in repair, "then the strip of land to be taken for the said railroad should be thrown open and become a part of the street or public avenue, without any assessment on the owners of the adjoining land or the public therefor." Certain general welfare clauses were included: one required the company to construct stone arches and bridges for all embankments or excavations on cross streets intersected by the company's road, which in the opinion of the common council needed to be arched or bridged for public convenience. Another provided that "a railing or other erection shall be made on the outer edges of the embankments or railroad path, and also such railing or fences on the edges of the excavations as the common council shall, from time to time, deem necessary to prevent accidents and loss of lives to our fellow-citizens."

By a resolution of the common council, signed by Mayor Bowne on January 30, 1832, the company was authorized " to take possession of the ground owned by the common council over which the line of railroad is ordered to be constructed." This land was to revert to the city when it ceased to be used for railroad purposes.[1]

Through a subsequent legislative amendment the mayor, aldermen and commonalty were empowered to permit the extension of the New York and Harlem railroad along Fourth avenue to Fourteenth street and through such other streets as the city officials and commonalty might from time to time authorize.[2]

The company desired to extend its lines below Twenty-

---

[1] Valentine, David T., *Ordinances of the Mayor, Aldermen and Commonalty of the City of New York* (N. Y., 1859), p. 623; *Ferry Leases and Railroad Grants* (N. Y., 1866), p. 202.

[2] *Laws of the State of New York, 1832*; ch. 93.

third street, and in May, 1832, the common council gave it permission to extend its tracks south to Prince street, through Union Place, Bloomingdale road and Broadway.[1] In addition to being subject to the conditions and restrictions previously imposed on the company with relation to its line above Twenty-third street, this extension grant provided that the track should be laid in such manner and' in such portions of the streets as should be approved by the street commissioner "so as to cause no impediment to the common and ordinary use of the streets for all other purposes." The railroad was not to obstruct the water-courses of the streets, and the company agreed to pave the roadway in and about the rails for a width of twenty-five feet in a satisfactory and permanent manner, and to keep this part of the streets in good repair. The permit further stipulated that the common council might require the company to remove the whole or any part of this extension and to replace the streets in good condition; also, that the company should have a single track constructed over the authorized route by May 1, 1834, and that it was "to charge and receive such tolls, rates, or fare for the carrying of passengers or effects upon said railroad tracks, south of Twenty-third street, as the common council may prescribe." The company accepted this franchise by an agreement dated May 18, 1832.[2]

Within a year after the signing of the contract the New York and Harlem Company had a portion of its road in operation.[3] The first car, the "John Mason," named in honor of the first president of the company, and built by

[1] Valentine, David T., *Ferry Leases and Railroad Grants*, pp. 203-5.

[2] *Proceedings of the Board of Aldermen*, vol. ii, pp. 419-420.

[3] Lamb, Martha J., *History of the City of New York: Its Origin, Rise and Progress*, vol. ii, p. 721; Haswell, C. H., *Reminiscences of an Octogenarian, 1816-1860* (N. Y., 1896), p. 265; Wilson, J. G., *Memorial History of the City of New York*, vol. iii, p. 375.

John Stephenson,[1] made its initial trip on November 26, 1832, from Prince street to Fourteenth street,[2] carrying Mayor Bowne, members of the common council and invited guests to witness the success of the experiment.[3] Two years later the road was in operation as far north as Murray Hill.[4]

It is interesting to observe that real-estate owners were anxious for the success of this new method of transportation; for instance, Mr. Samuel Ruggles, a prominent New Yorker and the owner of large tracts of real property between Third and Fourth avenues, in the vicinity of Irving Place and Lexington avenue,[5] was untiring in his efforts to obtain public support and approval of the enterprise. Mr. Ruggles's interest, however, was two-fold, for the reason that he, as well as being a large landholder, was also a director and one of the largest stockholders in the New York and Harlem Railroad Company.[6] His efforts were

[1] Stephenson received a patent on this car from President Andrew Jackson and members of his Cabinet; Lamb's *Biographical Dictionary*, vol. vii, p. 196. Stephenson built an extensive car factory in Harlem in 1836. Wilson, J. G., *op. cit.* The first horse-cars were a novelty as well as a convenience; they were like stage coaches hung on leather straps " with several compartments and side doors, the driver sitting above like a coachman and putting on the brakes with his feet;" Haswell, C. H., *op. cit.*; Lamb, Martha J., *op. cit.* Steam was used as a motive power below Fourteenth street for the first time in 1834; Haswell, C. H., *op. cit.*

[2] Wilson, J. G., *op. cit.*; Haswell, C. H., *op. cit.*

[3] *Ibid.*

[4] *Ibid.*; Wilson, Rufus R., *New York: Old and New, Its Story, Streets and Landmarks*, vol. i, p. 326.

[5] He had cut these avenues through his estate at his own expense; see King, Charles, *Progress of the City of New York During the Last Fifty Years*, p. 62.

[6] King, Charles, *Progress of the City of New York During the Last Fifty Years*, p. 62; Williams, Edwin, *New York As It Is in 1833*, p. 116; Appleton's *Cyclopaedia of American Biography*, vol. v, pp. 343-344.

well rewarded, for this new means of travel and communication was enthusiastically welcomed by practically the entire city. Even the mechanics and anti-monopolist parties, both of which vigorously protested against the granting of exclusive monopolies,[1] were in favor of the railroad,[2] which would be a vast improvement over the lumbering stages so slowly making their way over rough streets and roads.

This pioneer franchise, as well as the grants made during the decade preceding the Civil War, clearly recognized the interests of the public; a few of them reserved to the municipality the right to purchase or take over the roads at some future time. In this particular they were far more liberal in their provisions than the grants made during the period from 1860 to 1897, for these later grants usually gave not only the right of way for construction of the road, but were so drafted as to invest the grantees with special privilege which they regarded as a private property right subject to little or no public control. It is important to note here that the earlier franchises were very carefully drawn, explicit and detailed in their covenants, and were reduced to the form of a contract, signed and executed by the city and the grantees; while the later-day franchises were perpetual and were circumscribed by mere trivialities which imposed little restraint upon the grantees and practically freed them from responsibility to the public.

Bit by bit the New York and Harlem Railroad Company was authorized to extend its lines. On May 20, 1832, continuation of the road was permitted to Walker street;[3] in April, 1838, from the Bowery to Broome street, to Center

[1] Fox, D. R., *The Decline of Aristocracy in the Politics of New York* (N. Y., 1919), chs. xii and xiii, Columbia Studies, vol. lxxxvi.

[2] Myers, Gustavus, " History of Public Franchises in New York City," *Municipal Affairs*, vol. iv, 1900, p. 107.

[3] Valentine, David T., *Ferry Leases and Railroad Grants*, p. 206.

street, to Chatham street;[1] on November 13, 1848, the company received permission to construct a line in Canal street connecting with its road in Center street and running to a point seventy-five feet east of Broadway. This branch was to afford increased accommodation for the public in that it would serve as a connecting link with the New York and New Haven road,[2] which had its station and terminal at the corner of Canal street and Broadway.[3] Further extension was granted in 1850 through South street "to the rear of Tompkins' market, between Sixth and Seventh streets, for the conveyance of country produce";[4] and again on February 6, 1851, permission was given for the continuation of the road to the southerly end of what is now Park Row.[5] When this latter license was issued Alderman Oakley made a proposal for a three-cent fare covering the distance from City Hall to Third street, but it failed of adoption.[6]

By a resolution of December 14, 1844, the company was required to discontinue the use of steam-power on Fourth avenue below Thirty-second street on or before August 1, 1845,[7] but it apparently failed to comply with this demand, for a resolution of March 30, 1846, authorized the corporation attorney to "take legal measures to prevent the steam-power of the Harlem Railroad Company from plying below

[1] Valentine, David T., *Ferry Leases and Railroad Grants*, p. 206.
[2] Valentine, David T., *Ordinances of the Mayor, Aldermen and Commonalty of the City of New York*, p. 625.
[3] Frances, C. S., *The Stranger's Handbook for the City of New York* (N. Y., 1857), p. 97. The New York and New Haven road had another station at the corner of Fourth avenue and Twenty-seventh street; *ibid.*
[4] Valentine, David T., *Ferry Leases and Railroad Grants*, p. 212.
[5] *Ibid.*, pp. 215-219.
[6] *Proceedings of the Board of Aldermen*, vol. xli, p. 1389.
[7] Valentine, David T., *Ferry Leases and Railroad Grants*, pp. 208-209.

Thirty-second street on Fourth avenue as directed by the mayor and common council in December, 1844."[1]

A similar resolution adopted December 7, 1854, required the company to discontinue the use of steam-power on Fourth avenue south of Forty-second street within eighteen months,[2] and this action on the part of the city authorities ultimately resulted in the compulsory operation of a street-car line from the Astor House to Forty-second street. That the company strenuously endeavored to retain operation by steam-power is apparent from the resolution of February, 1858, to the effect that inasmuch as the New York and Harlem Railroad Company had

> failed to coerce the Common Council in repealing the existing ordinances of the corporation requiring them to discontinue the use of steam below Forty-second street; and in consequence of such failure, the company having determined to defy the acts of the Common Council, positively refuse to obey the ordinances of this body, and are now, through their paid agents, endeavoring to secure the passage of an act from the legislature of this State to continue their present nuisance, in violation of the existing ordinances and their agreement with the corporation,

the corporation counsel was directed to prepare a remonstrance against the passage of such act by the state legislature.[3]

The public became deeply suspicious of the councilmen when, in December of the same year, 1858, an ordinance, duly approved by the mayor and confirmed by act of the legislature, passed April 16, 1859,[4] authorized the company

---

[1] Valentine, David T., *Ferry Leases and Railroad Grants*, p. 209.
[2] *Ibid.*, p. 223.
[3] *Ibid.*, pp. 223-226.
[4] *Laws of the State of New York, 1859*, ch. 387.

to use steam-power on Fourth avenue below Forty-second street. Furthermore, the company's charters and franchises, having been granted originally for a period of thirty years, and being about to expire, were extended for a like period.[1] These same grants permitted the company to lay a double track on Madison avenue from Forty-second street to Seventy-ninth street for the use of their small cars only; no conditions were imposed and, seemingly, nothing whatever was demanded or required from the company for this extensive and extremely valuable privilege.

The people of New York city had every reason to be distrustful of the authorities, for in the fifties New York city politics sank to a very low ebb.[2] At that time the municipality fell into the grip of Tammany Hall, whose master-spirit was Fernando Wood, an able, resolute, unscrupulous demagogue of doubtful financial honesty who surrounded himself with a group of brutal rowdies and by means of force and fraud became the " boss " of the city. In 1854 he secured the mayoralty, and during the next four years he and his henchmen in the council resorted to all sorts of political debauchery.[3] In the municipal elections of 1857 Wood was defeated largely through the efforts of the reform element within Tammany. This group, of which Samuel J. Tilden was a prominent mem-

[1] *Proceedings of the Board of the Common Council*, vol. lxxii, p. 946; Valentine, David T., *Ferry Leases and Railroad Grants*, p. 227; *Laws of the State of New York, 1859*, ch. 387.

[2] Myers, Gustavus, *The History of Tammany Hall* (N. Y., 1907), pp. 198-231; Wilson, Rufus R., *New York: Old and New; Its Story, Streets and Landmarks*, vol. i, pp. 374-377; Roosevelt, Theodore, *New York*, p. 196; see also article by Richard Spillane in *The Evening Mail* (New York), January 30, 1918.

[3] *Ibid.* When first elected Wood made New York a "model" city for a few months by closing all saloons on Sunday, stamping out immoral resorts, and really cleaning the streets.

ber, with the endorsement of the Republicans and Native Americans, nominated Daniel F. Tiemann, a "Tammany-ite," who had, however, made a good record as an alderman and as governor of the almshouse. In the fall of 1858 an anti-Tammany council was chosen, which soon proved to be, for the most part, a body of "unreformed reformers." Mayor Tiemann, too, in his anxiety to satisfy all parties, satisfied none, and in 1859 he was defeated by Wood. The latter's return to power meant the indefinite postponement of reform, and this at a time when valuable franchise grants were being made.

The grant of 1859 really divided the road into two parts. That portion of the line running north from Forty-second street through Park or Fourth avenue now constitutes the main line of the New York Central and Hudson River Railroad Company and the New York, New Haven and Hartford Railroad Company entering the Grand Central Terminal. That part of the road running south from Forty-second street through Fourth avenue, the Bowery, Center street and other streets to the Post Office, and also that part of the road extending north from Forty-second street through Madison avenue and thence across the Harlem river constitutes the "city line" which was leased to the Metropolitan Street Railway Company in 1896.[1]

The next New York and Harlem extension after 1859 occurred in 1864, when the company was authorized to extend its horse-car line from Thirty-second street and Lexington avenue through Thirty-second street to the East Thirty-fourth street ferry.[2]

During this same year a bill was introduced in the legislature giving the company the right to extend its lines down Fourth avenue and Broadway to Whitehall street.

[1] *Infra*, ch. viii.
[2] *Proceedings of the Board of Aldermen*, vol. xciii, pp. 408-409.

THE FIRST STREET RAILWAY FRANCHISES

Among other things, the measure provided for the purchase by the company of the Broadway bus lines and the substitution therefor of a surface railway.[1] Although the

[1] An editorial in the *New York Herald* tersely describes the transportation difficulties at that time which are comparable to transportation on the present-day New York City Subway: " Modern martyrdom may be succinctly defined as riding in a New York omnibus. The discomforts, inconveniences and annoyances of a trip in one of these vehicles are almost intolerable. From the beginning to the end of the journey a constant quarrel is progressing. The driver quarrels with the passengers, and the passengers quarrel with the driver. There are quarrels about getting out and quarrels about getting in. There are quarrels about change and quarrels about the ticket swindle. The driver swears at the passengers and the passengers harangue the driver through the strap-hole—a position in which even Demosthenes could not be eloquent. Respectable clergymen in white chokers are obliged to listen to loud oaths. Ladies are disgusted, frightened and insulted. Children are alarmed and lift up their voices and weep. Indignant gentlemen rise to remonstrate with the irate Jehu and are suddenly bumped back into their seats, twice as indignant as before, besides being involved in supplementary quarrels with those other passengers upon whose corns they have accidentally trodden. Thus the omnibus rolls along, a perfect Bedlam on wheels.

"It is in vain those who are obliged to ride seek for relief in a city railway car. The cars are quieter than the omnibuses, but much more crowded. People are packed into them like sardines in a box, with perspiration for oil. The seats being more than filled, the passengers are placed in rows, down the middle, where they hang on by the straps, like smoked hams in a corner grocery. To enter or exit is exceedingly difficult. Silks and broadcloth are ruined in the attempt. As in the omnibuses pickpockets take advantage of the confusion to ply their vocation. Handkerchiefs, pocketbooks, watches and breastpins disappear most mysteriously. The foul, close, heated air is poisonous. A healthy person cannot ride a dozen blocks without a headache. For these reasons most ladies and gentlemen prefer to ride in the stages, which cannot be crowded so outrageously, and which are pretty decently ventilated by the cracks in the window frames. The omnibus fare is nearly double the carfare, however, and so the majority of the people are compelled to ride in the cars although they lose in health what they save in money. But it must be evident to everybody that neither the cars nor the stages supply accommodations enough for the public, and that such accommodations as they do supply are not of the

bill was warmly supported by certain business firms, including D. Appleton & Company and Lord & Taylor, the majority of the property-owners were opposed to the plan and the measure failed to pass.[1]

In 1872 the company was empowered to project its line from Seventy-ninth to Eighty-sixth street, through Eighty-sixth street to the Astoria ferry at Ninety-second street. It was also authorized to lay its tracks on Madison avenue as fast as that avenue should from time to time be opened. The company was not allowed to charge more than six cents for any distance below Forty-second street. The city was to receive such compensation for these rights and privileges as a commission of three, appointed by the State Supreme Court, should determine.[2]

In the meantime, 1866, the common council passed an ordinance granting to the New York and Harlem Railroad Company the right to construct a double-track line through One Hundred and Twenty-fifth street, St. Nicholas avenue, and Manhattan street, crossing what were then known as "all the grand Boulevards."[3] The company proposed to haul freight trains over these lines by means of steam locomotives. The resolution was vetoed by Mayor Hoffman,[4] but the aldermen intimated that they intended to pass the measure over the mayor's head.[5] As soon as this fact became known two hundred and twenty-six residents and

right sort. Both the cars and omnibuses might be very comfortable and convenient if they were better managed, but something more is needed to supply the popular and increasing demands for city conveyances." *New York Herald*, October 8, 1864.

[1] *New York State Senate Journal, 1864,* 87th session, p. 543.
[2] *Laws of the State of New York, 1872,* ch. 825.
[3] *Proceedings of the Board of Councilmen,* vol. cii, p. 632.
[4] *New York Times,* January 28, 1866.
[5] *Proceedings of the Board of Councilmen,* vol. cii, p. 718.

property-owners of the affected neighborhoods filed with the councilmen, June 24, 1866, a petition remonstrating and vigorously protesting against the plan. The petitioners pointed out that the contemplated railroad would be a dangerous obstruction to carriage traffic, a source of great offensiveness because of the transportation of cattle and swine across the island, an æsthetic eyesore, and, most important of all, it would greatly decrease the value of property and render that section unfit for residential purposes. In conclusion, they humbly prayed the councilmen to reconsider their action that " the public may be released from the apprehension of so great an evil." [1] On the evening of June 27, 1866, a meeting was held at the Adriatic Hotel, Eighth avenue and One Hundred and Twenty-fifth street, " to protest against the infamous scheme." [2] At this time One Hundred and Twenty-fifth street was considered the " grand " avenue north of Central Park. The city had laid out this thoroughfare at great expense and the residents of Harlem viewed it with a mingled feeling of jealousy and true civic pride. In the face of such unanimous opposition the councilmen did not repass the resolution.[3]

On December 28, 1874, the company filed a petition asking for an extension of its corporate life; the petition received favorable consideration and the charter was extended for a period of five hundred years, dating from April 16, 1889. No further franchise grants or alterations were made until May 11, 1893, when the company contracted with the city to complete the construction of their partly built road on Eighty-sixth street from Madison avenue, and on Eighty-fifth street to the transverse road in

[1] *Proceedings of the Board of Councilmen*, vol. ciii, pp. 22-23.
[2] *Ibid.*
[3] *Ibid.*, vol. civ, p. 326.

Central Park.[1] The city reserved the right to allow other railroad companies to operate over the completed road on equal terms with the New York and Harlem Company. The tracks, moreover, were henceforth to be the property of the city.

The city lines of the company were leased to the Metropolitan Street Railway Company on June 11, 1896, for a period of nine hundred and ninety-nine years,[2] and they are still operated under this lease which is now held by the New York Railways Company.[3] From a report submitted by the latter company to the Public Service Commission in March, 1908,[4] it would seem that all the street railway franchises of the New York and Harlem Company's surface lines within the city are now owned in perpetuity by that company, with the exception of the following: On the Bowery, from Grand street to Canal street; on Canal street, from Center street to Broadway; on Broadway, from Walker street to Fourteenth street; on Thirty-second street, from Park avenue to Lexington avenue; on One Hundred and Twenty-fifth street, from Park avenue to the Harlem river; and on Ninety-second street, from Avenue A to the Ferry.

The city has derived small financial benefit from the franchise grants to the New York and Harlem road. The five per cent on its gross receipts, which the Fourth avenue line now pays to the city, applies merely to the franchise extensions of 1872. The city has never exacted compensation for the franchise below Seventy-ninth street, and consequently has received nothing for this privilege.

[1] *Laws of the State of New York, 1888*; ch. 407; *ibid., 1892*, ch. 532; *Proceedings of the Board of Aldermen*, vol. 209, p. 312.

[2] *Infra*, ch. viii.

[3] *Annual Report of the New York Railways Company for the year ending June 30, 1918*, p. 1.

[4] See *Report of Public Commission, 1st District*.

2. THE GRANTS TO THE HUDSON RIVER RAILROAD COMPANY

Although the Hudson River Railroad Company cannot be considered as an integral part of the street railway system of New York city, nevertheless its franchise grants are worthy of consideration, not alone for the provisions therein contained, but for the manner in which they have been interpreted. For this reason, therefore, the grants to this road are here briefly considered.

The company was chartered by a legislative act passed May 12, 1846,[1] which provided, first, for the organization of a corporation known as the Hudson River Railroad Company; secondly, the company was authorized to construct a single, double or treble railroad between New York city and Albany; thirdly, it empowered the company to construct such branch or branches for depot and station accommodations as might be necessary; fourthly, it authorized the company " to transport, take or carry any property or persons upon the same by the power and force of steam, of animals, or of any mechanical or other power, or any combination of them, for the term of fifty years from the passage of this Act." The act also expressly provided that " the Legislature may at any time alter or repeal this Act," and it was provided that the Hudson River Railroad Company might " locate their railroad on any of the streets or avenues of the city of New York westerly of and including the Eighth avenue, and on or westerly of Hudson street, provided the assent of the corporation of said city be first obtained for such location." Pursuant to this act a resolution approved by Mayor Brady[2] on May 6, 1847, gave the company permission to construct a double track along the

---

[1] *Laws of the State of New York, 1846*, ch. 216.

[2] *Proceedings of the Board of Aldermen*, vol. xxxii, pp. 541-545; Valentine, David T., *Ordinances of the Mayor, Aldermen and Commonalty of the City of New York*, pp. 631-632.

Hudson river from Spuyten Duyvil creek to near Sixty-eighth street, using that part of Twelfth avenue which paralleled the shore; then winding from the river front so as to intersect Eleventh avenue at or near Sixtieth street; thence through the middle of Eleventh avenue to about Thirty-second street; thence on a curve to Tenth avenue, to West street, and thence to Canal street.

By the terms of this franchise certain fundamental restrictions were stipulated in behalf of public interest; for instance: the ordinance required the company to "lay their rails or tracks in the streets or avenues in such a manner as to cause no unnecessary impediment to the common and ordinary use of the street for all other purposes, and so as to leave all the water-courses free and unobstructed." It was also expressly provided that

it should be especially incumbent on the railroad company, at their own cost, to construct stone bridges across such of the streets intersected by the railroad as may, by the elevation of their grades upon the surface of said road, require to be arched or bridged whenever in the opinion of the Common Council the same shall be necessary for public convenience; and also to make such embankments or excavations as the Common Council may deem necessary to render the passage over the railroad and embankments at the cross streets easy and convenient for all the purposes for which streets and roads are usually put to.

The company was prohibited from carrying passengers below Thirty-second street and was to "be at all times subject to such regulations, with reference to the convenience of public travel through such streets and avenues as are affected by the said railroad as the Common Council shall, from time to time, by ordinance, direct." The company furthermore agreed to grade, pave and keep in repair a space twenty-five feet in width between and on either side of the tracks whenever in the opinion of the common council public interests required such paving to be done.

In an amendatory resolution dated August 12, 1847, the company expressly bound itself to abide by the terms and limitations of the ordinance of May 6, 1847.[1]

In 1849 the company was authorized to lay a double track from West street through Canal and Hudson streets to Chambers street, subject to all the restrictions and conditions laid down in the company's original grant.[2] In December of the same year the company was further empowered to extend a single track around the country market at the foot of Canal street which had been leased to the railroad corporation, so that it might make connections with the main line on West and Canal streets.[3] No additional provisions were prescribed in this franchise.

In 1869 the state legislature enacted a general law[4] authorizing the consolidation of railroad companies " whenever the two or more railroads of the companies or corporations so to be consolidated shall or may form a continuous line of railroad with each other." The act stipulated, however, that such consolidation " shall not release such new corporation from any of the restrictions, disabilities, or duties of the several corporations so consolidated."

The consolidation of the New York Central and the Hudson River railroads was effected under this act, which did not expressly extend the term or enlarge any of the rights of the Hudson River Railroad Company. In other words, the privileges of the company were not enlarged automatically by the result of mere consolidation. The extension of the fifty-year limit of the franchise of the Hudson River Rail-

[1] *Valentine*, David T., *Ferry Leases and Railroad Grants*, pp. 309-10.
[2] *Ibid.*, pp. 311-12.
[3] *Ibid.*, p. 312.
[4] *Laws of the State of New York, 1869*; ch. 917.

road Company occurred when the stockholders of the two consolidating companies entered into articles of agreement to form a corporation which should continue for a term of five hundred years.[1]

As the population of the city increased, protests against the New York Central and Hudson River Railroad Company's operation of locomotives and freight trains above Fourteenth street became more frequent. Their use became such a menace to life, limb and property on Tenth avenue that this street became notorious as "Death Avenue."[2] After 1880 the protests became more frequent and more vigorous; finally the legislature took action by passing the law of 1906.[3] This act proposed to terminate the use of the streets of New York city for railroads operating steam locomotives at grade. It authorized the Rapid Transit Commissioners to draft plans for the removal of the tracks, and provided that in case this official body could not come to an agreement with the railroad company within twelve months, it should " condemn all and any rights, privileges and franchises of any such railroad company or companies, to operate by locomotives using steam or other power . . . at grade." In case such condemnation was necessary, the board was instructed to direct the corporation counsel to proceed with such condemnation. Nothing was accomplished under this act.[4] After further attempts to solve the problem,[5] the board of estimate and apportionment on May

[1] See *Report of the Commission to Investigate the Surface Railroad Situation in the City of New York on the West Side*; appointed under Chapter 720, Laws of 1917. William H. Von Benschoten, Danforth E. Ainsworth, Charles A. Beard, Cyrus C. Miller, Ralph S. Rounds, Henry L. Stoddard, and Hiram C. Todd. Commissioners; p. 25.

[2] *Ibid.*, p. 26.

[3] *Laws of the State of New York, 1906*; ch. 109.

[4] *Report of Commission to Investigate the Surface Railroad Situation in the City of New York on the West Side*, p. 27.

[5] *Ibid.*

21, 1909, instructed the corporation counsel to report whether there were any substantial doubts as to the legal rights of the company and what action should be taken in order to have the question adjudicated.[1] In his reply to the board of estimate and apportionment the corporation counsel said:[2]

Applying the well recognized rule that franchises are construed most strongly in favor of the public, and as against the grantee, I am of the opinion that it cannot be successfully maintained that the act of 1869 contains a clear expression of legislative intention to extend the franchise of the Hudson River Railroad Company to use the streets without the assent of the city for the long period of five hundred years or in perpetuity.

Any doubt on the subject of what the Legislature intended by the act of 1869 should be resolved in favor of the public.

Therefore, to raise the question so that it may be judicially determined as speedily as possible, I advise you to instruct the Borough President to at once give notice to the company to remove its tracks from the streets on the West Side within thirty days from the receipt of such notice, and on failure to do so, the Borough President will immediately proceed to tear up such tracks and remove them from the streets, and the expense of such removal and the restoration of said streets to their former condition will be charged against the company.

President Ahearn of Manhattan Borough, acting upon this advice, served notice on the railroad company to remove its tracks within thirty days. The company at once took steps to prevent such action. Litigation on the subject culminated in a decision of the Court of Appeals,[3] May 19,

[1] *Minutes of the Board of Estimate and Apportionment of the City of New York: Financial and Franchise Matters, 1909*, p. 2313.
[2] *Ibid.*, pp. 2354-2370.
[3] New York Central and Hudson River Railroad Co. *vs.* The City of New York, 202 N. Y., 212.

1911, in which the court held that the fifty-year limitation in the act of 1846 applied "to the corporate existence of the Hudson River Railroad Company only (which might be extended), and not at all to the location of its tracks in the streets of New York," and moreover, the legislature "gave the city no authority to withdraw or cancel the franchise after it had once been made effective by the city's consent. Assuming the existence of that power in any one, it belonged, and still belongs to the Legislature and not to the corporation of the City of New York."

This opinion was concurred in by Judge Cullen, who said: "I concur in the opinion of Judge Willard Bartlett and also in the expression of his personal view as to the power of the Legislature to modify or regulate the franchise given by the state for the location of the plaintiff's railroad in the City of New York."

The New York Central and Hudson River Railroad Company considers its franchise to the streets of the city to be, therefore, perpetual, and in the numerous attempts to solve the perplexing West Side problem the company has always acted upon the assumption that the city was powerless to alter the company's grant.[1]

---

[1] For further details in regard to the West Side problem, see *Report of the Commission to Investigate the Surface Railroad Situation in the City of New York on the West Side,* 1918.

CHAPTER II

HISTORY OF RAILWAYS INCORPORATED BETWEEN 1850 AND 1860

1. THE SIXTH AND EIGHTH AVENUE RAILROAD COMPANIES

THE tide of immigration which had set in so strongly at the beginning of the second decade of the nineteenth century, reference to which has heretofore been made, continued to swell. Owing to the social, economic and political ills of Europe thousands of foreigners swarmed to America's shores, many of them to New York City, and these, together with the natural increase by birth, caused the population of the city rapidly to multiply.[1] By 1850 five hundred and fifteen thousand five hundred and forty-seven people were living on Manhattan Island, an increase of nearly three hundred and fifty thousand in twenty-five years. Consequently the geographical city expanded with enormous rapidity: Thirty-fourth street was now lined with city blocks, Madison Square, which a few years before had been an unsightly waste, was in a neighborhood of stately residences, and Fifth avenue below Forty-second street had been transformed from a country road into a paved thoroughfare flanked for miles by the homes of the

[1] Roth, Louis, *History of Rapid Transit Development in the City of New York*, p. 1; Wilson, Rufus R., *New York: Old and New, Its Story, Streets and Landmarks*, vol. i, pp. 325, 357; Roosevelt, Theodore, *New York*, p. 175; Holley, O. L., *A Description of New York in 1847*, p. 12; Richmond, J. F., *New York and Its Institutions, 1609-1871*, p. 103; *World Almanac*, 1918, p. 868.

refined and well-to-do.[1] With this northward expansion it was quite evident that the slow-going stages were no longer adequate to meet the growing demands of transportation.[2] It became apparent, therefore, that another railway, paralleling the New York and Harlem line, would be a profitable undertaking, and now the mad scramble for franchise privileges began. The common council, although without legal authority,[3] was disposed to act favorably upon the many applications presented, and among the first grants

[1] Roosevelt, Theodore, *op. cit.*, p. 183; Wilson, Rufus R., *op. cit.*, p. 357; Butler, W. A., *New York City, Its Growth, Misgovernment and Needs*, p. 22.

[2] In 1850 there were twenty-three stage lines operating a total of 550 licensed omnibuses; in 1851, there were 589 such conveyances. The rate of fare was usually two cents per mile. Belden, E. P., *New York, Past, Present and Future* (N. Y., 1849), p. 14; King, Charles, *Progress of the City of New York During the Last Fifty Years*, p. 75. Despite this rapid growth, the central and northern parts of the island were for the most part undeveloped. A graphic picture of Central Park as it was in the early fifties is given by Gen. Egbert L. Viele, the topographical engineer who had charge of laying out this pleasure ground: "It was for the most part a succession of stone quarries, interspersed with pestiferous swamps. The entire ground was the refuge of about five thousand squatters, dwelling in rude huts of their own construction, and living off the refuse of the city, which they daily conveyed in small carts, chiefly drawn by dogs, from the lower part of the city, through Fifth avenue (then a dirt road, running over hills and hollows). This refuse they divided among themselves and a hundred thousand domestic animals and fowls, reserving the bones for the bone-boiling establishments situated within the area. Horses, cows, swine, goats, cats, geese, and chickens swarmed everywhere, destroying what little verdure they found. Even the roots in the ground were exterminated until the rocks were laid bare, giving an air of utter desolation to the scene, made more repulsive from the odors of the decaying organic matter which accumulated in the beds of the old water courses that ramified the surface in all directions, broadening out into reeking swamps wherever their channels were intercepted." Wilson, J. G., *Memorial History of the City of New York*, vol. iv, p. 556.

[3] The first Railroad Act, passed in 1848, made no mention of street railways.

authorized we find those covering the Sixth and Eighth avenue roads.

These two avenues were the main arteries to the settled and more thickly populated districts of the West Side. By resolution of June 4, 1851, approved July 30, 1851, and embodied in agreements with the grantees on September 6, 1851, permission was given to lay a double track up West Broadway from Chambers street to Canal street to Hudson street, thence up Hudson street to Eighth avenue to Fifty-

PLATE III

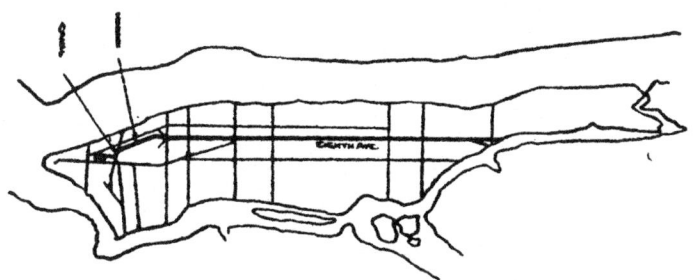

EIGHTH AVENUE RAILROAD COMPANY

first street, " said railroad to be continued through Eighth avenue to the Harlem river whenever required by the Common Council and as soon and as fast as the avenue is graded." The road, however, was to be completed to Forty-second street within one year and to the Harlem river within three years.[1] By the terms of the franchise the company was required to keep in good repair the space between the rails and outside the rails on either side for a distance of at least eight feet; the tracks were to be laid on

[1] Valentine, David T., *Ferry Leases and Railroad Grants*, pp. 262-281; *Ordinances of the Aldermen, Mayor and Commonalty of the City of New York*, p. 628; *Agreements between the Mayor, Aldermen and Commonalty of the City of New York and the Harlem, Hudson River, Sixth, Eighth, Second and Third Avenue Railroad Companies*, pp. 22-23.

a good foundation, with a grooved rail or such other rail as might be approved by the street commissioner; the pavement on either side of the rails was to be of square, grooved blocks of stone as far as Fifty-first street on the Eighth avenue road, and as far as Thirty-second street on the Sixth avenue line. New cars " with all modern improvements for the convenience and comfort of the passengers " were to be used, and they were to be operated in both directions as often as public necessity might require, subject to such schedule as the street commissioner and the common council should from time to time prescribe; long waits were to be minimized by allowing a headway of fifteen minutes in each direction between five and six o'clock in the morning, and between eight and twelve o'clock at night, and a headway of four minutes between six o'clock in the morning and eight o'clock in the evening. Motive power other than horses could not be used on the Eighth avenue line below Fifty-first street, nor on the Sixth avenue line below Forty-second street. The company agreed to make such connections with other roads in operation as the common council might from time to time direct; and its interest in the roads could not be assigned without consent of the common council. It was provided that a fare of not more than five cents should be charged for the entire length of the line; and a verified statement as to the monthly receipts of each road was to be filed with the comptroller. The common council reserved the right, should it seem beneficial to the interests of the city, to require the company to remove any portion of its tracks already laid; on failure to comply with this demand within ten days, the part of the tracks in question was to be removed by the street commissioner and the expense thereof charged to the railroad company. This is one of the few instances of a revocable street-railway grant in New York city prior to the creation of Greater New York.

In the grants to the Sixth and Eighth avenue roads will be found a partial exception to the limitless franchise whereby municipal ownership was made possible by the provision that the grantees

shall file with the Comptroller a statement, under oath, of the cost of each mile of road completed, and agree to surrender, convey and transfer the said road to the Corporation of the City of New York whenever required so to do, on payment by the Corporation of the cost of said road, as appears by said statement, with ten per cent advance thereon.

This franchise was originally known as the Sixth and Eighth avenue grant, but subsequently two distinct com-

PLATE IV

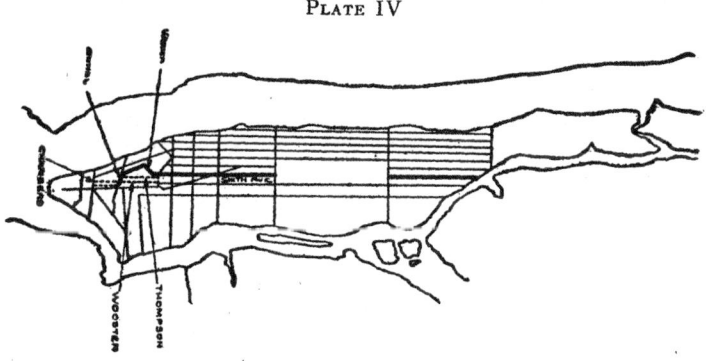

SIXTH AVENUE RAILROAD COMPANY

..... part of original route revoked by common council, June 23, 1852

panies, The Sixth Avenue Railroad Company and The Eighth Avenue Railroad Company, were organized by the grantees, the roads were separated and the route of the Sixth avenue line was changed to practically its present location, that is: through West Broadway from Chambers street to Canal street, along Canal street to Varick street, through Varick street to Carmine street, through Sixth avenue until it connected with the original line of the company. The grant for this new route provided that the West Broadway branch from Chambers street to Canal street should be built jointly by the two companies, both of which were made subject to the same conditions.[1]

Extensions were soon granted to both companies. In November, 1852, the Eighth Avenue Railroad Company was authorized to extend its system through Canal street to Broadway, upon which thoroughfare the only means of transportation was the stage-coach. This same resolution permitted the company to tap Broadway farther downtown by laying a track through Vesey street. The fare on the Eighth avenue line below Fifty-first street was to be not more than five cents and the same rate was prescribed for the Sixth Avenue Company on its line below Forty-third street.[2]

The fact that no compensation had been exacted from the railroad companies for these valuable franchises did not evoke any considerable outspoken criticism. Possibly the public entertained the same opinion toward the companies that was held when the original New York and Harlem grant was made. At that time the New York and Harlem Company maintained that in such a new and untried enterprise it was difficult to secure capital, that the whole project was merely a venture which if successful, would prove a valuable asset to the city as an artery connecting with the up-state sections. The company was of the opinion that the city and state, instead of driving a hard bargain, should

---

[1] *Proceedings of the Board of Aldermen*, vol. xlvi, pp. 638-639; Valentine, David T., *Ferry Leases and Railroad Grants*, pp. 262-263.

[2] *Proceedings of the Board of Aldermen*, vol. xlviii, pp. 421-422; Valentine, David T., *Ferry Leases and Railroad Grants*, pp. 263-264; *Ordinances of the Mayor, Aldermen and Commonalty of the City of New York*, pp. 629-630.

support the project in every possible way; indeed, it appeared that a majority of the inhabitants felt that the franchise defined fairly well, and sufficiently protected, the rights of the city.[1] In a report to the common council under date of February 16, 1852, the city comptroller, Mr. A. C. Flagg, suggested that for the monopoly enjoyed the railroads should be required to pave the avenues or streets from curb to curb and to keep them clean;[2] this, he stated, " would be a moderate compensation to the public for furnishing to the company not only a graded line for the road, but a thoroughfare already filled with more passengers than they can accommodate." The comptroller further suggested that in all future extensions of streets and avenues to the Harlem river each company should " be required to pay the expenses of grading and paving the avenue in proportion to the number of feet occupied by the double track. And the public ought to have the benefit of all revenues beyond ten per cent in a reduction of fare or a direct annual revenue might be exacted which would go to lessen taxation."

The board of aldermen did not heed this salutary advice; in fact, the communication received no attention whatever. Mayor Kingsland seems to have distrusted the aldermanic resolution of November, 1852, under which the extensions were granted, for on December 13 he returned it with neither approval nor objection,[3] but according to the provisions of the amended charter the resolution became a law.

It is of interest to note that the Eighth Avenue Company almost immediately broke faith with the city, by doubletracking College Place and Barclay street, contrary to the franchise provisions, and this move was checked only when

[1] *Morning Courier and New York Enquirer*, May 2, 10, 15, 1832.
[2] *Report of Comptroller Flagg to Common Council*, 1852.
[3] *Proceedings of the Board of Aldermen*, vol. xlviii, p 525.

the common council threatened to restore the streets to their former condition.[1] The Eighth Avenue line proved at once to be highly profitable; during the first year of its operation it paid six per cent dividends, and within four years the dividends were increased to eighteen per cent.[2] The validity of the Sixth and Eighth avenue grants, as well as those of other important street railways, was soon questioned. Franchises were being speeded through by the city fathers and on every hand rumors of aldermanic bribery were heard.[3] Finally James E. Coulter, a lobbyist, in an affidavit which appeared in the newspapers,[4] made the specific charge that there was an organized "ring to receive and distribute bribery money." In consequence, the grand jury, after carefully investigating these alleged malversations, handed down a presentment on February 26, 1853,[5] stating that

it was clearly shown that enormous sums of money had been expended for and toward the procurement of railroad grants in the city; and that toward the recession and procurement of the Eighth avenue railroad grant, a sum so large that it would startle the most credulous, but in consequence of the voluntary absence of important witnesses, the grand jury was left without direct testimony of the particular recipients of the different amounts.[6]

According to the testimony, the aldermen awarded the

[1] *Proceedings of the Board of Aldermen*, vol. xlviii, pp. 525-526.

[2] *New York Times*, December 26, 1865.

[3] *New York Tribune*, December 31, 1852; *New York Times*, December 31, 1852.

[4] *Ibid.*, February 26, 1853; Myers, Gustavus, *The History of Tammany Hall*, p. 198; Bowker, R. R., "The Piracy of Public Franchises," *Atlantic Monthly*, 1901, vol. 88, p. 465.

[5] *Documents of the Board of Aldermen*, vol. xxi, pt. ii, pp. 1333-1376.

[6] *Ibid.*, pp. 1219-1220.

grants to the party or parties paying the largest bribe. One John Pettigrew and his associates, anxious to secure the Eighth avenue franchise, bribed the aldermen, and a resolution was passed forthwith granting to the bribers the desired privilege; but when a group headed by one Solomon Kipp substantially increased its bribery bid over that of the Pettigrew faction, the common council deliberately revoked its former resolution and Pettigrew and his associates lost both the franchise and the bribe money.[1] One of the witnesses, Theodore Martine, testified before the grand jury:

I know Solomon Kipp . . . one of the grantees of the Eighth avenue railroad . . . ; he has frequently admitted to me that he had to pay large sums of money to members of the Common Council to procure the passage of those several grants and has frequently admitted that he has expended for said purpose upwards of fifty thousand dollars.[2]

The Third avenue grant (see pages 59-62) was acquired under similar circumstances. James W. Flynn, one of the grantees of this franchise, testified:

Before procuring the grant there was money raised by the company for procuring it, but in what way it was to be used I do not know of my own knowledge. I do not know the exact amount raised, I gave something over two thousand dollars towards the fund. . . . I was given to understand by Mr. Dewey [3] all my associates except Mr. Van Schaick and Mr. Reynolds paid the same as I did; those two gentlemen were not in the habit of attending our meetings. . . . My impression, derived from what passed, was that the sum of ten thousand dollars was to be placed where one of the assistant

[1] *Documents of the Board of Aldermen*, vol. xxi, pt. ii, pp. 1371-1373.
[2] *Ibid.*, p. 1573.
[3] Horace M. Dewey, a lawyer and promoter, acted as treasurer for the company.

aldermen could get it; there was more money raised after it passed the Board of Assistants; it was raised for the purpose of assisting it through the Board of Aldermen. My impression, derived from what passed, that the sum was to be placed in the hands of Mr. Dewey, who was to place it where one of the aldermen could get it. I think the first sum raised after it passed the Board of Assistants was between nine thousand and ten thousand dollars and afterwards a further sum of from seven thousand to eight thousand; I did not ask how this money was disposed of, and he advised me not to ask any questions; I think this most likely was Mr. Dewey; I think Mr. Dewey told me he had given Aldermen Tweed three thousand dollars to get the grant through the Board of Aldermen; . . . there was in the neighborhood of from twenty-eight to thirty thousand raised.[1]

Other grantees of the Third avenue franchise corroborated Flynn's testimony.[2] Notwithstanding these revelations made by the grand jury, the Eighth avenue railroad franchise, and, as a matter of fact, all the other railroad grants made at this time remained intact.

This wholesale bribery and robbery aroused the city to fever heat.[3] Taxes were soaring [4] and on every hand there was public criticism. One of the direct results of the prevailing condition of affairs was the formation of the City Reform Party,[5] which elected a substantial majority to the

[1] *Documents of the Board of Aldermen*, vol. xxi, pt. ii, pp. 1333-1335.

[2] *Ibid.*, pp. 1336-1337, 1338-1341, 1343. Every department of the city government was corrupt; Myers, Gustavus, *The History of Tammany Hall*, p. 202.

[3] *New York Tribune*, January 3, 1853; February 26, 1853.

[4] *Ibid.*, January 3, 1853; January 4, 1854.

[5] *Ibid.*, November 8, 1854; *New York Times*, November 8, 1854; Myers, Gustavus, *loc. cit.*, pp. 203-206; Scisco, Louis D., *Political Nativism in New York State* (N. Y., 1901), see ch. ix, "Local Nativism in New York City, 1854-1860," especially pp. 204-210.

common council in 1854. While the character of conciliar legislation improved somewhat and the municipal authorities endeavored to make the surface railroad companies[1] fulfill their contract obligations with the city, the people, and especially the property-owners, demanded greater protection. Relief was seemingly obtained when the state legislature enacted on April 4, 1854, the first general law authorizing the construction of street railways.[2] By this act the common council of any city was forbidden to authorize the construction in the streets of the city of "a railroad for the transportation of passengers which commences and ends in said city without the consent thereto of a majority in interest of the owners of property in which said railroad is to be constructed being first had and obtained." After such consent had been obtained, the council had the right to award grants for the construction of a street railway upon such terms and conditions as it might see fit to prescribe. This freedom of aldermanic action was limited, however, for no grant could be made except to a person or persons who would give adequate security to comply in all respects with the conditions prescribed by the common council, and who would agree to carry passengers at the lowest rate of fare. The act further required that notice of the time and conditions of the proposed grant be published in the newspapers and that all interested be invited to submit bids for the proposal. The rights of all companies which had commenced the construction of their roads under the authorization of the local authorities were validated by section three of the act, which read as follows:

This act shall not be held to prevent the construction, extension, or use of any railroad in any of the cities of this

[1] Myers, Gustavus, *op. cit.*, p. 207; *New York Tribune*, May 3, 1854.
[2] *Laws of the State of New York, 1854*, ch. 140.

state which has already been constructed in part; but the respective companies and parties by whom such roads have been in part constructed, and their assigns, are hereby authorized to construct, complete, extend, and use such roads in and through the streets and avenues designated in the respective grants, licenses, resolutions or contracts under which the same have been so in part constructed; and to that end the grants, licenses and resolutions aforesaid are hereby confirmed.

These original franchises have been the subject of much litigation. When granted they were invalid, for the reason that the legislature, at the time the grants were made, had not delegated authority to the city government to grant franchises. Judge Hoffman of the Superior Court of New York City, in the case of Hope & Co. v. The Sixth and Eighth Avenue Railroad Companies,[1] held that the Eighth avenue charter was a *license* from the city and not a *grant* from the state. It is interesting to note that in his judgment the legislature "has no more power to establish a railroad in a street in the City of New York without the assent of the corporation, than to run it through the house of an individual owner without his consent." But more to the point:

... The Common Council have reserved the power to cause the road, or any part thereof, to be taken up at any time they shall see fit; have provided that the road shall be transferred to them whenever they demand it, upon payment of the costs and ten per cent added, and that the parties on being required

---

[1] See compilation entitled *The City and the Eighth Avenue Railroad*, p. 18. This compilation contains the contract of 1851 between the City and the Eighth Avenue Railroad Company, showing its important terms and the nature of the contractual relations between the parties thereto; the opinions of the courts in the various litigations in which the contract has been involved to May 25, 1897. It also sets forth the interests of the city in the road by reason of the contract and the attitude of the legal advisers of the city.

at any time by the corporation, and to such extent as the Common Council shall determine, shall take up at their own expense said rails, or such part thereof as they shall be required, and upon failure so to do the same may be done at their expense by the Street Commissioner.

In words, then, the power to purchase for the use of the city, and thus to extinguish a monopoly in others, the power to remove such portions as may be found injurious to public convenience and absolute power to annul the license is reserved. When the companies accepted the permission thus conferred, they were bound to know that the law was, as it is now pronounced to be, that the corporation could not give them an irrevocable right; and hence, that the power to take up the rails was not an unmeaning or contradictory reservation, but a declaration of legal rights and position of the parties.

In the opinion of Judge Hoffman, an enabling statute by the legislature was unnecessary.[1]

In the case of The Mayor, Aldermen and Commonalty of the City of New York v. The Eighth Avenue Railroad Company,[2] decided in 1890, the Court of Appeals held that the company was bound to pay car licenses as required under its franchise and contract of 1851. Mr. Justice Haight, in rendering the opinion of the court, stated that the contract between the company and the city had been ratified by the confirmatory act of 1854, and hence was binding.

In the words of the learned Justice, the act of 1854 " ratified and confirmed the grants, licenses, resolutions and contracts made by the Common Council, so that thereafter they became good, valid and binding. It is under the provisions of this act that the grant to construct and operate a railroad in the streets named was made valid. It is the act

[1] *The City and the Eighth Avenue Railroad*, p. 20.
[2] 118 N. Y., 389.

under which the defendant was incorporated and took title to its property and franchises. The same words which confirmed the grant confirmed the contract, and if one is made valid the other must be also."

The language is clear and unmistakable; yet in 1898, when an action was brought to test the right of the city to purchase the property of the Eighth Avenue Railroad Company [1] under the provisions of its original agreement with the common council, the Court of Appeals held that the city had no such right. Justice Gray, who wrote the opinion, held that only the " grants, licenses and resolutions " were confirmed by the act of 1854—not the contract. It is most difficult to understand the logic by which the court arrived at such a conclusion. Apparently, moreover, the court failed to take into consideration the fact that provisions reserving to the city the right to purchase the road on certain terms were contained not only in the original resolution granting the franchise but also in the contract. The practical effect of this decision was to confirm the privileges of the company granted under the original resolution of the common council, but to release it from the obligations imposed by the same resolution. This curious decision is probably best explained by Mr. Delos F. Wilcox when he points out that " this particular case was decided just at the time when the Metropolitan Street Railway Company, under the astute counsel of Elihu Root and the executive direction of William C. Whitney, was bringing together the magnificent system of street railways, with unlimited capitalization based upon perpetual rights in the streets of New York. . . . The decision of the Eighth Avenue Railroad case against the contention of the city was absolutely necessary at that time for the furtherance of the plans of the Metropolitan Company." [2]

[1] Potter *v.* Collis, 156 N. Y., 16.
[2] Wilcox, D. F., *Municipal Franchises*, vol. ii, p. 109.

On November 23, 1895, the company's franchises and property were leased to the Metropolitan Street Railway Company for a period of ninety-nine years [1] at an annual rental of two hundred and fifteen thousand dollars and all taxes. This lease, which is still in force, is now held by the New York Railways Company.[2]

Although they are of no great importance, mention should, nevertheless, be made of the special franchises which have been granted to the Sixth Avenue Company. By resolution of the common council, approved October 8, 1892, a franchise was granted for the construction of a double-track line on Fifty-third street from Sixth avenue to Seventh avenue.[3] A similar resolution, approved October 29, 1892, authorized the company to build a double track on West Third street from Sixth avenue to Sullivan street to connect with the extension of the Metropolitan Cross-Town Railway Company.[4] A franchise for a similar extension on Fiftieth and Fifty-first streets from Sixth avenue to a point eight hundred feet west of Sixth avenue was approved December 1, 1892.[5] By resolution of the common council, approved by the mayor on April 27, 1894, the company was required " as soon as practicable, to construct and operate its railroad from One Hundred and Tenth street to Lenox avenue and along Lenox avenue to the Harlem river." [6] This part of the route was incorporated in the original grant of 1851, and therefore the resolution was merely an order rather than a franchise.

[1] *Infra*, ch. viii; *Annual Report of the New York Railways Company for year ending June 30, 1918*, p. 28.
[2] *Ibid.*
[3] *Proceedings of the Board of Aldermen*, vol. 207, p. 162.
[4] *Ibid.*, pp. 374-377.
[5] *Ibid.*, vol. 208, p. 162.
[6] *Ordinances, Resolutions, &c., adopted by the Common Council and approved by the Mayor, 1894*, vol. lxii, p. 51.

On February 1, 1892, the Sixth Avenue Company leased its road to the Houston, West Street and Pavonia Ferry Railroad Company,[1] the consideration being payment of all taxes and an annual rental of one hundred and forty-five thousand dollars. This lease is still in force and is now in the hands of the New York Railways Company.[2]

2. THE SECOND AVENUE RAILROAD COMPANY

Provision for the franchise of the Second Avenue Railroad Company was made by resolution of the common council on December 11, 1852.[3] Four days later this reso-

PLATE V

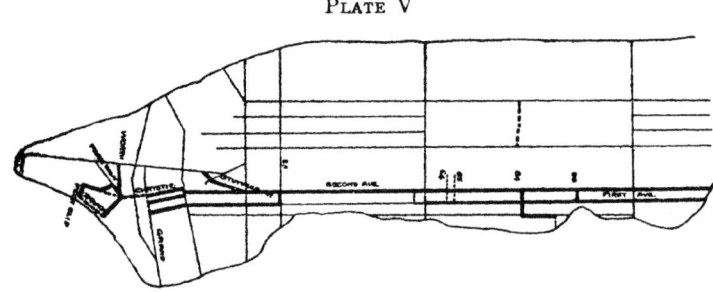

SECOND AVENUE RAILROAD COMPAFY
- - - - - trackage rights obtained on tracks of other companies
. . . . . franchise routes neither constructed nor used by this company

lution was embodied in an agreement [4] which gave permission to Denton Pearsall, Joseph C. Skaden, A. P. Rapelyea, William L. Hall, Richard T. Mulligan, and others to construct a railway line through the following named streets, viz.: A double track down Second avenue from Forty-

[1] *Annual Report of the New York Railways Company for year ending June 30, 1918*, p. 28.
[2] *Ibid.*, p. 1.
[3] *Proceedings of the Board of Aldermen*, vol. xlviii, p. 363.
[4] Valentine, David T., *Ferry Leases and Railroad Grants*, pp. 173-178.

second street to Twenty-third street, through Twenty-third street with a single track to First avenue; thence to Allen street, to Grand street, to the Bowery; down the Bowery across Chatham, through Oliver, through South across Roosevelt, through Front street to Peck Slip, the terminus. The grant also provided for a return loop as follows: From Peck Slip to Pearl street, through Chatham, through the Bowery, through Grand street, through Chrystie street to Second avenue to Twenty-third street, and thence back to its upper terminal opposite the Harlem river. Very few restrictions were placed upon the grantees; the rails were to be laid in such a manner that the watercourses of the streets would be left free and unobstructed; the company was to pave the streets in and about the rails "in a permanent manner" and to keep the same in repair satisfactory to the street commissioner; no motive power other than horses could be used below Forty-second street;[1] the fare below this street was to be not more than five cents, and the common council reserved the right to regulate the rate for the entire length of the road, when completed, to the Harlem river.[2] The mayor refusing to approve or veto the resolution, it nevertheless became a law in conformity with the provisions of the amended charter of the city. Subsequently it was mutually agreed that the company should pay annually one-half of one per cent of its gross receipts into the city treasury.[3]

[1] Apparently no other motive power was employed on any street surface road, with the exception of the New York and Harlem road and the Hudson river road, prior to the introduction of cable power.

[2] Another clause provided that cars were to be operated at stated intervals for the convenience of the public and according to such directions as the common council might from time to time prescribe.

[3] *Report of the Public Service Commission for the First District of New York State*, 1913, vol. v, p. 1148.

Property-owners and taxpayers sought to prevent the construction of the road; the Supreme Court granted injunctions on the ground that the corporate authorities were guilty of a breach of trust in that they had given away property which, if offered for sale, would have yielded large profits.[1]

Such proceedings simply delayed construction; minor changes and extensions were soon made. By resolution of the Board of Aldermen, July 18, 1853, approved by the mayor on July 20, 1853, the route was changed from Front, between Roosevelt street and Peck Slip, to South street between the same points.[2] In 1855 the company was authorized to construct bridges over the Harlem and Bronx rivers in order that its lines might tap the territory outside of Manhattan.[3] Two years later the legislature permitted the company to discontinue that part of its road running through Oliver street and South street to Peck Slip; the same act, however, provided for a double-track extension, as follows: "Through that part of the Bowery extending from Chatham Square to Pearl street, to Peck Slip, and thence through Peck Slip to South street, together with the necessary turn-outs or switches in Peck Slip for the convenient operation and working of said railroad."[4]

The city officials took the position that the legislature had no right to grant franchises to railroad companies for the use of the streets of the city without the consent of the local authorities. This opinion was expressed in a resolution of the board of aldermen under date of April 28, 1857, passed by the board of councilmen on May 25, 1857, and

[1] Stuyvesant *vs.* Pearsall *et al.*, 15 N. Y., 244.
[2] Valentine, David T., *Ferry Leases and Railroad Grants*, p. 178.
[3] *Laws of the State of New York, 1855*, ch. 373.
[4] *Ibid., 1857*, ch. 551.

approved by the mayor two days later,[1] which stated that "should the Second Avenue Railroad Company undertake to lay rails in any of the streets of the city by the authority thus conferred upon said company by the said legislature, the counsel of the corporation is hereby authorized and directed to restrain said company by injunction, and further, if necessary, to test the validity of the said act." This threat was without avail and the company was soon able to take refuge behind the general act of 1860, which deprived the local authorities of franchise-granting power.[2]

On November 22, 1867, the common council, notwithstanding the legislative act of 1860, authorized the Second Avenue Railroad Company " to lay down and use the necessary turn-outs, switches, and sidetracks extending from their present tracks in Second avenue to and along their property in Sixty-third and Sixty-fourth streets, between the First and Second avenues."[3] This resolution, after having been favorably reported by the committee on railroads, was transmitted to the mayor for his approval.[4] There is no indication in the records of the council that the resolution was returned with the executive veto, and no trace of it is to be found among the papers as having gone into effect.

Just prior to the enactment of the constitutional amendment forbidding special legislation for surface railroads, the state legislature granted an important extension to the company.[5] This act made possible the operation of a line in Second avenue from Twenty-third street to Houston street, to Forsyth street, to Division street, to Chatham

[1] Valentine, David T., *Ferry Leases and Railroad Grants*, p. 179.
[2] See ch. iii.
[3] *Proceedings of the Board of Aldermen*, vol. 108, p. 143.
[4] *Ibid.*, p. 159.
[5] *Laws of the State of New York, 1872*, ch. 240.

Square. It also provided for an extension through Stuyvesant street across Third avenue, Eighth street and Fourth avenue to Astor Place, and through Astor Place to the easterly side of Broadway. Provision also was made for a double track from First avenue through and along Sixty-third and Sixty-fourth streets to within two hundred feet of Third avenue. The act further authorized the construction of a double-track line in Eighty-sixth street from Second avenue to Avenue A to Ninety-second street and thence to the East river, and a connecting link in Worth street between Chatham Square and Broadway. Other minor extensions were also allowed. This act also contained a provision empowering the Second Avenue Railroad Company to use the tracks of other railroad companies, or to cross the same, provided compensation was arranged therefor. Few restrictions were embodied in this act, although it contained a stipulation to the effect that the company should pay to the city a sum to be determined upon by three commissioners appointed by the Supreme Court. These commissioners reported on February 4, 1873, that the company should pay for its extension franchises the sum of one thousand dollars for the remainder of the current year ending September 30, 1873, and annually thereafter a sum equal to one-third of one per cent of the gross receipts of the company.[1]

Another extension was granted in 1884 for a double-track line along First avenue from the Harlem river to Fifty-seventh street, and along Fifty-seventh street to Second avenue; also for a double-track line through Ninety-sixth street to connect the Second avenue road with a proposed Fifth avenue route.[2] By the terms of this ordinance the

[1] *Report of the Public Service Commission, First District of New York State*, 1913, vol. v, p. 1148.
[2] *Proceedings of the Board of Aldermen*, vol. 184, p. 743.

company was to comply with all the provisions of the general street railroad law.

From 1893 to 1897 the company operated over the tracks of the New York and Harlem Railroad Company known as Transverse Road No. 3 in Central Park from Eighth avenue to Central Park East, and thence along Eighty-fifth street. Transverse Road No. 3 was built under a contract with the department of public works of the city of New York. Permission for the Second Avenue Company to operate over it was obtained through the Department of Parks. After 1897 the Second Avenue Company ceased to use the road and the consent of the department of parks was revoked by the board of estimate and apportionment in December, 1910.[1]

The company during its corporate existence entered into many trackage agreements with other railroad companies,[2] but such arrangements in no way affected its franchise grants. On June 28, 1898, the company leased its lines to the Metropolitan Street Railway Company.[3] The road is now being operated, through an agreement, by the New York Railways Company.[4]

3. THE THIRD AVENUE RAILWAY COMPANY

The franchise for the Third avenue railroad was granted by resolution of the board of aldermen December 18, 1852,[5] to Myndert Van Schaick, H. M. Dewey, Elijah P. Purdy,

---

[1] *Minutes of the Board of Estimate and Apportionment*, 1910; *Financial and Franchise Matters*, pp. 4300, 5007.

[2] *Report of the Public Service Commission, First District, State of New York*, 1913, vol. v, pp. 1150-1155.

[3] *Infra*, ch. viii.

[4] *Annual Report of New York Railways Company for the year ending June 30, 1918*, p. 1.

[5] *Proceedings of the Board of Aldermen*, vol. xlviii, pp. 529-530.

James W. Flynn, James McElvaney and seven others, all of whom were reputed to be politicians and omnibus owners.[1] The mayor returned the resolution on December 31st without approval or rejection, but, in accordance with the charter, it became operative and binding.[2] By the terms of the contract the grantees were authorized to construct a double-track road from the corner of Park Row and Broadway to Chatham street, thence along this thoroughfare to the Bowery to Third avenue, and thence to the Harlem river.

In building the road, the grantees were to lay the tracks upon a good foundation with a grooved rail or such other type of rail as the common council and street commissioner might approve; they were also obligated to keep in good repair the space inside the tracks and for a distance of two feet beyond either outer rail. Steam power was prohibited; the cars were to be new and up-to-date in every particular in order that the passengers might enjoy the greatest comfort and convenience when traveling thereon, and were to run "as often as public convenience may require, under such prudential directions as the common council and the street commissioner may, from time to time, prescribe." Passengers were to be charged not more than a five-cent fare for any distance between the southern terminus of the road and Sixty-first street, and a six-cent fare for the entire length of the road. The grantees were to pay an annual license fee as prescribed by law for each car. The grant provided for a track through the Bowery and Grand street in order to connect the Third avenue road with the Second avenue line in the event that the latter road should be con-

[1] *New York Tribune*, December 20, 1852; *New York Times*, Dec. 20, 1852; Bowker, R. R., "The Piracy of Public Franchises," *Atlantic Monthly*, 1901, vol. 88, p. 465.
[2] Valentine, David T., *Ferry Leases and Railroad Grants*, p. 181.

structed. Both companies were to enjoy the common use of the double-track line through the Bowery to Chatham street. This grant was justly and severely criticized,[1] for the franchise was not only given away but was also made exclusive and perpetual; even the railroad company itself was to exist in perpetuity.

PLATE VI

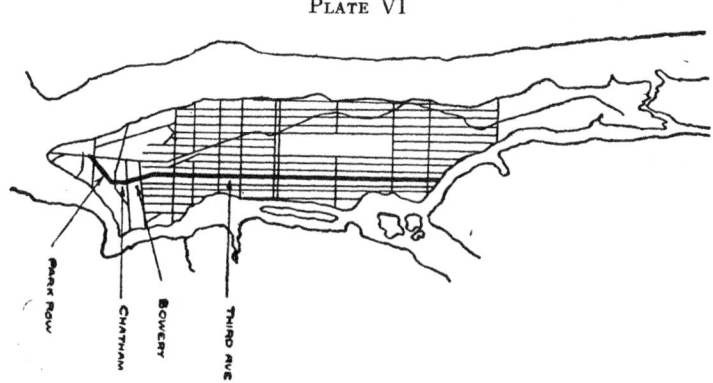

THIRD AVENUE RAILROAD COMPANY

Numerous extensions were made: in 1864 the common council authorized the railroad company to extend its lines on Sixty-sixth and Seventieth streets to the East river by way of Third avenue and Thirty-fourth street. This resolution, although vetoed by the mayor, was passed,[2] only to be later declared unconstitutional under the act of 1860.[3] Another short extension was authorized in 1867 which enabled the company to connect its tracks on Third avenue with its depot on One Hundred and Thirtieth street.[4] Under the terms of the act the company was prohibited

[1] *New York Tribune*, December 20, 1852; *New York Times*, December 20, 1852.
[2] Valentine, David T., *Ferry Leases and Railroad Grants*, pp. 195-196.
[3] People v. Third Avenue Railroad Co., 45 Barb., 63.
[4] *Laws of the State of New York, 1867*, ch. 237.

from laying more than two tracks on One Hundred and Thirtieth street for any distance exceeding one hundred and fifty feet; in other respects this special franchise stipulated the same conditions as the original grant.

It was not until August 14, 1884, that the company made its next application for additional trackage. At that time it filed with the secretary of state a certificate of extension for a single-track line through East Twenty-first and East Twenty-second streets to Lexington avenue; thence by a double track through Lexington avenue to Ninety-seventh street, and thence along said Ninety-seventh street to the Harlem river. In its petition to the board of aldermen the company made no offer of compensation for such extension.[1] Two months later, October 13, 1884, a further application was presented to the aldermen for permission to extend the road from its southern terminus in Park Row across Broadway, through Vesey street to Church street; the company then proposed to operate to South ferry over the tracks of the South Ferry Railroad Company with which it had an agreement;[2] the sole inducement offered was a single fare for continuous passage from South ferry to the Harlem river. This application, like its predecessor, died in the aldermanic committee on railroads.[3]

After 1890 the Third Avenue Railroad Company made every possible effort to extend its system; in fact, it became the keen rival of the Metropolitan Street Railway Company (see chapter viii). From 1893 to 1898 a number of certificates for extensions were filed with the secretary of state;[4] of these extensions the franchise for the

[1] *Report of Public Service Commission, First District, State of New York*, 1913, vol. v, pp. 1290-92.

[2] *Proceedings of the Board of Aldermen*, vol. 176, pp. 180-182.

[3] *Ibid.*, p. 182.

[4] *Report of the Public Service Commission of First District, State of New York*, 1913, vol. v, pp. 1291-1294.

so-called "Kingsbridge line" is of greater importance, not alone for the actual terms of the grant but also for the method of obtaining it and its interpretation by the courts.

The proposed Kingsbridge route extended from One Hundred and Twenty-fifth street to Yonkers. The Third Avenue Railroad Company and the Metropolitan Street Railway Company each petitioned for a franchise covering this road.[1] Hearings pursuant to law were accorded both applicants.[2] The aldermanic committee on railroads to whom the petitions were referred reported in favor of the Third Avenue Railroad Company,[3] although at the various public hearings the preponderance of sentiment was markedly in favor of the competing company.[4] Various reasons were assigned by the railroad committee for its decision;[5] in the first place, the existing route of the Third Avenue Company together with the proposed extension would enable the people of the city to have access to greater urban territory. Again, the Third Avenue Company, because of its previous occupation of a large portion of the territory to be affected by the new grant, was in a position to contribute materially in building up that portion of the city. Further, the Third Avenue Company was the first to make application—a rather flimsy argument—and, lastly, the city would gain more financially by awarding the franchise to the Third Avenue Railroad Company. After considerable delay, largely due to the efforts of the Metropolitan Street Railway Company to secure the grant,[6] the award was made, by a vote of twenty to eleven, to the Third Avenue

[1] *Proceedings of the Board of Aldermen*, vol. 218, pp. 297-299.
[2] *Ibid.*, pp. 301, 404.
[3] *Ibid.*, p. 298.
[4] *Ibid.*, p. 298.
[5] *Ibid.*, pp. 298-299.
[6] *Ibid.*, pp. 309-14; 374-391; 467-485, 520-528.

Railroad Company.[1] Mayor Strong, although approving of the extension, vetoed the resolutions on the ground that they did not afford equal opportunity for competing companies to bid for the right to construct the line.[2] The mayor's communication was laid over;[3] in the meantime the council was besieged with petitions urging that the franchise be granted to the Third Avenue Railroad corporation.[4] Finally the grant was repassed and approved by the mayor, the company agreeing to pay thirty-eight and one-half per cent of the gross receipts in addition to the minimum required by law and a cash bonus of two hundred and fifty thousand dollars.[5]

According to the stipulated conditions, the company was required to have the cars properly heated, to provide proper fenders and wheel-guards, to pave the street in and on either side of the tracks for a distance of two feet, and to keep the street free from dirt and snow; a five-cent fare was to be charged and transfers to branch lines were to be issued.

The Metropolitan Street Railway Company, questioning the legality of the above-mentioned grant, began court proceedings, and, after two years of litigation, the Court of Appeals, in June, 1897, set aside the sale on technical grounds.[6] The court held that the sale in reality covered two separate extensions, which was contrary to section ninety-three of the Railroad Law;[7] that the common

[1] *Proceedings of the Board of Aldermen*, vol. 218, p. 538.
[2] *Ibid.*, pp. 582-583.
[3] *Ibid.*, p. 588.
[4] *Ibid.*, pp. 317-341.
[5] *Ibid.*, vol. 227, p. 586.
[6] Beekman *v.* The Third Avenue Railroad Company, 153 N. Y., 144.
[7] *Laws of the State of New York*, 1890, ch. 565; amended 1892, chs. 306, 676; 1893, ch. 434.

council had no power to impose a cash payment in addition to the percentage of gross receipts required by law. Anticipating this legal obstacle, the Third Avenue Company, in November, 1895, purchased the Forty-second street, Manhattanville and St. Nicholas Avenue Railroad [1] (see chapter v). No sooner had the decision in Beekman v. The Third Avenue Railroad Company [2] been rendered than the Third Avenue Railroad Company petitioned for an extension of the Manhattanville line along identically the same streets named in the ordinance so recently declared invalid by the courts. The Metropolitan Street Railway Company also petitioned a second time.[3] Hearings were had upon the applications and the aldermanic committee on railroads again reported in favor of making an immediate grant to the Third Avenue Company.[4] The committee took occasion to explain "the imperative necessity" for the speedy construction of the line and incidentally stated that the Third Avenue Railroad Company had been placed in an unjust position by the "illiberal mandamus proceedings which involved the company in heavy expense pending the consideration of the application by this Board." The committee stated that it was not unmindful of the provisions of the new charter of the Greater City (see chapter ix) which stipulated a limited period for franchise grants, but their recommendation was simply "a renewal of an old grant." Many taxpayers thought otherwise, and so secured an injunction restraining the mayor and aldermen from further action in the matter.[5] This restraining order was

[1] *Report of the Public Service Commission, First District, State of New York*, 1913, vol. v, chart ii, nos. 21 and 18.
[2] *Supra*, p. 64.
[3] *Proceedings of the Board of Aldermen*, vol. 227, pp. 586, *et seq.*
[4] *Proceedings of the Board of Aldermen*, vol. 227, pp. 586-592.
[5] *Ibid.*, pp. 702-704.

later upheld by the Appellate Division of the Supreme Court.[1] Various rumors of aldermanic bribery were circulated.[2] Alderman Charles A. Parker, chairman of the railroad committee, openly charged that the Metropolitan Railway Company had promised a "handsome" contribution to Tammany Hall if the Tammany members of the board would vote against the award to the Third Avenue Company.[3] Other reports were circulated to the effect that Tammany was solidly behind the Metropolitan Street Railway Company, while the Republicans were a unit for the Third Avenue Company.[4] Report had it that all Tammany men in the employ of the Third Avenue Company would be dismissed unless the Tammany aldermen fell into line.[5] The Kingsbridge franchise was made a party issue. Alderman Parker was quoted as saying: "We Republicans recognize that our political existence depends upon our vote on that franchise."[6]

In an investigation made by the Citizens' Union it was asserted that the executive and administrative officers of the regular Republican and Tammany organizations were in control of the surface railways of New York city and Brooklyn.[7] James B. Reynolds, chairman of the executive committee of this organization, boldly stated that "the day of granting franchises in perpetuity in the City of New York is over." The Union in its platform demanded "that

---

[1] Gilgrist v. 42nd St., Manhattanville &c., 23 N. Y. (App. Div.), 625.
[2] *New York Times*, Sept. 28, 1897; *New York World*, Sept. 24-28, 1897; *New York Tribune*, Sept. 28, 1897.
[3] *Ibid.*
[4] *Ibid.*
[5] *Ibid.*
[6] *New York World*, September 28, 1897.
[7] *New York Times*, September 28, 1897.

the City shall retain the ownership of its franchises and that all grants thereof be for limited periods in order that the increases of value shall accrue to the people; we demand stringent supervision of gas and railroad companies and of all other corporations using city franchises, so as to insure adequate service at reasonable rates."[1] The *New York World*, in a sweeping editorial, said it was a case between the people of New York City and a " gang of thieves, robbers, and their pals in the Board of Aldermen," who sought to give away a franchise worth a million dollars.[2]

Two years elapsed before action of any consequence was taken on the Kingsbridge grant; meanwhile the Third Avenue Railroad Company attempted to construct a double track in Amsterdam Avenue, paralleling the tracks of the Ninth Avenue Railroad Company, a subsidiary of the Metropolitan Street Surface Railway Company.[3] Property-owners and others remonstrated,[4] and finally the Third Avenue Company was forced by the legislature to abandon the project.[5] Just at this time the Metropolitan Street Surface Railway Company conceived the plan to absorb the Third Avenue system, and consequently the competing companies reached an agreement as to the Kingsbridge grant. The Metropolitan Company was allowed to operate over the tracks of the Third Avenue Company on the Boulevard between Fifty-ninth and Sixty-fifth streets as well as on certain other specified streets, in consideration of which privilege it withdrew its opposition to the Kingsbridge extension. However, before this arrangement was concluded

[1] *New York World*, September 25, 1897.
[2] *Ibid.*, September 28, 1897.
[3] See leading New York newspapers under date of September 14 and 30, 1897.
[4] See leading New York newspapers under date of September 30, 1897.
[5] *Laws of the State of New York, 1899*, ch. 371.

the Kingsbridge Railway Company had been incorporated by Henry Hart, Edward Lauterbach and others, all identified with the Third Avenue Railroad Company;[1] in fact, from the day of its inception the Kingsbridge Company has been a subsidiary of the Third Avenue Railroad Company. This new corporation at once petitioned the municipal assembly for the Kingsbridge franchise.[2] A resolution embodying the grant was drafted which, after having been favorably reported by the aldermanic railroad committee,[3] and after having been submitted to the board of estimate and apportionment for amendment and approval, was adopted December 30, 1899.[4]

This franchise, instead of being given in perpetuity, was granted for twenty-five years with the privilege of a renewal at the end of that period for another twenty-five years upon a revaluation basis. Other important conditions provided that the company pay to the city the statutory three per cent of its gross receipts during the first five years, and five per cent thereafter; a further payment of one per cent during the first and second five years, three per cent during the third five years, and five per cent for the remaining years. The road was to be operated by means of underground electric current or by any other motive power except steam or overhead electricity. Overhead electric power might, however, be employed between the south side of the bridge over the Harlem ship canal and the northern city limits. The company was to keep the streets in repair between the tracks and for a distance of

[1] *Report of the Public Service Commission, First District of the State of New York*, 1913, vol. v, p. 555.
[2] *Proceedings of the Board of Aldermen of the Greater City of New York*, vol. iv, p. 1123.
[3] *Ibid.*, p. 740.
[4] *Ibid.*, pp. 739-744; 1123-1130.

two feet on either side; the fare was to be not more than five cents for one continuous ride with transfers to branch lines; the usual requirements were expressed in regard to cars, &c.

By a resolution of the board of estimate and apportionment, under date of January 29, 1909, approved by the mayor February 1, 1909, and embodied in a contract dated March 4 of the same year, the company obtained a franchise for a double-track extension [1] " beginning and connecting with the existing double-track street surface railway on Amsterdam avenue, at or near the intersection of said avenue with Fort George avenue; thence northerly, westerly, southerly in, upon and along said Fort George avenue as it winds and turns to its intersection with Audubon avenue, with a loop terminal at such intersection, to be constructed within the present roadway of said Fort George avenue."

This grant was made for the short term of three years with the privilege of renewal for two more; it was not exclusive and could not be transferred.[2] The franchise stipulated that the company should pay to the city the sum of three hundred dollars in cash within thirty days, and three per cent of the gross receipts based on a proportion of the extension of the entire route of the company; *i. e.*,

$$\frac{\text{gross earnings of extension}}{\text{gross earnings of entire line}} = \frac{\text{extension}}{\text{entire length of line}}.$$

In no case should it be less than eleven hundred dollars annually. At the expiration of the term of the contract, or the renewal thereof, the tracks and equipment of the com-

[1] *Minutes of Board of Estimate and Apportionment of the City of New York: Financial and Franchise Matters, 1909;* pp. 403-413, 766, 963.

[2] The company was to keep in repair the streets between the tracks and for a distance of two feet on either side thereof and, when necessary, to sprinkle the streets.

pany, constructed on the streets provided for in the extension, were to revert to the city free of cost. Due to financial difficulties, the road was not completed within the specified time and by resolution of the board of estimate and apportionment, adopted March 14, 1912, and approved by the mayor on the following day, an extension of the two-year limit was granted in which to complete the road.[1]

In 1896 the Third Avenue Company obtained an important lease of land under water; by an agreement entered into on November 23 of that year with the department of docks[2] it leased the Harlem river front from Two Hundred and Sixteenth street to Two Hundred and Eighteenth street; this lease was for ten years with the privilege of two renewals of ten years each. The annual rental for the original term was twenty-two hundred and fifty dollars with an increase of ten per cent for each subsequent renewal. The company agreed to maintain at its own expense the land under the water and the structures thereon, and to rebuild any portion of the latter which might be destroyed or injured by fire, floating ice, collisions, or by action of the elements. No portion of the leased premises was to be sublet without permission of the board of docks. In case the dock commissioners wished to rebuild the walls, piers, or bulkheads on the premises, the lease of such portion of the property on which such rebuilding was to be done could be terminated upon written notice of a resolution adopted by the board of docks to that effect.

In 1889 the company applied to the state railroad commission for permission to change the motive power on the Third avenue line from One Hundred and Thirtieth street to Ann street and Broadway; the application was granted

---

[1] *Minutes of the Board of Estimate and Apportionment of the City of New York: Financial and Franchise Matters, 1909*, pp. 550-552, 928.

[2] See *Report of Department of Docks, 1897*.

but the commissioner of public works refused to allow the company to make the change on the ground that the constitutional amendment of 1875 [1] required the consent of the municipality to constitute a valid franchise. The railroad commission maintained that a grant of permission to change the motive power was not a franchise grant. This opinion was upheld by the Court of Appeals.[2]

The company has made many important trackage and transfer agreements with other surface railway companies of the city,[3] but these arrangements have not impaired its franchise rights. It has also been the parent of many subsidiary companies.[4] The property of the entire Third Avenue system—the Third Avenue Railroad Company and the companies controlled by it—was leased April 13, 1900, to the Metropolitan Street Railway Company for nine hundred and ninety-nine years. The Third Avenue Company was already in the hands of a receiver;[5] shortly afterward the Metropolitan Street Railway Company's scheme collapsed and on January 6, 1908, Mr. F. W. Whitridge was appointed receiver for the Third Avenue Railroad Company and its subsidiaries. On March 1, 1910, the property was sold at auction to James W. Wallace, Adrian Iselin and Henry Bromner, acting as a committee for certain bondholders. The purchasers incorporated the Third Avenue Railway Company and took over the lines formerly operated by the Third Avenue Railroad Company.[6]

[1] Article 3, Section 18.
[2] *In re* Third Avenue Railroad Company, 121 N. Y., 536.
[3] *Report of the Public Service Commission, First District, State of New York*, 1913, vol. v, pp. 1299-1308, 1314.
[4] *Infra*, ch. viii.
[5] *Report of Public Service Commission, First District, State of New York*, 1913, vol. v, pp. 1298, 1308.
[6] *Ibid.*, p. 1315.

4. THE NINTH AVENUE RAILROAD FRANCHISES

The franchise for the Ninth avenue railroad was speeded through the common council over the mayor's veto, December 28, 1853, and was accepted by the grantees on December 30, 1853.[1] During the year previous an effort had been made to obtain the grant when a resolution to this effect was adopted by the board of assistant aldermen on December 20, 1852, and by the board of aldermen on January 5, 1853.[2] Various attempts were made to amend the resolution in the interest of the city, but to no avail.[3] One of these proposals embodied a three-cent fare;[4] the resolution was vetoed by Mayor Westervelt on the ground that the terms for which such exclusive privileges were granted were wholly inadequate.[5] An examination of the grant substantiates the mayor in his conclusions. The franchise gave to James Murphy, William Radford and Miner C. Story the right to build a railroad from Fifty-first street to the Battery and back through the following streets, viz.: Ninth avenue to Gansevoort street, through Greenwich street to the Battery; through Gansevoort street to Washington street, and through that street to Battery Place. It was provided that the line should be continued from Fifty-first street north along Ninth avenue to Bloomingdale Road, to Tenth avenue to the Harlem river, whenever required by the common council and "as soon and as fast" as these avenues were graded; no other conditions were expressed.

Murphy and Radford, two of the grantees, were instrumental in incorporating the Ninth Avenue Railroad Com-

[1] Valentine, David T., *Ferry Leases and Railroad Grants*, pp. 294-296.
[2] *Ibid.*, 296.
[3] *Proceedings of the Board of Aldermen*, vol. xlviii, pp. 423-431.
[4] *Ibid.*, p. 428.
[5] *Ibid.*, vol. xlix, pp. 165-166.

pany, December 28, 1853. On July 30, 1859, they and their associates assigned their franchise rights to this company. The validity of the grant was soon questioned on the ground that the legislature had not yet delegated to the common council the power to grant franchises, with the result that property-owners along the proposed line secured injunctions against the company.¹ A resolution of the

PLATE VII

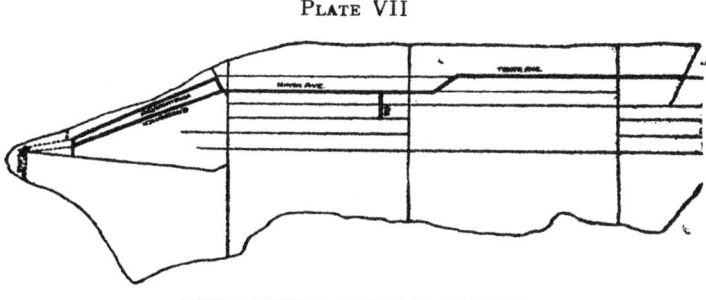

NINTH AVENUE RAILROAD COMPANY

‑ ‑ ‑ ‑ ‑ ‑ ‑ ‑ ‑ ‑ trackage rights obtained on tracks of other companies
. . . . franchise routes neither constructed nor used by this company

common council in 1859, after reciting that Murphy and his associates had laid railroad tracks from Fifty-fourth street to Canal street and Ninth avenue, but had been prevented " by legal difficulties interposed by property-owners below Canal street " from completing their railroad as originally planned, stated that the necessary accommodation of the public required that the grantees should be allowed an outlet or terminus for the road in the southern and business section of the city and that they should be compelled to put the line in operation, and the company was thereby authorized to connect its tracks with the tracks of the Hudson River Railroad Company and the Sixth

¹ *Proceedings of the Board of Aldermen*, vol. 74, p. 1110.

and Eighth Avenue Railroad Companies in and below Canal street, and to operate their cars over any portion of the same.[1]

In 1859 the road was purchased by George Law and his associates, who were also in control of the Eighth avenue line, for seven hundred and twelve thousand, four hundred and forty-six dollars;[2] thenceforth both companies had practically the same officials. Law, fully aware of the past troubles of the Ninth Avenue Company, lost no time in appealing to the state legislature for confirmation of the conciliar grant of 1853,[3] even though the franchise had been ratified and confirmed by the general law of 1854.[4] He was eminently successful in his effort, for the franchise was reconfirmed by special act in 1860.[5]

Numerous extensions were subsequently authorized.[6] In 1866 the Ninth Avenue Company was given authority to use jointly with the Dry Dock and East Broadway and Battery Railroad Company an extension granted to the latter company for the following streets: On Desbrosses street from Greenwich street to the North river, double tracks; on Cortlandt street from Greenwich street to the North river, double tracks; on Fulton street from Washington street to Greenwich street, single tracks; and on Fulton street from Greenwich street to Broadway, double tracks.[7] In consideration of this extension the Ninth Ave-

[1] *Proceedings of the Board of Aldermen,* vol. 74, p. 1110; see also Wetmore *v.* Story, 22 Barb., 414.
[2] *New York Times,* December 26, 1865. See editorial and more especially article on last page entitled "Our City Railroads."
[3] *New York State Assembly Journal, 1860;* 83rd session, p. 174.
[4] *Laws of the State of New York, 1854,* ch. 140.
[5] *Ibid., 1860;* ch. 411.
[6] Valentine, David T., *Ferry Leases and Railroad Grants,* pp. 300-304.
[7] *Laws of the State of New York, 1866;* ch. 868.

nue Company was to pay interest on one-half the cost of construction and a proportional sum towards maintenance. In case the Dry Dock Company failed to construct these extensions within six months, the Ninth Avenue Railroad Company was authorized to build the same, in which event the Dry Dock Company was to enjoy trackage rights subject to the same charges as previously arranged for the Ninth Avenue Company.

On December 5, 1882, by the unanimous resolution of the common council, the company was required as soon as practicable to continue its railroad from the existing terminus in Ninth avenue, at or near Sixty-fourth street, to the Grand Boulevard (formerly known as Bloomingdale Road, now Broadway), thence along that thoroughfare to Tenth avenue to One Hundred and Twenty-fifth street. Moreover, " when Tenth avenue shall be properly regulated and graded for the convenient operation of a horse railroad, said railroad, as soon thereafter as public convenience may require, shall be further extended and continued from time to time along Tenth avenue to the Harlem river." [1] Mayor Grace vetoed this resolution,[2] principally for the reason that the question of this extension was being litigated. The company believed it already had the right to continue its tracks without any further action on the part of the common council. In the opinion of the corporation counsel two points were involved in this litigation: (1) whether the railroad company under any circumstances had any right to construct its tracks without being directed so to do by the aldermen; (2) whether the common council could invest the company with any right to make such extension inasmuch as (a) lapse of time had worked a for-

[1] *Proceedings of the Board of Aldermen*, vol. 168, pp. 1043-1044.
[2] *Ibid.*, pp. 1202-1203.

feiture of the original franchise, and (b) it was a mooted question whether or not the resolution of 1853 was still effective in view of the fact that the Bloomingdale Road, having been replaced by the Grand Boulevard, had practically gone out of existence. The mayor expressed an opinion that no action should be taken until the court had rendered its decision. The resolution was objectionable on other grounds, namely, that it failed to make adequate provision for requiring the railroad company to keep its tracks in proper order, to maintain paving on either side of the rails at its own expense and to regulate and keep the grades in conformity with the direction of the commissioner of public works. Despite these objections the resolution was passed over the mayor's veto.[1]

In 1892 another special franchise was granted by resolution of the common council for the construction of a double-track railroad on its route as extended on Fifty-third street from Ninth avenue to Seventh avenue.[2] It was stipulated that this franchise be sold at public auction pursuant to the state Railroad Law. Horse, steam or overhead trolley power was forbidden; the work was to be done under the direction of the commissioner of public works of the city; cars were to run as often as public convenience might require; and no passenger was to be charged more than a five-cent fare. At the time of sale the purchasing company had to deposit with the city comptroller five hundred thousand dollars as a guarantee of good faith that the road would be constructed: otherwise this sum would be forfeited to the city.

In addition to these franchises the Ninth Avenue Company has trackage rights, but no franchise, for the north

[1] *Proceedings of the Board of Aldermen*, vol. 168, p. 1383.
[2] *Ibid.*, vol. 208, pp. 73-78.

track on Fulton street, between Greenwich and Washington streets.[1]

The company on March 12, 1892, leased its property and franchises to the Houston, West Street and Pavonia Ferry Railroad Company for a term of ninety-nine years at an annual rental of six per cent on its eight hundred thousand dollars capital stock for the first five years and eight per cent thereafter;[2] and further agreed to pay all taxes, including a corporation tax of twenty-five hundred dollars. On December 12, 1893, the Houston, West Street and Pavonia Ferry Railroad Company was merged in the Metropolitan Street Railway Company.[3] The property of the Ninth Avenue Company is now operated under lease by the New York Railways Company.[4]

[1] *Report of the Public Service Commission, First District, State of New York*, 1913, vol. v, p. 1032.

[2] *Annual Report of the New York Railways Company for the year ending June 30, 1918*, p. 28.

[3] *Cf. infra*, ch. viii.

[4] *Annual Report of the New York Railways Company for the year ending June 30, 1918*, pp. 1, 28.

CHAPTER III

THE FIGHT FOR BROADWAY
1852 TO 1884

BROADWAY, the principal residential and business street of the city, was, of all the streets and avenues, the one most sought after by the crafty franchise-seekers. On July 16, 1852, Jacob Sharp, William Menzies, D. R. Martin, Freeman Campbell and twenty-six others petitioned the common council for permission to construct a surface railroad on Broadway from South ferry to Fifty-ninth street.[1] The property-owners along Broadway, fearing a railroad would ruin them, protested vigorously.[2] After a few months the agitation subsided, and the board of aldermen, on November 19, 1852, and the board of assistant aldermen, on December 6 of the same year, passed the ordinance[3] notwithstanding the fact that no less than half a dozen other applications, each of which proposed terms more favorable to the interest of the city, had been submitted.[4]

Alexander T. Stewart and others agreed not to charge a greater fare than three cents to each passenger and in addition to pay a license fee for each car which was not to exceed one thousand dollars per year. Thomas A. Davies and others were willing to give the city one cent for every

---
[1] *Proceedings of the Board of Aldermen*, vol. xlvii, p. 117.
[2] *Ibid.*, vol. xlviii, pp. 13, 62-69, 108-109, 124-125, 156, 187, 196, 269, 532.
[3] Valentine, David T., *Ferry Leases and Railroad Grants*, pp. 243-248.
[4] *Proceedings of the Board of Aldermen*, vol. xlviii, pp. 530-537.

five-cent fare collected. In another petition Davies, D. H. Haight, Stephen Storms and others offered to carry passengers for three cents each, or to pay the city ten thousand dollars per year for ten years with the privilege of charging each passenger a five-cent fare. William McMurray and Henry Hilton solicited the grant at a five-cent fare with a bonus to the city of one hundred thousand dollars a year. John La Farge and his associates offered a three-cent fare. Watts Sherman and others agreed to pay the city one cent for every five-cent fare. A wave of indignation swept over the city when these facts became known.[1]

Mayor Kingsland in vetoing the resolution, December 18, 1852, reviewed the offers of the competing petitioners and pointed out that any one of them would result in a far greater financial return to the city than the grant which had been authorized by the council. He also plainly stated that if the community demanded the construction of a railroad through any one of the thoroughfares of the city, it was the duty of the councilmen to grant that accommodation, but added that it was equally their duty not to lose sight of the rights and interests of the city, by refusing to grant it to those who would construct it on the most favorable terms and who would be willing to pay the largest amount for the privilege.[2]

In spite of public opposition and the praiseworthy veto of the mayor, the councilmen threatened to repass the resolution.[3] To prevent this action, Thomas A. Davies and Courtlandt Palmer brought suit in the Superior Court against the mayor, aldermen, and commonalty.[4] As a re-

[1] *New York Evening Post*, July 17, 1852; November 20, 23, 1852.
[2] *Proceedings of the Board of Aldermen*, vol. xlviii, p 533.
[3] *New York Evening Post*, December 30, 1852; *New York Tribune*, December 30, 1852.
[4] Davies *v.* The Mayor &c. of New York City, New York Superior Court, Duer's Cases, vol. viii, p. 464.

sult a restraining injunction was issued by Judge William W. Campbell,[1] a copy of which was duly served on each member of the common council. The councilmen, however, did not heed this injunction, for two days later, on December 29, 1852, the ordinance was repassed by a vote of fifteen to three, Alderman Alonzo A. Alvord not voting.[2]

As soon as this action had been taken, Alderman Oscar W. Sturtevant presented a preamble and resolutions stating that Judge Campbell, "without color of law or justification, assumed the prerogative of directing and controlling the municipal legislation of this city. . . . [If] such . . . unwarrantable interference be submitted to or tolerated without just rebuke . . . the whole municipal legislation of this city [will] be subjected to the caprice or interested views of any judge. . . ."[3]

The public was astounded at this action and steps were at once taken to punish the aldermen for contempt.[4] The case was bitterly contested, the able array of counsel for the aldermen vainly advancing every argument in favor of their clients.[5] Alderman Sturtevant, as the author of the resolution, was sentenced to a term of fifteen days in the city prison and fined two hundred and fifty dollars, to be paid to the city treasury, together with court costs. The other aldermen with the exception of Alderman Wesley Smith, who expressed regret and apologized to the court, were likewise fined. This decision of the Superior Court was sustained by the Court of Appeals.[6]

[1] Davies v. Mayor &c., *op. cit.*, vol. viii, pp. 468-469.
[2] *Proceedings of the Board of Aldermen*, vol. xlviii, p. 641.
[3] *Ibid.*, p. 643; Davies v. The Mayor &c. of New York City, New York Superior Court, Duer's Cases, vol. viii, pp. 469-470.
[4] *Ibid.*, p. 463.
[5] *Ibid.*, pp. 473-478.
[6] The People v. Compton *et al.*, New York Superior Court, Duer's Reports, vol. viii, pp. 545-573.

THE FIGHT FOR BROADWAY

This first Broadway grant was afterward declared invalid by the Court of Appeals [1] on the ground that construction had not been commenced in time to bring it under the general confirmatory act of 1854. Thus the work of the "forty thieves," as the councilmen were known in those early days, was without result and the attempt to construct a surface railroad on Broadway had failed for the time being.[2]

[1] Milhau v. Sharp, 27 N. Y., 611.

[2] It is interesting to note the conditions laid down in this abortive grant to Jacob Sharp and his associates in 1852. In the first place, the tracks were to be laid under the direction of the street commissioner, in or near the middle of the streets, the outer rails to be not more than twelve feet six inches apart and to be laid flush with the pavement; that the inner portion of the rails should be equal in height with the outer, and that the groove should not be more than one inch wide unless some other type of rail was approved by the street commissioner or the city council; the space between the rails and for one foot on each side was to be kept in repair by the grantees. New cars were to be used and were to be equipped with all modern improvements; passengers were not to be permitted to stand in the aisle or on the platform, and any car having all its seats occupied was not to take on other passengers. Cars with horses attached were not to exceed forty-five feet in length, and in making stops they were not to obstruct crossings; only one stop in each block was permitted, unless the blocks should be of "extraordinary length" or the weather should be rainy. An attendant was to be present at every appointed stopping place in the crowded streets and his duty was to assist passengers in and out of the cars. The grantees were to keep in readiness "a number of sleighs adequate to the public accommodation" when the travel of the cars might be obstructed by snow. Broadway, south of Fourteenth street, was to be swept and cleaned every morning, except Sundays, and the sweepings carried away before eight o'clock during the summer season, and before nine o'clock in the winter. North of Fourteenth street the sweeping was to be done as often as twice a week when weather conditions permitted. The fare was to be five cents from one point to another on the route and on such combined systems of routes as might thereafter be adopted by means of cars and transient omnibuses. As compensation the city was to receive for the first ten years the car license fee allowed by law at the date when the franchise was granted. At the expiration of this period a further license

The opposition to a Broadway surface railroad below Union Square continued to be so persistent and powerful that the franchise-grabbers resolved to make application for a railroad paralleling it. Accordingly, Assemblyman Dixon on March 19, 1857, introduced a bill at Albany authorizing John A. Kennedy and others to lay a road on Seventh avenue, from Fifty-ninth street to Broadway, thence down Broadway to University Place; down University Place, Green and Canal streets to West Broadway, and thence through College Place to Park Place.[1] Several petitions were filed in opposition to the measure [2] and it failed to pass. When the council learned of the introduction of this bill they virtuously resolved that public emergency did not necessitate the construction of such a road, that the citizens of New York city were wholly opposed to it, and that its legislative authorization would be unwise.[3]

By this time it was clearly evident that the mass of the people as well as the property-owners were determined to keep Broadway clear. Broadway was the "Fifth Avenue" of the mid-nineteenth century; it was the notable route for all civic and military processions.[4]

The second attempt to steal Broadway was made in 1859. On October 20 of that year the New York and Yonkers Railroad Company, which had been organized under the

fee could be prescribed by the common council with permission of the legislature. Should the grantees refuse to consent to the increased payment, the road with all its equipment and appurtenances was to be surrendered to the city at a fair and just evaluation. Valentine, David T., *Ferry Leases and Railroad Grants*, pp. 243-247.

[1] *New York State Assembly Journal, 1857*, 80th Session, p. 783.
[2] *Ibid.*, pp. 1070, 1157; *Senate Journal*, pp. 767, 801.
[3] *Proceedings of the Board of Aldermen*, vol. lxvi, pp. 25-26.
[4] *New York State Assembly Journal, 1857*; 80th Session, pp. 1070, 1157; *Senate Journal*, pp. 767, 801.

General Railroad Act of 1850,[1] petitioned the common council for permission to lay tracks in certain streets of the city. To conceal their purpose the projectors of the new road widely advertised it as the "Yonkers Road" which was to connect Yonkers with New York. As a matter of fact the road was to be constructed by the New York and Harlem Railroad Company and all cars were to run over the tracks of the latter company to Eighth avenue. From Eighth avenue they were to operate a double track to be laid through Fifty-ninth street to Seventh avenue to Greenwich avenue to Sixth avenue to Eighth street; thence a single track was to extend to Greene street to Waverly Place to Wooster street to Canal street to West Broadway; along West Broadway to College Place to Barclay street to Broadway. The ordinance also authorized a double-track line up Green street to University Place to Broadway to Forty-fourth street.[2]

This route was extremely valuable even though it did not include lower Broadway. Undoubtedly the petitioners hoped that at some future time the opportune moment would present itself for securing the whole of lower Broadway. The "Yonkers Road" scheme enabled its promoters to evade the law of 1854, which required the consent of property-owners along the proposed route. By commencing the road in Westchester county, north of Spuyten Duyvil, they were able to get around the statute which related only to railroads "commencing and ending within the city limits." It was currently reported that a mile or two of track was to be laid outside the city limits, that being sufficient in the opinion of the company to circumvent the law.[3]

[1] *Laws of the State of New York, 1850*; ch. 104.
[2] *Proceedings of the Board of Councilmen*, vol. lxxvi, pp. 658-659.
[3] *Ibid.*, p. 995.

The state legislators, ably supported by lobbyists, were eager to grant this franchise and a spirited race took place between City Hall and Albany. The aldermen won by rushing the ordinance through both branches on December 7, 1859.[1]

The conditions attached to the grant were trifling. Improved patterns of grooved iron rails were to be laid along the proposed route so as not to impede or obstruct the ordinary use of the streets and the avenues, nor to interfere with the water-courses. The company was to relay all pavements which might be taken up for the purpose of laying the rails, and to keep the same in good repair. It was further provided that no motive power except horses could be used below the intersection of Exterior street and Eighth avenue. Cars were to be operated in both directions as often as public convenience might require and in accordance with such " reasonable directions " as the common council might from time to time prescribe. The company was authorized to arrange with the Sixth and Eighth avenue railroad companies for the use of their tracks wherever feasible. The rate of fare was not to exceed five cents, and the company was to pay such annual license fee for each car as the council might determine. This annual tax was subsequently fixed at fifty dollars.

This grant was immediately vetoed by Mayor Tiemann on several grounds: First, that it had been hurriedly adopted by the board of councilmen and the board of aldermen on the same night, contrary to law; secondly, that it was an indirect means of stealing Broadway; thirdly, that the people of Westchester county were amply provided for by the Hudson River Railroad and there was, therefore, no necessity for any further grant in that direction. In the

[1] *Proceedings of the Board of Councilmen*, vol. lxxvi, pp. 920-923 *Proceedings of the Board of Aldermen*, vol. lxxvi, p. 507.

fourth place, no right was reserved, as in the case of the grants to the Sixth and Eighth avenue roads, to take over the property at cost. And, lastly, the only part of the proposed line needed within the city limits was on Broadway from Barclay street to Fifty-ninth street. This part, however, in the opinion of the mayor, ought to yield a large annual revenue to the city, and he appended to his message two communications in which attractive financial offers were made for a franchise for this route. D. Henry Haight, Edwin Hoyt, Amos B. Eno, Aaron Arnold, Nicholas Ludlow and John B. Phelps, all responsible men, offered a million dollars or an annual license fee of seventy thousand dollars. The second communication was from D. R. Martin and others who offered fifty thousand dollars a year for the privilege. The resolution was not passed over the mayor's veto.

By 1860 the wave of municipal reform which had begun a few years earlier had spent itself without dislodging the undesirable elements in the city government. The "Tweed Ring," instead of being ousted, was expanding its operations; it controlled the primaries and carried the elections.[1] Honest councilmen were a rarity.

This was the situation when Governor Morgan, in his message to the legislature on January 3, 1860, pointed out the necessity of more surface railways in Upper Manhattan to accommodate the rapidly increasing population. He advised that franchise grants be made a source of revenue to the city, and further recommended that the council of New York city be stripped of all control over future grants.[2] Already the relations between the state legislature and the local authorities of the Metropolis were strained to the

[1] Myers, Gustavus, *History of Tammany Hall*, pp. 233-234.
[2] *New York State Assembly Journal, 1860*, 83rd Session, pp. 33-34.

breaking point, hence the legislators were not slow to act upon the governor's suggestion. A bill to this effect was introduced in the Assembly on January 16, 1860, and its passage by that body by a vote of 60 to 0 [1] indicated to some degree at least the consensus of public opinion in regard to the common council. This measure was rejected by the Senate,[2] which proceeded to enact an amended bill, more sweeping in its content. This Senate bill was adopted by the Assembly [3] and approved by Governor Morgan on February 6, 1860.[4]

By this act the legislature directed that it should not be lawful thereafter to lay, construct, or operate any railroad on any of the streets or avenues of New York city, "wherever such railroad may commence or end, except under the authority and subject to the regulations and restrictions which the legislature may hereafter grant and provide." [5] This act, however, was not to affect the operation "as far as laid" of any railroad then constructed or in process of construction and duly authorized. Furthermore, it was not to impair any valid grant for a railroad in New York city previous to January 1, 1860.

The councilmen naturally frowned upon this action of the state legislature. Even before the act became a law the aldermen in a resolution passed January 30, 1860, resolved that the home-rule privileges of the city were being grossly violated, and that the bills before the legislature were an indirect contravention of the guaranteed rights, privileges, and immunities of the citizens of this city; the said bills by their

[1] *New York State Assembly Journal, 1860*, 83rd Session, p. 226.
[2] *New York State Senate Journal, 1860*, 83rd Session, pp. 116, 139.
[3] *New York State Assembly Journal, 1860*, 83rd Session, p. 226.
[4] *New York State Senate Journal, 1860*, 83rd Session, p. 179.
[5] *Laws of the State of New York, 1860*; ch. 10.

provisions having in contemplation the deprivation of the inhabitants of this city of all control, right, title and interest over the streets, avenues, and public places and highways located in said city, . . . without the sanction or consent of its corporate authorities, the agents and representatives of its citizens, thus virtually creating companies or corporations possessing powers and privileges superior to the representatives of the people by conferring upon said companies or corporations a monopoly of our principal streets and highways.[1]

This protest made little impression either upon the governor, to whom a copy was transmitted,[2] or upon the people of the city. They had been fleeced so many times by the city legislators that they were once more turning to the state legislature for relief.[3] Even from this source they were not at all certain that they would secure the desired results. This feeling was voiced by the daily press, for, as one editor wrote: " It is of very little consequence to the people by which class of robbers they are despoiled. That they will be plundered by one or the other is certain; and it is only a choice of evils of which it is very hard to choose the best."[4] At any rate, the scene of franchise-granting was transferred for the time being from the city hall to the state capitol.

In 1859, before the franchise power was taken out of the hands of the council, a number of bills providing for valuable railroad grants in New York city were passed by the Assembly,[5] only to be killed in the Senate by a handful of resolute, inflexible rural senators.[6]

[1] *Proceedings of the Board of Aldermen*, vol. lxxvii, pp. 173-174.
[2] *Ibid.*, p. 175.
[3] They had sought relief from the legislature in 1854.
[4] *New York Herald*, February 2, 1860.
[5] *New York State Assembly Journal, 1859*; 82nd Session, pp. 1100-1102; 1111, 1131-1132.
[6] *New York State Senate Journal, 1859*; 82nd Session, p. 639.

During the opening days of the session of 1860 various representatives of the interests concerned in supplying the city with transportation facilities came forward with a number of additional projects for street railroads. The legislature was soon confronted with a multitude of railroad schemes. By the middle of March no less than twenty-four projects, which included practically all the remaining thoroughfares of any value, had been incorporated into bills. These measures proposed street surface railroads for Avenues A and B,[1] Avenue C and Thirty-fourth street,[2] Avenue D,[3] from Barclay street to South ferry,[4] Broadway,[5] Eleventh avenue and Twenty-third street,[6] Grand street,[7] Houston street,[8] Greenwich street,[9] Lexington avenue, [10] South and West streets,[11] Seventh avenue,[12] Tenth avenue and Forty-second street,[13] and many other streets.[14]

Various schemes were resorted to in order to avoid public attention and criticism; for instance, Assemblyman Jaques of New York city introduced a bill entitled "An Act for the better protection of strangers and citizens in the City of New York, and to incorporate the New York Passenger and Baggage Line Company." [15] The true purpose of this act was disclosed when Mr. Jaques reported it out of the judiciary committee amended so as to read " An Act for the better protection of strangers and citizens in the City of New York, and to incorporate the New York Pas-

[1] *New York State Assembly Journal, 1860*; 83rd Session, p. 194.
[2] *Ibid.*, p. 871.
[3] *Ibid.*, p. 351.
[4] *Ibid.*, p. 769.
[5] *Ibid.*, pp. 422-485.
[6] *Ibid.*, p. 271.
[7] *Ibid.*, p. 347.
[8] *Ibid.*, p. 739.
[9] *Ibid.*, p. 666.
[10] *Ibid.*, p. 420.
[11] *Ibid.*, p. 287.
[12] *Ibid.*, p. 230.
[13] *Ibid.*, p. 350.
[14] *Ibid.*, pp. 93, 227, 495, 373-387, 512, 524.
[15] *Ibid.*, p. 543.

senger and Baggage Line Company by the construction of a surface railroad on Broadway, and other streets and avenues."[1]

Of the two dozen New York city railroad bills introduced, the most important was the "Gridiron Bill."[2] This measure was identical with the "Yonkers Road" franchise, which Mayor Tiemann had vetoed, except that it granted the additional right to lay tracks down Broadway from the Astor House to South ferry. This bill was no sooner introduced than property-owners,[3] civic bodies,[4] and the press[5] began to protest against its passage. The legislature was also urged at this time to enact in the interest of the taxpayers a law providing for the sale of all public franchises at auction. While this suggestion passed unheeded, public opinion was so aroused that the "Gridiron Bill" was dropped.[6]

Of the many New York city street-railway franchise bills which poured into the legislature in 1860 only five were favorably reported by the Assembly Committee on Cities and Villages, and each of these was almost devoid of essential conditions. Chairman Pond in reporting the measures, after expanding on the supremacy of the legislature, endeavored to justify the committee's action: he explained the rapid growth of the city, called attention to the fact that the surface cars of the city were carrying twenty-five millions of passengers annually, and that the existing roads were wholly inadequate to meet the city's constantly increasing demands on transportation. He further advocated

[1] *New York State Assembly Journal, 1860*, 83rd Session, p. 603.
[2] *New York State Senate Journal, 1860*, 83rd Session, p. 67.
[3] *New York State Assembly Journal, 1860*, 83rd Session, p. 597.
[4] *New York Tribune*, January 31, 1860.
[5] *Ibid.*, January 27, 1860.
[6] *New York State Assembly Journal, 1860*, 83rd Session, p. 641.

constructing railroads in such parts of the city as were then without sufficient means of access to the business sections; and, in conclusion, declared that public interest demanded the construction of the proposed surface railroads.[1]

Governor Edwin D. Morgan was a courageous and sagacious man, whose personal and public life was of the highest character; although of the same political faith as the majority party in the legislature,[2] he vetoed all five grants. He took occasion to rebuke the legislators for their failure to impose suitable conditions, and especially in not providing for a substantial financial return to the city. He emphasized the fact that the legislators should not have sacrificed permanent interests for temporary advantages, and added that the privileges proposed to be conferred in these acts were deemed to be of great pecuniary value and that

responsible individuals stand ready to pay a large bonus into the treasury of the city of New York for the franchises conferred upon the persons named in these bills without cost or equivalent. . . . The bills to which I am constrained to interpose my objections are grants of power in perpetuity.

Ordinary prudence would suggest that this should be avoided. Powers that are useful today, under the changing circumstances of communities and of municipal operations, may, a few years hence, become objectionable. Hence it is that the exclusive benefits of patents are limited, the existence of corporations circumscribed within certain periods, ferry franchises defined and restricted. The whole genius of our government requires that privileges granted, especially those of pecuniary value, or affecting the public convenience, shall,

---

[1] *New York State Assembly Documents*, 83rd Session, Doc. no. 106, pp. 1-7.

[2] Alexander, D. S., *A Political History of the State of New York* (N. Y., 1906-1909), vol. ii, p. 248; Appleton's *Cyclopedia of American Biography*, vol. iv, p. 398.

after a certain time, cease, and the power of revision and amendment be exercised in accordance with the requirements of public interest.[1]

Lobbyists, railroad agents, and other interested individuals anxiously and impatiently listened to this message. A thrill of satisfaction must have penetrated their ranks as they listened to the bitter attacks on the Governor by the "people's representatives." All five measures were enacted into law over Governor Morgan's veto, April 17, 1860.[2] There is little doubt that the legislators were bribed; just what the various members received will probably never be known. Various estimates of the cost to the promoters of from twenty-five thousand dollars to five hundred thousand dollars have been made.[3] One of the leading New York newspapers which had given generous support to the election of the legislature of 1860, stated at the close of the session that it did not believe it possible "that another body so reckless, not merely of right but of decency—not merely corrupt, but shameless—will be assembled in our halls of legislation within the next ten years."[4] The value of the five grants was estimated at the time to be from fifteen million to twenty million dollars.

These acts authorized surface railways in South, West and other avenues;[5] in Avenue D, East Broadway and other streets and avenues;[6] Seventh avenue;[7] Fourteenth

---

[1] *New York State Assembly Journal, 1860*, 83rd Session, pp. 1339-1341.
[2] *New York State Assembly Journal, 1860*; 83rd Session, pp. 1363-66.
[3] *New York Herald*, April 19, 1860.
[4] *New York Tribune*, April 18, 1860.
[5] *Laws of the State of New York, 1860*; ch. 511.
[6] *Ibid.*, ch. 512.
[7] *Ibid.*, ch. 513.

street;[1] Tenth avenue and Forty-second street.[2] All five roads covered by these grants were subsequently constructed; they became the property of the Bleecker Street and Fulton Ferry Railroad Company, the Broadway and Seventh Avenue Railroad Company, the Central Park, North and East River Railroad Company, the Forty-second Street and Grand Street Ferry Railroad Company, and the Dry Dock, East Broadway and Battery Railroad Company.[3]

Each of the original acts named a group of individuals as grantees. They were given the right to convey passengers and freight and were required to run cars as frequently as public convenience should demand, subject to reasonable regulations of the common council. They were also required to pay the same license fee for passenger cars as that being paid by other New York city railroads. The same requirement was made in regard to fares. The acts further directed and required the common council to grant permission to the several grantees and their assigns for the construction and operation of the railroads along the streets enumerated. The persons named in the acts were authorized to use any portion of other railroad tracks already laid in the streets mentioned in these grants. Compensation for the use of the tracks of other railroad companies was to be determined by agreement with the owners, or by court proceedings such as were available to railroad companies for the condemnation of land. Each act stipulated that " in all cases the use of said streets and avenues for the purposes of said railroad, as herein authorized, shall be considered one of the uses for which the Mayor, Aldermen and Commonalty of said city hold said streets and avenues."

[1] *Laws of the State of New York, 1860*; ch. 514.
[2] *Ibid.*, ch. 515.
[3] *Infra*, ch. iv; Wilcox, Delos F., *Municipal Franchises*, vol. ii, p. 113.

Another specific requirement was that the mayor, common council, and other officers of the city should " do such acts within their respective departments, as may be needful to promote the construction and protect the operation of the said railroad as provided in this law." No stipulation as to time or mode of construction was made.

The common council at first refused to recognize the legality of these franchise acts, and both branches on April 20, 1860, directed the counsel of the corporation to take proper legal steps " to restrain and prevent the use or occupation of any street for a railroad without the consent of the corporation." However, in a resolution adopted January 4, 1862, the council petitioned the legislature to repeal the grants.[1] The legislature paid little attention to the request and the several repeal bills which had previously been introduced in both houses [2] failed of passage.

In the autumn of 1862 the Seventh Avenue Railroad Company began to lay tracks on Seventh avenue and other streets. The board of councilmen at once directed the corporation counsel to apply for a restraining writ.[3] The property-owners, in the meantime, had obtained a temporary injunction restraining the Seventh Avenue Railroad Company from proceeding with its work. This injunction, however, was dissolved [4] and the case was carried to the Court of Appeals, where the franchise grant was declared to be constitutional.[5] This decision virtually settled the question of the constitutionality of the other grants.

[1] *Proceedings of the Board of Councilmen*, vol. lxxxiv, pp. 756-757.
[2] *New York State Senate Journal, 1861*; 84th Session, pp. 121, 183-204; *New York State Assembly Journal, 1861*; 84th Session, pp. 71-72.
[3] *Proceedings of the Board of Councilmen*, vol. lxxxviii, p. 94.
[4] *Proceedings of the Board of Aldermen*, vol. lxxxviii, p. 396.
[5] Mayor &c. of New York City *v.* The Second Avenue R. R. Co., 32 N. Y., 261.

A relatively small number of New York city surface railway franchise bills were introduced in either house of the legislature in 1861 [1] and not a single one was enacted into law. The legislators were thoroughly aware of the tremendous opposition created by the action of their predecessors; they were also cognizant of the fact that petitions were being circulated throughout the state asking for an investigation of the means by which the New York city franchises were passed.[2] The feeling of indignation was so great in the metropolis that Mayor Fernando Wood in his annual message argued for a separation of the city from the state. In his opinion, the city would be justified in the eyes of the country in " seeking a separation from a political association that has proved so emphatically a yoke, as grievous as it is dishonorable." [3]

In 1863 the effort to appropriate Broadway was again attempted. On February 27th of that year a measure was introduced in the Assembly [4] granting to George Law and others, the owners and managers of the Eighth avenue line, a surface railway franchise for Broadway. This bill made no provision for revenue to the city nor for keeping the streets in repair, nor did it subject the grantees to the usual laws governing corporations. Despite vigorous opposition,[5] there were indications that it would pass.[6] The city authorities, believing the measure to be unconstitutional and un-

[1] *New York State Senate Journal, 1861*; 84th Session, p. 324; *New York State Assembly Journal, 1861*; 84th Session, pp. 121, 424, 583-584.

[2] *New York Times*, January 3, 1861.

[3] *Documents of the Board of Aldermen, 1861*, pt. i, no. 1, pp. 6-8.

[4] *New York State Assembly Journal, 1863*; 86th Session, p. 329.

[5] *Ibid.*, pp. 420, 477, 533, 561, 571, 667, 691, 822, 865.

[6] *Ibid.*, pp. 914, 1274; *New York State Senate Journal, 1861*; 86th Session, pp. 288, 337, 352, 461; *New York Tribune*, Apr. 21, 22, 1863; *Proceedings of the Board of Aldermen*, vol. xc, p. 23.

just,[1] resolved to forestall it. Mayor George Opdyke, in a special message to the council on April 2, 1863, said that the great value attached to this franchise was well known, and that "parties of undoubted responsibility have offered two millions of dollars for it, while it is estimated to be worth at least double that amount"; that these same parties had offered to carry passengers for three-fifths of the rate of fare named in the bill then before the legislature, or, instead of this reduction, were willing to pay into the city or state treasury two hundred thousand dollars annually for a term of ten years.[2]

Having this information before them the common council, with the mayor's support, immediately prepared to rush through an ordinance issuing to the New York and Harlem Company a franchise for the much-coveted Broadway route. The promoters of the legislative bill, who were in favor of granting the franchise to the Eighth Avenue Company, procured injunctions restraining the aldermen from issuing *any* franchise for this particular line; but when a deputy-sheriff attempted to serve the injunctions upon the city fathers he was summarily expelled from the room; the doors were locked and guarded,[3] while the aldermen and councilmen proceeded to award the grant to the New York and Harlem Railroad Company. As their authority for issuing this franchise, the councilmen turned to the original charter of the New York and Harlem Company as amended in 1832, which empowered the mayor, aldermen and commonalty to extend the tracks of this company through such streets of the city as they from time to time might see fit.

[1] Certain persons felt that the city councilmen were simply jealous of the legislators for selfish reasons; see *New York Times*, April 22, 1863.
[2] *Proceedings of the Board of Aldermen*, vol. xc, pp. 23-25.
[3] *New York Tribune*, April 23, 1863; *New York Herald*, April 22, 1863.

In addition to the usual provisions regarding construction, rate of fare, motive power, type of car, and the convenience and comfort of passengers, this franchise required the New York and Harlem company to pay an annual license fee of twenty-five dollars for each car operated and ten per cent of the entire gross receipts. To all intents and purposes this grant was made in perpetuity.[1] The mayor in approving the measure stated that despite the well-known objections to a railroad on Broadway, he, nevertheless, felt constrained to sign the conciliar grant, especially in view of the fact that a bill then before the legislature, concerning a franchise for this same street, utterly disregarded the interests of the city; in his judgment there should be no hesitancy in making a choice between the two proposals. Under the conciliar grant to the New York and Harlem Company the road was expected to yield an annual revenue of thousands of dollars to the city treasury; up to that time no grant had been made which in any way approached this particular one in protecting the city's welfare.[2] In spite of the unanimous opposition to a railroad on Broadway, the public under the circumstances quite generally approved the action of the city officials.[3]

The legislators were greatly chagrined when they learned of the issuance of the franchise by the common council,[4] and April 23, 1863, the very day on which Mayor Opdyke signed the resolution granting the franchise to the New York and Harlem Company, the Assembly at Albany passed the Broadway bill with an amendment repealing that portion of the New York and Harlem Company's charter

---

[1] Valentine, David T., *Ferry Leases and Railroad Grants*, pp. 230-234.

[2] *Proceedings of the Board of Aldermen*, vol. xc, pp. 93-94.

[3] *New York Tribune*, April 23, 1863; *New York Times*, April 24, 1863; *New York Herald*, April 23, 1863.

[4] *New York Times*, April 22, 1863; *New York Tribune*, April 22, 1863.

which permitted extension of its road through the city streets under the direction of the city authorities.[1] At Albany the measure finally passed both houses [2] amid charges of gross corruption.[3] The truth of these charges was shown later when, upon complaint of Theodore McNamee, Assemblymen William Brown, of Monroe County, and Gideon Searles, of Cattaraugus County, were arrested on April 23 and hailed into court on the charge of receiving a bribe for their votes on the Broadway bill. According to the testimony of James R. Thompson, before the court, Brown was to receive four hundred dollars for his vote: two hundred dollars down and two hundred dollars after the bill had been passed. Other members who were under the influence of Brown were to be paid three hundred dollars each for casting their votes in favor of the bill.[4]

On April 24 a lengthy memorial was sent to Governor Horatio Seymour, signed by thousands of influential New York citizens, asking for the veto of the legislative bill.[5]

[1] *New York State Assembly Journal*, 1863, 86th Session, p. 1192.

[2] *Ibid.*, p. 1274; *New York State Senate Journal, 1863*, 86th Session, p. 787.

[3] *New York Tribune*, April 23, 1863; *New York Herald*, April 23, 1863.

[4] *New York Tribune*, April 25, 1863; *New York Times*, April 24, 1863.

[5] *New York Tribune*, April 24, 1863. The supporters of the bill urged Governor Seymour to approve the legislative measure on the ground that it would prevent the future passage of injurious legislation by the city authorities. He forcefully answered this argument as follows: "I am now urged to approve this act for the purpose of preventing improper action by the city government, and thus, by a vicious reasoning, two public measures, each improper in itself, are to receive the sanction of two official bodies because each is apprehensive that the other is to consummate a wrong. The dangerous facility which such reasoning lends to the adoption of bad measures, under the color of preventing worse by the others, how it misleads the conscience of those who entertain it, how it creates a scramble between public authorities, in the distribution of valuable franchises under the pretext of the public good, how demoralizing the tendency upon legislative bodies and upon all incumbents of public trust, is sufficiently obvious.

The governor promptly took such action on the ground that the measure was clearly an invasion of the corporate rights of the city and wholly unconstitutional in that it permitted the use of streets and avenues without the consent of the proper city officials, and without compensation to the city. He made an urgent plea for home rule for cities and pointed out, among other things, the great evils resulting from legislative interference in matters of local self-government; that measures of the greatest concern and importance were determined by men who had little or no knowledge of, and who often were not directly interested in, the localities for which they legislated. The transferring of appointments and jurisdiction from the locality to Albany tended to create a body of parasitic lobbyists who by their corrupt methods affected the character of much legislation.[1] In conclusion, the governor earnestly urged that the policy of legislative interference with local affairs be abandoned, for "the assumption of local and municipal jurisdiction and the centralization of power have proved destructive to the purity of our legislation and endangered the preservation of our rights and the maintenance of our political institutions."[2]

Meanwhile both the Eighth Avenue Railroad Company and the New York and Harlem Railroad Company began the struggle for possession of Broadway. The Eighth Avenue Company commenced laying tracks at the Battery, Fourteenth street and Broadway, and other places along the line. The New York and Harlem Company started

[1] "Much of the odium which frequently attaches to the character of representatives is due to the fact that they are the unconscious instruments of those skilled in the art of procuring or preventing the passage of laws."

[2] Lincoln, Charles Z., *Messages from the Governors of the State of New York* (Albany, 1909), vol. v, pp. 517-520.

THE FIGHT FOR BROADWAY

their line on Broadway at Union Square, between Thirteenth and Fourteenth streets, and near the Battery in Whitehall street, but this work was summarily stopped by service of an injunction granted by Judge Barbour of the New York City Superior Court on application of the Eighth Avenue Railroad Company.[1] The Eighth Avenue Company also was forced to suspend its work for the reason that it was then too late for the legislature to repass the franchise bill over the governor's veto.[2]

The next attempt to obtain a right of way on Broadway was made by the Dry Dock, East Broadway and Battery Railroad Company in 1866. This company was organized in 1863.[3] In addition to the usual franchise conditions it agreed to pay into the city treasury five per cent of the net proceeds of the company together with a license fee of fifty dollars for each two-horse car and twenty-five dollars for each one-horse car operated. Subsequently this company acquired the franchise for a railroad along certain streets and avenues, including Washington and Greenwich streets on the west, and Park Row to Broadway on the east.[4] By an act of the legislature passed May 1, 1866, this company was authorized to extend its lines.[5] Inasmuch as this road was a crosstown line, handling the heavy traffic from the North and East rivers, the company was determined to link up its east and west branches. Accordingly, on October 28, 1866, workmen began construction in Broadway by laying tracks from Ann to Fulton streets, it being the evident intention of the Dry Dock and East Broadway and Battery Company to extend its track from Fulton to Wash-

[1] *New York Tribune*, April 25 and 27, 1863.
[2] The legislature adjourned on May 10, 1863.
[3] *Infra*, ch. iv.
[4] *Laws of the State of New York, 1860*, ch. 512.
[5] Valentine, David T., *Ferry Leases and Railroad Grants*, pp. 418-419.

ington streets and thence to the Cortlandt street ferry. This short extension would greatly increase the value of the original franchise.

The city authorities at once took action, and an opinion submitted by Corporation Counsel O'Gorman to Mayor Hoffmann, November 9, 1866, declared that the company had no legal right to connect the Park Row and Fulton street termini. He further advised that the street department, through the police authorities, compel the removal of the rails. The company reluctantly complied with such an order.[1]

A bold and dishonest attempt, which eclipsed all others, was made to secure Broadway in 1869. On February 16th of that year Senator Genet introduced a bill entitled, "An Act to authorize the construction of a railroad in Broadway, Lexington Avenue, and certain other streets and avenues in the City of New York."[2] The grantees named in the bill were John Murphy, Joseph G. Jennings, Isaac Bell, Henry Leet, and fifteen others. They were authorized to operate a railroad along the following streets: commencing at South ferry, through Whitehall street and Broadway to Union Square, then to and through Fourth avenue to Twenty-third street to Lexington avenue with branch lines along Seventy-second and One Hundred and Tenth streets to Central Park. They were also to make connections with the Broadway and Seventh Avenue Railroad Company at Union Square. When a bill for supposedly the same purpose came from the Assembly many senators were astonished to find it entirely changed, even as to title.[3] It named

[1] *Proceedings of the Board of Aldermen, 1866*; vol. 104, pp. 86-91.

[2] *New York State Senate Journal, 1869*; 92nd Session, p. 162; *New York Tribune*, February 17, 1869.

[3] *New York State Assembly Journal, 1869*; 92nd Session, p. 329. This bill is printed in full in the New York Tribune of April 10, 1869.

as grantees John Kerr, John Cosgrove, John S. Martin and dozens of others, many of whom were obscure and unknown. This bill, which its sponsors proposed to rush through, authorized the construction and operation of a railroad on Broadway to Twenty-third street, to Lexington avenue, to Thirty-fourth street, to North river and on parts of Fifty-ninth, Seventy-second, Fourteenth, Duane, Chambers, and Fulton streets, Burling Slip, John street, Maiden Lane, Pearl and Wall streets, to the Wall street ferry and through Dey and West streets to Cortlandt street ferry. Near the conclusion of the measure was a provision allowing the construction of a road through Fifth avenue, provided the written consent of property-owners along that thoroughfare was obtained. A six-cent fare was practically allowed by the provision that the company was to charge the same rate as other companies which " should not be increased beyond one cent for each passenger without the consent of the legislature." Only two other conditions of importance were made: steam as a motive power was not to be used on any part of the line and the company was to reimburse the coach companies for their loss of business. The city was to receive no compensation whatever and the grant was made in perpetuity. The measure was bitterly opposed both within and without the legislature; several senators were especially antagonistic toward it. Senator O'Donnell moved to assess the capital stock of the company in the same manner and at the same rate as other real estate.[1] Not successful in this effort, the same senator offered an amendment requiring the consent of property-owners along the route.[2] Senator Morgan proposed an amendment for the sale of the franchise at public auction by the city comptroller, the proceeds to go into the city

[1] *New York State Senate Journal, 1869*; 92nd Session, p. 549.
[2] *Ibid.*, p. 550.

treasury.[1] Senator O'Donnell moved to amend the act so as to require the consent of the city council to make it effective. This motion was lost by a vote of two to one.[2] Another amendment was offered by Senator Morgan requiring the grantees to pay two million dollars into the city treasury in consideration of the franchise privilege; this amendment met the fate of its predecessors.[3]

Senator Folger, in the course of the debate, declared the franchise was worth five million dollars, yet the Senate was asked to *give* this privilege to a few men forever. He proposed that the measure should not go into force for thirty days after becoming a law. For the first twenty days of this period the incorporators of the bill should have the privilege of paying two million dollars to the city; if they failed to do so, then for the remaining ten days any person or persons should have the same privilege, and the deposit being made, such party or parties should be entitled to the franchise. If at the expiration of the thirty-day period no deposit had been made, the incorporators named in the bill were to enjoy full possession of the grant. This amendment was likewise defeated.[4]

As soon as the contents of the bill became known in New York city, Alexander T. Stewart, one of the city's leading merchants, immediately sent a public message to W. W. Campbell, chairman of the Senate Railroad Committee, offering to pay at least two million dollars for the franchise then under consideration. This offer was ignored.[5]

The opposition to the measure did not diminish. It was currently rumored that the "Tweed Ring" wanted the

---

[1] *New York State Senate Journal, 1869*; 92nd Session, p. 550.
[2] *Ibid.*, p. 550.
[3] *Ibid.*, p. 552.
[4] *Ibid.*, pp. 551-552; *New York Tribune*, April 10, 1869.
[5] *New York Tribune*, April 10, 1869.

franchise for themselves and that the bill before the legislature did not give them the desired control.[1] At any rate the act was shelved by the Senate [2] and the Broadway railway project was again postponed.

The city of New York instead of securing relief from the legislature, was for fifteen years, 1860-1875, subjected to the most wilful and evil laws relating to railroad franchises. Indeed conditions were so bad that the Constitutional Commission of 1874 resolved to curb the unlimited power of the legislature in respect to city railroad grants.[3] Accordingly an amendment was framed which forbade the state legislators to pass any law authorizing the construction of street railways except with the consent of the local authorities having control of the streets and the majority of the owners of property. In case, however, that the majority of the owners whose property abutted upon that portion of each street in which the railway was to be constructed, failed to consent to such construction, application might then be made to the general term of the Supreme Court for the appointment of three commissioners to take testimony as to the necessity of constructing the proposed railway. If the report of these commissioners was favorable, and upon confirmation thereof by the court, their findings would be taken in lieu of the majority consents of the property-owners.

This amendment, which met with the voters' approval,

---

[1] See New York City press, April 10, 1869.

[2] *New York State Senate Journal, 1869*; 92nd Session, p. 743.

[3] Prince, L. B., *The Proposed Amendments of the Constitution of the State of New York (1874): Their History, Nature and Advantages* (N. Y., 1874), pp. 9-10; Goodnow, F. J., *Municipal Problems* (N. Y., 1907), pp. 80-81. In 1867 a pamphlet entitled "Communications to the Constitutional Convention on Special Railway Legislation," by H. B. Willson, urged that the legislature be stripped of power to grant railway franchises.

produced a lull in the granting of railway franchises in the cities of this state.¹ Nevertheless it did not prevent promotion schemes for railroads in the more important thoroughfares of New York city.² The metropolitan public was still thoroughly antagonistic to a privately owned railway on Broadway, and it is interesting to note that Theodore E. Tomlinson and others petitioned the board of aldermen, February 11, 1879, " to cause a surface railroad to be constructed on Broadway, to be run by or under the supervision of the corporate authorities, so that they derive the benefit of the franchise." ³

Just a month later, March 11, the question of a Broadway railway was again brought up in the board of aldermen. Alderman William R. Roberts, after explaining the importance of the Broadway railroad project to the property-owners and to the public in general, offered a set of resolutions whereby no franchise for a railroad on Broadway would be approved by the board of aldermen unless it embodied the following propositions: (1) a continuous line from the Battery to Central Park, at a rate of fare not to exceed five cents for the entire length of the road; (2) the sale of the franchise at public auction to the highest bidder, on such terms and with such restrictions as shall be for the best interests of the city, the property-owners along the line and the traveling public. These salutary resolutions were lost by a vote of fifteen to three.⁴ Alderman William Sauer then proposed to give the franchise to the Broadway and Seventh Avenue Railroad Company. This corporation would be required to operate the most improved horse-cars

---
[1] Wilcox, Delos F., *Municipal Franchises*, vol. ii, p. 121.
[2] *Proceedings of the Board of Aldermen, 1879*; vol. 153, p. 389.
[3] *Ibid.*, p. 225.
[4] *Ibid.*, pp. 357-359.

THE FIGHT FOR BROADWAY

as often as public convenience might demand, and not more than a five-cent fare was to be charged for the entire route. As a consideration for the franchise, the company was to pay semi-annually to the city treasury five per cent of the gross receipts from fares "collected on the extension." The company was also to be required to remove all snow from the carriage-way on Broadway from Fourteenth street to Bowling Green, and to keep the pavement in good repair between the tracks and for two feet on the outer side of each rail. These resolutions further proposed to allow the Twenty-third Street Railway Company, which was practically controlled by the same men who owned the Broadway and Seventh avenue road, to connect the tracks leased by it from the Bleecker Street and Fulton Ferry Railroad Company at the junction of Bleecker street and Broadway with the new tracks to be laid on Broadway. Also, "for the further accommodation of the public," the New York and Harlem Railroad Company was empowered to extend its horse-car line on Fourth avenue so as to connect with the authorized Broadway tracks. It has already been shown that the Broadway and Seventh avenue line was controlled by the New York and Harlem Company.[1] This plan proposed, therefore, to give different companies, controlled by the same individuals, the most valuable surface railway franchises which were within the power of the councilmen to bestow. This set of resolutions never went beyond the committee on railroads.[2]

At this same meeting of the board, Alderman Nicholas Haughton presented resolutions granting a Broadway franchise to the Forty-second Street, Manhattanville and St. Nicholas Avenue Railroad Company. The conditions imposed were identical with those laid down in the resolutions

---
[1] *Cf. supra*, p. 83.
[2] *Proceedings of the Board of Aldermen, 1879*; vol. 153, pp. 360-364.

offered by Alderman Sauer: a five-cent fare for each passenger; three per cent of gross receipts to be paid to the city; the streets to be kept in good repair and snow removed from Fourteenth street to Battery Place.[1]

At this meeting of March 11, 1879, a communication from John B. Haskin, on behalf of a reform group, set forth the arguments in favor of a municipal railway on Broadway. In the opinion of Mr. Haskin any railroad through Broadway should be managed and operated in the interests of the city; if, however, the city did not deem it wise to construct such a line, then the franchise should be sold at public auction to the highest responsible bidder. He further stated that if the council was determined to sell the franchise without putting it up at public auction, he would pay in gold therefor one million dollars within ten days from the making of the legal grant. If neither of these propositions was acceptable, he and others would form a corporation, similar to the organizations of August Belmont, William H. Appleton, and others, and of John Sloane, Pierre A. Lorillard and others, who had already made applications for a Broadway franchise. The new corporation would not charge more than five cents per passenger; would operate the most modern and up-to-date cars at public convenience; keep the whole of Broadway clean and in repair; and also pay into the city treasury, weekly, all over ten per cent of the net profits of the road, or twenty-five per cent of the net profits, whatever they might amount to, over and above the running expenses of the road, and upon a basis of seven per cent interest on the cost of building and equipping it. This resolution evidently was never reported by the committee on railroads.[2] No further action was taken by the councilmen during 1879; the promoters besieged the state legislature, but without results.[1]

[1] *Proceedings of the Board of Aldermen, 1879*; vol. 153, pp. 365-368.
[2] *Ibid.*, pp. 388-392.

THE FIGHT FOR BROADWAY

On November 6, 1880, the councilmen made another attempt to give the Broadway franchise to John Sloane, Pierre A. Lorillard, Albert Gallatin Stevens, Lawrence Kip and others. Their proposed line was to extend from South ferry to Seventeenth street; the company was to pay in to the city treasury five per cent of its gross receipts, and was to keep the pavement between the tracks in good repair. This resolution met the same fate as its predecessors.[2]

Thus in spite of many years of planning and scheming lower Broadway[3] was still without a railroad, and so continued until 1884. It is interesting to note that all the franchises that had thus far been proposed for this route were without time limit; they were, in other words, to all intents and purposes, granted in perpetuity.

[1] See *Senate and Assembly Journals for 1879 and 1880.*
[2] *Proceedings of the Board of Aldermen, 1880,* vol. 160, pp. 499-501.
[3] A franchise for Broadway, from Union Square north to Forty-fifth street, had been secured by legislative grant in 1860. *Infra*, pp. 119 *et seq.*

CHAPTER IV

HISTORY OF RAILWAYS INCORPORATED BETWEEN 1860 AND 1875

IT has already been noted that the legislative act of January 30, 1860, deprived the common council of the city of New York of its power to grant franchises for street surface railways,[1] and that thereafter such grants were to issue from the state legislature. The legislature continued to make such grants until January 1, 1875. During this period of fifteen years numerous railroad measures were introduced, having for their purport the obtainment of valuable franchise rights.[2] Of the many New York city railroad franchise bills introduced during this time twelve important ones were enacted into law, and it is the purpose of this chapter briefly to trace the franchise history of the companies receiving such grants.

1. THE CENTRAL PARK, NORTH AND EAST RIVER RAILROAD COMPANY

The Central Park, North and East River Railroad Company was incorporated on July 19, 1860, for a period of one hundred years with a capital stock of one million two hundred and fifty thousand dollars.[3] Its original franchise

---

[1] *Supra*, ch. iii.
[2] See index to *New York State Senate and Assembly Journals* for this period, and especially for 1860 and 1873.
[3] *Report of Public Service Commission, First District of New York State*, 1913, vol. v, p. 271.

was granted by a special legislative act passed on April 17, 1860,[1] which gave Charles W. Durant, Myron S. Clark, John Butler, Jr., and fifteen others, or their assigns, authority to build a railroad for the conveyance of passengers and freight along the following route: commencing at the intersection of Tenth avenue and Fifty-ninth street, along Tenth avenue to West Twelfth street to Greenwich street to Bat-

PLATE VIII

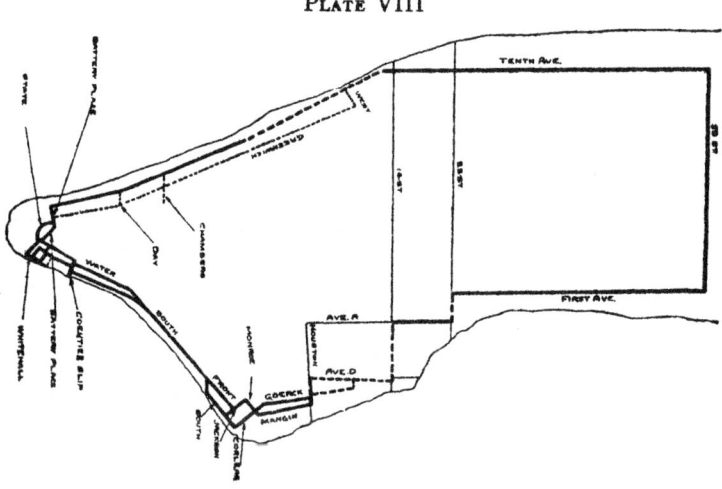

CENTRAL PARK, NORTH AND EAST RIVER RAILROAD COMPANY

- - - - - trackage rights obtained on tracks of other companies
. . . . . franchise routes neither constructed nor used by this company

tery Place; from Battery Place to State street, to Whitehall street, to South ferry; thence returning along Whitehall street to State street, to Bowling Green to connect with the line in Battery Place, " with the right to construct and maintain and use a double track " from West street through Chambers street to its intersection with Hudson street. A

[1] *Laws of the State of New York, 1860*, ch. 511.

branch was permitted to begin at the corner of Tenth avenue and Fifty-ninth street, running along Fifty-ninth street to First avenue to Twenty-third street to Avenue A to Fourteenth street to Avenue D to Houston street to Mangin street to Grand street to Corlears street to South street to Montgomery street to the junction of Front and South streets; from this point along South street to Old Slip to Water street to Whitehall street to South street to Coenties Slip to Front street. The act further provided for a branch in Broad street from Water to South streets to Houston street to Goerck street to Grand street to Monroe street to Jackson street to Front street. The company was to lay all necessary turnouts, switches, and to make connections with other surface railway lines. The conditions embodied in the grant were simple: the road was to be constructed in the most approved manner, cars were to run as often as public convenience might require, and the company was to be subject to "such reasonable rules and regulations in respect thereto" in the transportation of freight and passengers as the common council might by ordinance prescribe; the rate of fare and car licenses were to be the same as were then paid by other railroads operating in the city. The common council was authorized and required to grant permission to the persons named in the act for the construction and operation of the proposed road.

This act was one of several, affecting New York city street-railway measures, passed over Governor Morgan's veto. The governor insisted that the interests of the city were not properly safeguarded by a franchise which was granted in perpetuity and which guaranteed scarcely any financial remuneration to the municipality.[1]

The common council, pursuant to the provisions of the

[1] *New York State Assembly Journal, 1860*; 83rd Session, pp. 1339-41.

act, protestingly adopted a resolution on December 28, 1861, granting a franchise for this " belt line " route.¹

It was not until 1896 that any further franchise privileges were granted to this company. On April 14th of that year the common council passed a resolution over the mayor's veto granting an extension on the following streets:² commencing at the intersection of Dry street and West street and running easterly to Greenwich street and thence northerly to West Broadway (formerly College Place) with a double-track line to Vesey street to connect with an extension of the Metropolitan street railway. No additional stipulations were made in this franchise except that cable or underground electricity was to be the motive power used. Mayor Strong vetoed the grant because he felt that the company ought to be responsible for removing all accumulations of snow from streets through which the extensions were to be built, and that such work should be done under the immediate supervision of the commissioner of street cleaning.³

The Central Park, North and East River Railroad Company, like practically all the other street surface railway companies of New York city, has had an interesting, though somewhat stormy, career. From its inception it has entered into many trackage agreements with other companies which, however, have affected its financial rather than its franchise status.⁴

On October 14, 1892, the company leased its property for the remainder of its corporate existence to the Metropolitan Crosstown Railway Company at an annual rental

¹ *Proceedings of the Board of Aldermen*, vol. lxxxiv, pp. 448-51.
² *Ibid.*, vol. 222, pp. 60-62.
³ *Ibid.*, vol. 222, p. 61.
⁴ *Report of Public Service Commission, First District of the State of New York*, 1913, vol. v, pp. 277-279.

of eight per cent on its capital stock of one million eight hundred thousand dollars for the first five years, and nine per cent thereon thereafter.[1] The Metropolitan Crosstown Company afterward became merged in the Metropolitan Street Railway Company,[2] and when the latter company went into bankruptcy the Central Park, North and East River Railroad Company went into the hands of a receiver and the road and its franchises were ultimately sold, November 14, 1912, under a mortgage foreclosure, to Edward Cornell. Cornell and his wife in turn sold the property to the Belt Line Railway Corporation, which was simply the Central Park, North and East River Railroad Company reorganized. No new franchises have been received by it and the road is operated at present under an agreement with the New York Railways Company.[3]

2. THE FORTY-SECOND STREET AND GRAND STREET FERRY RAILROAD COMPANY

This company was incorporated on February 16, 1863, in accordance with the provisions of the General Railroad Law of 1850; it was capitalized at six hundred thousand dollars for a corporate life of one thousand years.[4] Like the Central Park, North and East River Railroad Company, just described, its original franchise was granted to John T. Conover and others by special legislative enactment over the veto of Governor Morgan.[5]

The line commenced at the Forty-second street ferry and

[1] *Report of Public Service Commission, op. cit.*, p. 276.
[2] *Infra*, ch. viii.
[3] *Annual Report of the New York Railways Company for the year ending June 30, 1918*, p. 1.
[4] *Report of the Public Service Commission, First District of the State of New York*, 1913, vol. v, p. 424.
[5] *Laws of the State of New York*, 1860, ch. 515.

extended eastward to Tenth avenue, thence along Tenth avenue to Thirty-fourth street to Broadway, down that thoroughfare to Twenty-third street, thence to Fourth avenue to Union Place to Fourteenth street to Avenue A to First street to Hudson street to Cameron street to Grand street ferry on the East river; returning through Grand street to Goerck street to Houston street and Second street to connect with the main line in Avenue A. Other provis-

PLATE IX

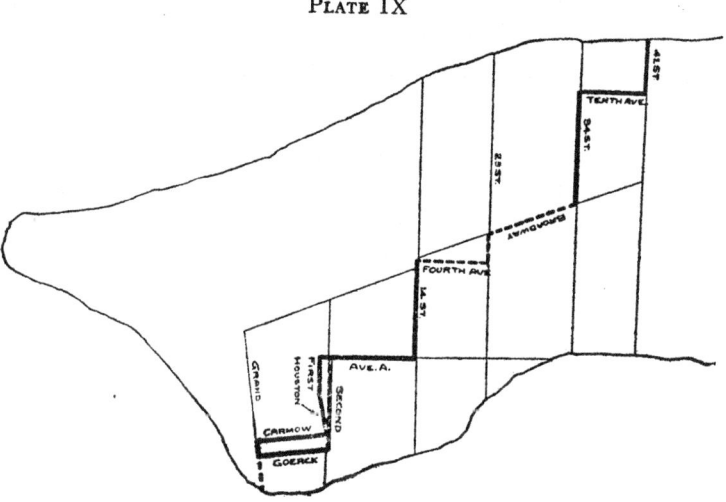

FORTY-SECOND STREET AND GRAND STREET FERRY RAILROAD COMPANY
- - - - - trackage rights obtained on tracks of other companies

ions of the act are identical with those contained in the Central Park, North and East River franchise.

The company has entered into several intercorporate relationships which have not affected its franchise. Its property was leased on April 6, 1893, to the Metropolitan Crosstown Railway Company for the remainder of the corporate life of the lessor company. Just before the execution of the lease, ownership of a majority of the capital stock was acquired by the Metropolitan Traction Company of New York. On May 28, 1894, the Metropolitan Crosstown Railway Company was amalgamated with the Lexington and Pavonia Ferry Railroad Company and the original Metropolitan Street Railway Company to form the second Metropolitan Street Railway Company.[1] The original lease of the Forty-second Street and Grand Street Ferry Company is now in the hands of the New York Railways Company which pays an annual rental of eighteen per cent on the par value of seven thousand four hundred and eighty shares of capital stock, all taxes and corporate expenses.[2]

3. THE DRY DOCK, EAST BROADWAY AND BATTERY RAILROAD COMPANY

On December 8, 1863, the Dry Dock, East Broadway and Battery Rail Road Company was incorporated by Charles Curtis, John Kerr, John E. Devlin, and others, for one thousand years, with a capital stock of one million two hundred thousand dollars.[3] The original franchise acquired by the company was one of the five special franchise measures enacted over the governor's veto in 1860.[4] The charter route of about sixteen miles provided for a road commencing at the north end of Avenue D, running thence to Eighth street to Lewis street to Grand street to East Broadway to Chatham Square, Chatham street and Park row; also from the corner of Avenue D and Eighth street along Avenue D to Houston street to Goerck street to Grand street; also connecting with the double track in East Broad-

[1] *Infra*, ch. viii.
[2] *Annual Report of the New York Railways Company for the year ending June 30, 1918*, p. 28.
[3] *Report of the Public Service Commission, First District of the State of New York*, 1913, vol. v, p. 354.
[4] *Laws of the State of New York*, 1860, ch. 512.

way through Canal street to the westerly side of Broadway. Several other short branches and connecting lines were mentioned in this act. The conditions were the same as for the Forty-second Street and Grand Street Ferry Railroad company: the grantees were to pay the city an annual

PLATE X

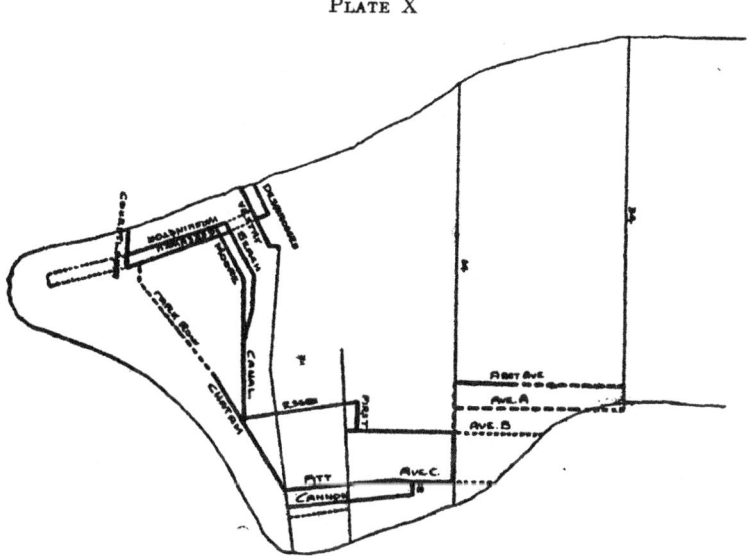

DRY DOCK, EAST BROADWAY AND BATTERY RAILROAD COMPANY

- - - - - trackage rights obtained on tracks of other companies
. . . . . franchise routes neither constructed nor used by this company

license fee for each car; the same rate of fare was authorized as that charged by other roads; if necessary, their lines might intersect tracks already built; and they were given permission to operate their cars upon any portion of such tracks, upon paying compensation to the owners thereof. Interference by the local authorities with the construction and operation of the road was prohibited; this provision, it should be noted, was an exception to the two previous legislative charters above mentioned.

In 1866 three extensions were authorized by the legislature. On May 1st of that year the company received authority to construct a single-track line [1] from Avenue B through Second street to Avenue A to Essex street and Rutgers street to East Broadway; from Avenue D across Houston street through Columbia street to Grand street. This franchise imposed no new conditions; it simply facilitated a change of route, for when constructed it would enable the company to abandon its line in Goerck street. Within one year the company was to abandon and remove one of its tracks in Avenue B and Clinton street from Second street to East Broadway. Permission for the second extension was granted on the same day, May 1st, 1866,[2] authorizing the construction of a double track from Greenwich street through Desbrosses street to Cortlandt street to the North river, and through Fulton street to Broadway, with a single track from Washington street to Greenwich street, and a double track from Greenwich street to Broadway. The conditions of this franchise have been explained.[3] On May 10, 1866, a double-track extension was authorized from the junction of East Broadway and Grand street to Sullivan street to Canal street to Vestry street to the Hudson river.[4] This act empowered the company to purchase the equipment "used by the Telegraph Stage Company in running a line of stages to and from Grand street ferry through Grand street, Broadway and certain other streets." The franchise stipulated that the ex-

[1] *Laws of the State of New York, 1866*, ch. 866.
[2] *Ibid.*, ch. 868.
[3] *Supra*, ch. viii.
[4] *Laws of the State of New York, 1866*, ch. 883.

tension be constructed within one year; the fare was limited to five cents per person, and the company was to pay the city five per cent of the net proceeds from the operation of the extension. The company paid this percentage but questioned its liability as to the car-license fee under the act of 1860; it finally maintained that the act of 1866 repealed the license provision of the act of 1860. The Court of Appeals, however, held that the act of 1866 was not in any sense amendatory of the former law and held that the company was, therefore, subject to both.[1]

It was not until 1912 that any additional franchise rights were obtained by this company. On May 9th of that year the board of estimate and apportionment granted a franchise for a single track connecting with the existing tracks of the company in Canal street and extending across Broadway to Canal street to Church street, thence southerly to Lispenard street, connecting at that point with the company's tracks already built.[2] This franchise was granted in accordance with the provisions of the charter of Greater New York.[3] The contract was for twenty-five years with a renewal upon revaluation for a similar period. The company agreed to make an initial payment of one hundred dollars within three months after the date of the contract and in addition to pay annually three per cent of the proportional gross receipts during the first five years, or not less than one hundred and twenty-five dollars per year; and five per cent during the remainder of the original term with minimum payments of two hundred and twenty-five dollars

[1] *The Mayor, Aldermen and Commonalty of the City of New York v. The Dry Dock, East Broadway and Battery Railroad Company*, 112 N. Y., 137.

[2] *Minutes of the Board of Estimate and Apportionment of the City of New York: Financial and Franchise Matters*, 1912, pp. 2063-73.

[3] *Infra*, ch. ix.

during the second five years; two hundred and forty dollars during the third five years; two hundred and sixty-five dollars for the fourth five-year period, and three hundred dollars for the last five-year period. In the event of renewal, payments were to be no less than the minimum required for the last year of the original term. The company was not to have exclusive railway privileges in the streets mentioned, and the extension was not to be leased or assigned without the consent of the city. This franchise stipulated that the company should abandon its single track on Lispenard street, between Broadway and Church street, and also the connection on Broadway from Canal street to Lispenard street.

The company has from time to time entered into trackage agreements with the Third Avenue Railroad Company, the New York and Harlem Railroad Company, The Second Avenue Railroad Company, Avenue C Railroad Company, The Houston, West Street and Pavonia Ferry Railroad Company, The Christopher and Tenth Street Railroad Company, The Forty-second Street and Grand Street Ferry Railroad Company, Central Park, North and East River Railroad Company, The Twenty-third Street Railway Company, Forty-second Street, Manhattanville and St. Nicholas Avenue Railway Company, The Broadway and Seventh Avenue Railroad Company, The Twenty-eighth and Twenty-ninth Street Railway Company, The Metropolitan Street Railway Company, and the New York City Railways Company.[1] At the present time it is operated under an agreement by the New York Railways Company.[2]

[1] *Report of the Public Service Commission, First District of the State of New York*, 1913, vol. v, pp. 361-370.
[2] *Annual Report of the New York Railways Company for the year ending June 30, 1918*, p. 1.

4. THE BROADWAY AND SEVENTH AVENUE RAILROAD COMPANY

This company, which acquired one of the five franchises rushed through the legislature in 1860, was incorporated May 26, 1864, for one thousand years with a capital stock of two million one hundred thousand dollars.[1] Frequent reference has been made in the previous chapter to the company and its relations to the various attempts which were made to get control of Broadway. The original franchise for this road was granted in perpetuity, with absolutely no safeguard to the city, to Jacob Sharp, Peter B. Sweeney, John Kelley, John Kerr, and others.[2]

In 1866 the company was authorized to change that part of its route running through Fourth and Thompson streets so as to connect with the company's track in Canal street. That part of the line in Thompson street was to continue "until Thompson street shall be widened in the manner provided by law."[3] The following year another legislative act required the company to run its cars on MacDougal street in the same direction as the cars of the Bleecker Street and Fulton Ferry Railroad Company.[4]

On June 5, 1892, the company, in conjunction with the Metropolitan Crosstown Railroad Company, petitioned the common council for a franchise extending its lines [5] on Twenty-third street from Broadway to Lexington avenue to Twenty-seventh street, also across Canal street to South Fifth avenue to Broome street.

On April 14, 1896, another extension franchise was ob-

[1] *Report of the Public Service Commission, First District, State of New York*, 1913, vol. v, p. 45.
[2] *Laws of the State of New York, 1860*, ch. 513.
[3] *Ibid., 1866*, ch. 500.
[4] *Laws of the State of New York, 1867*, ch. 904.
[5] *Proceedings of the Board of Aldermen*, vol. 207, pp. 7-8.

tained from the common council [1] for a short extension on Broome street to connect with the tracks of the Bleecker Street and Fulton Ferry Railroad Company, and on University Place from Eighth street to Wooster street to West

PLATE XI

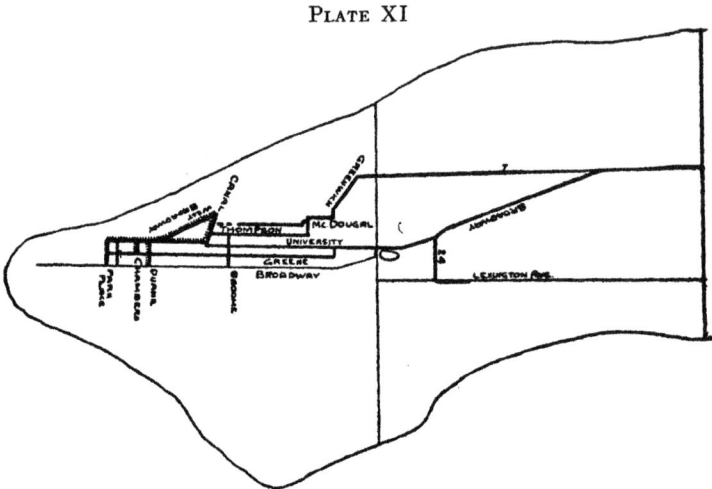

BROADWAY AND SEVENTH AVENUE RAILROAD COMPANY

- - - - - trackage rights obtained on tracks of other companies
. . . . . franchise routes neither constructed nor used by this company

Fourth street to connect with a branch of the Metropolitan Street Railway Company; permission was also granted for a slight extension on Third street. No new conditions were imposed in any of these extensions.[2]

[1] *The City Record*, vol. xxiv, pt. ii, pp. 1119-1122.

[2] An interesting question grew out of the refusal of the Broadway and Seventh Avenue Company to pay the car license fee authorized by the act of 1860, which granted the original franchise, on the ground that such payment was no longer obligatory. It appears that by an ordinance of the common council passed December 31, 1858, every street surface railway company was to pay an annual license fee of fifty dollars for two-horse cars and twenty-five dollars for one-horse cars. On April 24, 1867, this ordinance became inoperative by act of

The Broadway and Seventh Avenue Railroad Company has played an important rôle in the street surface railway consolidation of New York city. On May 13, 1890, its lines were leased to the Houston, West Street and Pavonia Ferry Railroad Company for the unexpired term of its charter for an annual rental of ten per cent on the par value of its capital stock of twenty-one thousand shares and, in addition, interest on its funded debt as well as all taxes and corporate expenses.[1] The Houston, West Street and Pavonia Ferry Railroad Company, on December 12, 1893, became an integral part of the Metropolitan Street Railway Company. Thereafter, February 14, 1902, all the lines of the Metropolitan Street Railway Company were leased to the Interurban Street Railway Company.[2] The Broadway and Seventh Avenue road is now operated under lease by the New York Railways Company.[3]

5. THE BLEECKER STREET AND FULTON FERRY RAILROAD COMPANY

The original franchise for this company, which was incorporated by Stephen R. Roe, Hugh Smith, Peter B. Swee-

the common council, but this resolution was subsequently repealed, October 28, 1867. The Broadway and Seventh Avenue Company maintained that the resolution of the board of aldermen, April 24, 1867, absolved it from any license payment stipulated in the franchise act of 1860. The Court of Appeals, however, ruled that the repealing act of October 28, 1867, restored the ordinance of December 31, 1858, and that it, therefore, continued in full force and effect. *Proceedings of the Board of Aldermen*, vol. lxxii, p. 826; Mayor, Aldermen and Commonalty of the City of New York v. The Broadway and Seventh Avenue Railroad Company, 97 N. Y., 275.

[1] *Annual Report of the New York Railways Company for the year ending June 30, 1918,* p. 28.

[2] *Infra,* ch. viii.

[3] *Annual Report of the New York Railways Company for the year ending June 30, 1918,* p. 1.

ney and others on December 12, 1864, for a period of one thousand years, with a capital stock of nine hundred thousand dollars,[1] was granted by the legislature in 1860[2] to the incorporators. The route covered Fourteenth street from the corner of Eleventh avenue to Hudson street to Troy street to Fourth avenue to MacDougal street to Bleecker street to Crosby street to Howard street to Elm street to Reade street to Center street to Chatham street and Park row to Broadway with a branch line from Reade street through Center street to Leonard street to connect with the main line in Elm street. Another branch was to run from the corner of Hudson and Troy streets to the southerly end of Abington Square and Bleecker street and through that street to connect with the line in MacDougal street. The company was further authorized to construct a road beginning at Park row along Beekman street to South street to Fulton street to William street to Ann street, back to Park row and Broadway. Numerous other branches and connections were provided for. The conditions of the franchise were practically the same as those required in the other four similar street surface railway acts of 1860, the most important being the clause stipulating that the same rate of fare be charged and the same license fee be paid as by other railroad companies of the city.

On April 11, 1873, the legislature authorized certain other extensions.[3] The company was permitted to use the tracks already laid by other companies should it deem such usage necessary upon making proper compensation therefor; the company was further required to pay an annual license fee of fifty dollars for every car used on the extension,

[1] *Report of the Public Service Commission, First District, State of New York*, 1913, vol. v, p. 265.
[2] *Laws of the State of New York, 1860*, ch. 514.
[3] *Laws of the State of New York, 1873*, ch. 199.

was to pave and keep in repair the surface of the streets within the tracks, and the same rate of fare was to be charged on the extension as was being charged on the main line, but there was to be no duplication of fares. The company was authorized to make transfer arrangements with other railway companies intersecting the tracks of the

PLATE XII

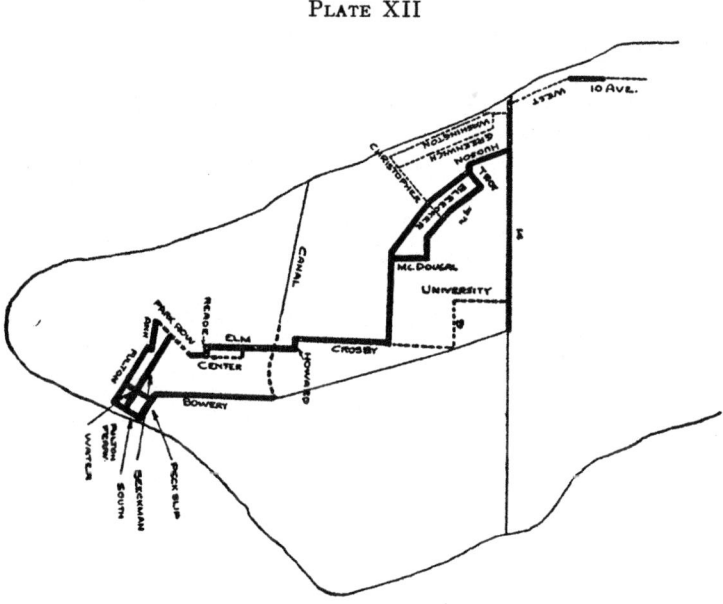

BLEECKER STREET AND FULTON FERRY RAILROAD COMPANY

- - - - - trackage rights obtained on tracks of other companies
. . . . . franchise routes neither constructed nor used by this company

Bleecker Street Company, but any additional charge for a transfer was not to exceed three cents. Lastly, the act authorized the company to lease its road, or any portion thereof.

The financial return to the city was modified a month later when the legislature provided that the company should pay one per cent of its gross receipts in lieu of the annual license fee of fifty dollars per car.[1] Later it became necessary for the city to institute judicial proceedings to collect this percentage.

In 1875, by legislative act, the company was permitted to lease its property to any other street surface railway corporation,[2] and subsequently a lease was made on January 10, 1876, with The Twenty-third Street Railway Company for a term of ninety-nine years, the consideration being fifty thousand dollars, which was to be applied in liquidating the floating debt of the lessor, and an annual rental equal to one and one-half per cent of the capital stock of the Bleecker Street Company. The Twenty-third Street Railway Company also agreed to pay the principal and interest on the seven-hundred-thousand-dollar first-mortgage bonds which had been issued by the lessor company; it also took the property subject to "every act passed and to be passed amendatory thereof."[3]

Prior to the execution of this lease, the city had on May 1, 1866, leased to the Bleecker Street and Fulton Ferry Company the land and buildings in the block bounded by Tenth Avenue, Little West Twelfth street, Washington street, Gansevoort street and West street, to be used as a car-barn, for a period of fifteen years with the privilege of renewal for a like term. The railway company failed to make payment of rent for the property, and also failed to pay the car-license fee authorized by law. The city brought suit and the company filed a counter claim for alleged damages sustained through the interference of the city with the company's operations on Eleventh avenue, where a sewer

[1] *Laws of the State of New York, 1873*, ch. 647.
[2] *Ibid.*, *1875*, ch. 389.
[3] The Mayor, Aldermen and Commonalty of the City of New York v. The Twenty-third Street Railway Company, 113 N. Y., 311.

was then being constructed.[1] The city obtained a judgment against the company for the unpaid rent, but, after hanging fire for some years, an adjustment was made on June 12, 1878, whereby the company surrendered its lease covering the car-barn property, and the city released the company from all payments under the judgment or any pending litigation; an exception, however, was made for the one per cent gross receipts provided by the law of 1873. The Twenty-third Street Railway Company refused to make the payments on the ground that the act of 1873, which modified the original franchise, was unconstitutional, and therefore imposed no obligation on the Bleecker Street and Fulton Ferry Railroad Company. It further maintained that there was nothing in the terms of its lease with the Bleecker Street Company which obligated it to pay the percentages. The Court of Appeals held [2] that it was wholly within the power of the legislature to alter and amend the charter and franchise of a company, and that the amendatory act of 1873 was constitutional. The court also held that, while it was not actually stipulated in the lease that the Twenty-third Street Company should pay the percentage, inasmuch as the lessee had taken the place of the lessor as to its charter rights, powers and privileges, it therefore took its place as to its charter obligations and duties, and was not entitled to exercise the former without discharging the latter.

The franchise for the Mail street extension was granted by resolution of the board of aldermen on December 20, 1884.[3] A similar resolution had previously been vetoed by

[1] People *ex rel* Bleecker St. and Fulton Ferry Railroad Co. *v.* Commissioner of Taxes &c. of New York City, 60 N. Y., 638.

[2] Mayor &c. of New York City *v.* The Twenty-third St. Ry., 113 N. Y., 311.

[3] *Proceedings of the Board of Aldermen*, vol. 176, pp. 1082-1088.

Mayor Edson because it failed to incorporate any provision for compensation to the city.[1] The conditions were: (1) not more than a five-cent fare for one continuous ride to any point on the road of the company " or any road, line, or branch operated by it or under its control " within the limits of the city; (2) the company was required to keep in repair the pavement between the tracks and for two feet on either side thereof; (3) the city was to receive three per cent of the gross receipts during the first five years, and five per cent thereafter. These payments were to be made on that proportion of the entire gross receipts of the company which the extension should bear to the entire road. This was seemingly an unimportant extension, but it effectually furthered the elaborate gridiron system of street surface railways which Jacob Sharp and his associates had in view.

Another franchise grant was obtained in 1896. By resolution of the common council, adopted April 14th, the company was given permission to extend its tracks in Broome street to connect with the Broadway and Seventh Avenue road.[2] No additional fare was to be charged, transfers were to be given, the motive power was to be cable or underground electricity, or any motive power except steam or overhead electricity, and the usual percentages were to be paid annually to the city.

The Bleecker Street and Fulton Ferry Railroad Company has had a varied career. For the first ten years of its existence it was, according to the report of Alvan S. Southworth, receiver for the company,[3] a sort of golden oasis

[1] *Proceedings of the Board of Aldermen*, vol. 176, pp. 981-983.

[2] *Ordinances and Resolutions &c.*, adopted by the Common Council and approved by the Mayor, *1896*, vol. lxix, pp. 64-68.

[3] See Report filed in County Clerk's office of New York County on January 27, 1876; *New York Times*, January 27, 1876; *New York Tribune*, January 27, 1876.

used for the enrichment of its officials and their friends. For years it had been " preyed upon by evil-minded and unscrupulous men with a view to depress its value and then lease or otherwise acquire its chartered rights." Southworth's report shows that four hundred and thirty-four thousand dollars of the company's bonds were given away gratuitously. J. T. Conover, who became president of the company in 1866, never paid a dollar for his stocks and bonds; the same was true of Jacob Sharp and other officials of the company. Receiver Southworth alleged not only that Conover did not build the extension permitted by the legislative act of 1873, but that he made a corrupt bargain with other crosstown railway companies in which he pledged the company not to lay a rail over the route covered by this valuable grant; Southworth claimed that these competing companies were attempting to vitiate the franchises of the Bleecker Street Company. The receiver estimated that for an expenditure of fifty thousand dollars he could put into operation three miles of railway which would earn more than one hundred and ten thousand dollars annually—" a sum more than sufficient to pay the bonded debt of the road and a fair dividend on the stock in the course of two years."[1] He also added that " were the present roads properly managed four hundred and fifty thousand dollars a year could be collected, or nearly two hundred thousand dollars in excess of the present earnings. With the use of the new franchises the earnings could be increased to seven hundred and thirty thousand dollars per annum, making it one of the most valuable franchises in the city."[2]

The Twenty-third Street Railway Company,[3] which ob-

[1] See Report filed in New York County Clerk's office, January 27, 1876; *New York Times,* January 27, 1876; *New York Tribune,* Jan. 27, 1876.
[2] *Ibid.*
[3] *Infra,* p. 130.

tained its franchise for a lump sum, leased the Bleecker Street and Fulton Ferry Railroad Company's property on January 10, 1876, and operated the two roads as one. This was quite natural inasmuch as the officers and principal stockholders of the two companies were almost identically the same, as the following comparison clearly shows:[1]

BLEECKER STREET AND FULTON FERRY RAILROAD COMPANY.	TWENTY-THIRD STREET RAILWAY COMPANY.
President: Jacob Sharp.	*President:* Jacob Sharp.
Secretary: Thomas H. McLean.	*Secretary:* Thomas H. McLean.
Treasurer: David James King.	*Treasurer:* Lewis May.
Directors: Jacob Sharp.	*Directors:* Jacob Sharp.
Eugene S. Ballin.	Eugene S. Ballin.
Isaac Hendrix.	Isaac Hendrix.
David James King.	David James King.
John Downey.	John Downey.
Henderson Moore.	Henderson Moore.
S. B. H. Vance.	S. B. H. Vance.
Thomas B. Kerr.	L. Marx.
Joseph Jacobs.	Lazarus Rosenfeld.
John H. Selmes.	James Lynch.
Alex. E. Kursheedt.	John R. Flanagan.
William Mangies.	James Flanagan.

Mayor Edson in a message to the board of aldermen dated October 13, 1884, pointed out that the receipts of the two companies were so intermingled that it was impossible to determine what proportion of the joint receipts was earned by either road.[2] Mr. Jacob Sharp, in an interview with a deputy collector of city revenue, said that "if he [the collector] would pick out or distinguish the particular nickels or coins received from the cars of the Bleecker Street and Fulton Ferry Railroad Company, he [Sharp] would pay the percentage demanded thereon, but otherwise he would not."[3] Thus for years the city received no revenue from this particular source.

[1] *Proceedings of the Board of Aldermen*, vol. 176, pp. 245-257.
[2] *Ibid.*, p. 248.   [3] *Ibid.*

On December 22, 1909, the attorney-general of the state, at the suggestion of the Public Service Commission of the First District, instituted proceedings against the Bleecker Street and Fulton Ferry Company for the forfeiture of its franchises covering such portions of its route as were not already constructed or being regularly operated.[1] After considerable negotiation a settlement was finally reached on January 10, 1913, by which the company surrendered its franchises to various streets.[2] Such surrender, however, in no way affected the franchise rights of the company to those thoroughfares over which its road was in actual operation.

In addition to several trackage agreements, this company has leased various portions of its lines from time to time to other railroad corporations.[3] The Twenty-third Street Railway Company released a part of the Bleecker Street and Fulton Ferry road on November 10, 1876, to the Christopher and Tenth Street Rail Road Company for a period of ninety-eight years; subsequently the latter company was leased to the Central Crosstown Railroad Company, which in turn was leased to the Metropolitan Street Railway Company.[4] The remaining portion of the Twenty-third Street Company's road and holdings was leased on April 25, 1893, to the Houston, West Street and Pavonia Ferry Railroad Company.[5] The Bleecker Street and Fulton Ferry road is now operated under lease by the New York Railways Company which pays an annual rental of one and one-half per cent on its nine thousand shares of capital stock,

[1] *Report of the Public Service Commission, First District of the State of New York*, 1913, vol. v, p. 35.
[2] *Ibid.*
[3] *Ibid.*, p. 34.
[4] *Infra*, ch. viii.
[5] *Infra*, ch. viii.

together with interest on the first mortgage bonds, and all taxes and corporate expenses.[1]

6. THE TWENTY-THIRD STREET RAILWAY COMPANY

The history of this company, as heretofore shown, was intimately associated with that of the Bleecker Street and Fulton Ferry Railroad Company. The Twenty-third Street Railway Company was first incorporated on June 10, 1869; its corporate life was to extend for a thousand years, and its entire capital stock was stated to be two hundred and fifty thousand dollars. Three years later the company was virtually reorganized with a capital stock of six hundred thousand dollars.[2] The method by which this company obtained its franchise was in marked contrast to the earlier legislative grants. It has already been noted that there had been repeated protests from many sources against the granting of exclusive franchise rights which brought little revenue to the city; to overcome this criticism the legislature on May 10, 1869, passed an act authorizing the construction and operation of a double-track surface railroad on Twenty-third street from the North to the East rivers.[3] The franchise for this road was to be sold at public auction to the highest bidder by the city authorities; it was purchased by Sidney A. Yoemans for one hundred and fifty thousand dollars; he in turn, with legislative sanction,[4] transferred his rights to the Twenty-third Street Railway Company for one hundred and thirteen thousand dollars. Aside from the manner in which it was awarded, this franchise does not

[1] *Annual Report of the New York Railways Company for the year ending June 30, 1918*, p. 27.

[2] *Report of the Public Service Commission, First District, State of New York*, 1913, vol. v, p. 1332.

[3] *Laws of the State of New York, 1869*, ch. 823.

[4] *Ibid., 1872*, ch. 521.

differ materially from the usual legislative street-railway grant. The particular type of rail was designated, cars were to be run to suit the public convenience, the rate of fare was to be no more than that charged by other railroads operating in the city, and the company was to be subject to such reasonable rules and regulations as the common council

PLATE XIII

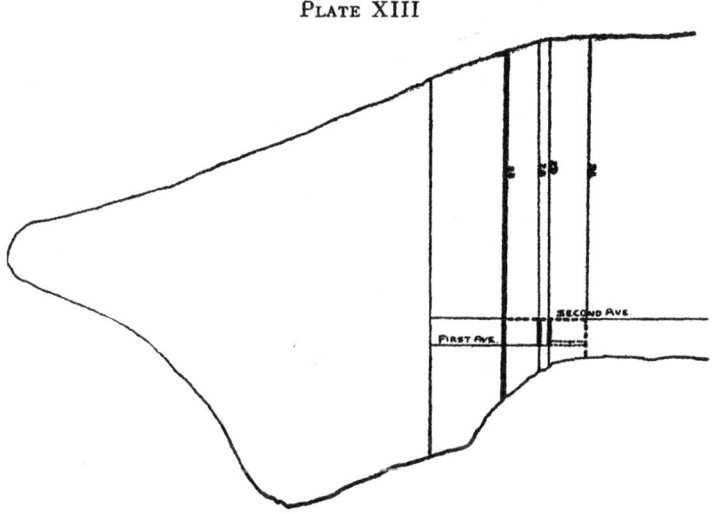

TWENTY-THIRD STREET RAILWAY COMPANY
- - - - - trackage rights obtained on tracks of other companies
. . . . . franchise routes neither constructed nor used by this company

might prescribe. The act further allowed the company to intersect the lines or make use of the tracks of other companies.

In 1873 another legislative franchise [1] permitted the company to extend its lines on Second avenue from Twenty-third to Twenty-ninth streets; on Twenty-eighth street from Second to First avenues; on Twenty-ninth street from Second to First avenues; and on First avenue from Twenty-

[1] *Laws of the State of New York, 1873*, ch. 109.

eighth to Thirty-fourth streets. The company was to exercise the same rights and privileges as those enjoyed under its original franchise.

The intercorporate relations of this company have already been noted. The road is now leased to the New York Railways Company under an agreement dated April 25, 1893, for the unexpired term of its charter in consideration of the payment of an annual rental of eighteen per cent on its six thousand shares of capital stock, par value; all taxes, assessments, water rents and charges, including interest on one million five hundred thousand dollars improvement and refunding mortgage five-per-cent bonds, with a sinking fund of two thousand two hundred and five dollars and seventy cents per annum.[1]

7. THE AVENUE C RAILROAD COMPANY

The franchise for this road was granted on May 6, 1868, to Alfred B. Darling and forty-six others.[2] The road was to commence at Duane and West streets, thence through Duane street to Greenwich street to Charlton street to Prince street to the Bowery to Stanton street to Pitt street to Avenue C to Third street, and from this point to the northern extremity of Avenue C; also a line was to run through Third street to First street to East Houston street to the Bowery to West Houston street to Washington street and back to Duane street. The usual conditions were prescribed, but in addition to the car-license fee the grantees were to pay one thousand dollars annually to the sinking fund commissioners of the city. The expense of laying the track in Greenwich and Washington streets was to be borne

---

[1] *Annual Report of the New York Railways Company for the year ending June 30, 1918*, p. 27.

[2] *Report of the Public Service Commission, First District, State of New York*, 1913, vol. v, p. 18.

equally by the grantees or their assigns and any other company which might thereafter be authorized to construct a road in those streets. The grantees were to keep the tracks clear of snow and ice.

The company was incorporated on December 8, 1868, for a period of ninety-nine years with a capital stock of five hundred thousand dollars. In 1871 the legislature granted an extension through certain streets;[1] the act also empowered the use of other railroad tracks upon proper compensation to their owners and the Avenue C Company was authorized to lease its lines or consolidate them with other roads. Compensation to the city was to be determined by commissioners appointed by the Supreme Court pursuant to the General Railroad Act of 1850; otherwise the terms of the franchise were the same as in the original grant.

On May 26, 1874, the franchise and property of this company were sold under foreclosure.

8. THE HOUSTON, WEST STREET AND PAVONIA FERRY RAILROAD COMPANY

This company was a reorganization of the Avenue C Railroad Company, the property of which had been purchased by Ebenezer Beadleston and others under mortgage foreclosure proceedings. Beadleston and his associates on June 3, 1874, organized the Houston, West Street and Pavonia Ferry Railroad Company. The corporate life of the company was to extend for ninety-three years and its capitalization was stated to b two hundred and fifty thousand dollars.[2] The Houston, West Street and Pavonia Ferry Company, by deed dated June 9, 1874, received from Beadleston and his associates the former property of the Avenue C

[1] *Laws of the State of New York, 1871*, ch. 19.
[2] *Report of the Public Service Commission, First District, State of New York*, 1913, vol. v, p. 486.

Railroad Company, including all rights and franchises; it also acquired by the same transaction all trackage rights entered into by the Avenue C company.[1]

Since its incorporation the Houston, West Street and Pavonia Ferry Company has obtained only one additional franchise; this grant was made by the common council and approved by the mayor on October 8, 1892, for certain short extensions.[2] No new provisions were embodied in this grant.

PLATE XIV

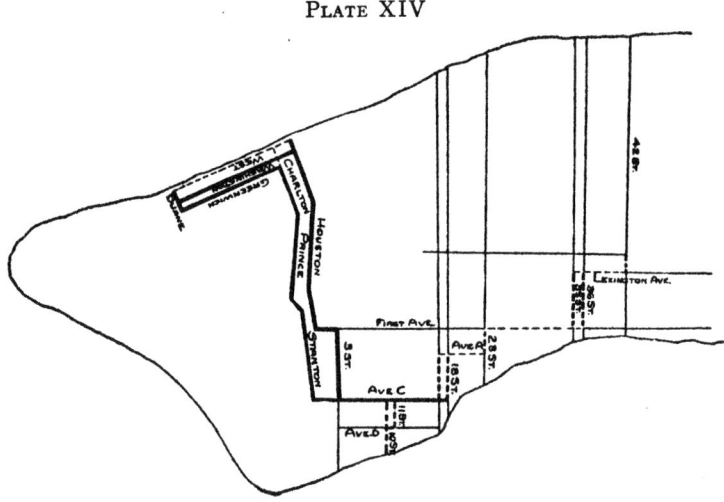

HOUSTON, WEST STREET AND PAVONIA FERRY RAILROAD COMPANY
- - - - - trackage rights obtained on tracks of other companies

This company, after securing control of several New York city street railways, was merged with the Broadway Railway Company and the South Ferry Railway Company to form the first Metropolitan Street Railway Company.[3]

[1] *Report of Public Service Commission, op. cit.*, pp. 486-487.
[2] *City Record*, vol. xx, pt. iv, pp. 2999-3001.
[3] *Infra*, ch. viii.

9. THE ONE HUNDRED AND TWENTY-FIFTH STREET RAILROAD COMPANY

This company, which soon became a subsidiary of the Third Avenue Railroad Company, was chartered November 26, 1870, by Robert Squires and others for the purpose of constructing a surface railroad on the following streets: Beginning at the Hudson river at the foot of One Hundred and Thirtieth street, to Manhattan street, to One Hundred and Twenty-fifth street to the Harlem river; also from One Hundred and Twenty-fifth street along Third avenue to the Harlem bridge, and from the corner of One Hundred and Twenty-fifth street and Tenth avenue, along Tenth

PLATE XV

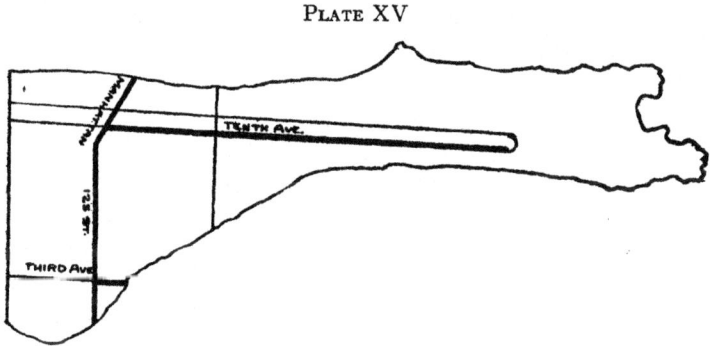

ONE HUNDRED AND TWENTY-FIFTH STREET RAILROAD COMPANY

avenue to its northern terminus. The capital stock of the company was one hundred and fifty thousand dollars, and it was incorporated for a period of one thousand years.[1]

The franchise for this road was framed by the legislature in 1870. That body directed the commissioners of the sinking fund of the city of New York to " sell at public auction to the highest bidder the right, privilege and franchise to

[1] *Report of the Public Service Commission, First District of the State of New York*, 1913, vol. v, p. 1054.

construct, operate by animal power, and use a railroad with a single or double track " in the streets above mentioned.[1] The act provided that notice of this sale should be published in at least five daily papers for a period of six weeks prior to such sale. This notice was to specify the day, hour and place of sale, which was to be conducted in the ordinary manner of auction sales, namely, that the franchise should be sold to the person or corporation offering to pay the largest sum into the city treasury. A certificate of purchase was to be issued to the highest bidder provided the amount so bid was paid into the city treasury within ten days thereafter. In addition, the purchaser was required to execute a bond to the " Mayor, Aldermen and Commonalty " for such a sum as the commissioners might determine, to the effect that the road would be in operation at the end of two years. An exception was made for Tenth avenue, and there it was to be completed as fast as the street was " opened, graded and paved." The commissioners were allowed to reject all bids and to re-advertise the sale if, in their judgment, it was for the best interests of the city. The other conditions were the same as the previous legislative grants of this period. In arranging for the sale of this franchise the legislature seems to have taken a broader view respecting franchise grants.

This franchise was sold to Robert Squires and others on July 20, 1870, for sixty-seven thousand dollars.[2] In the following November Squires turned the franchise over to the newly incorporated One Hundred and Twenty-fifth Street Company.[3] Just one month later this company's property, rights, and franchise privileges were leased to the

[1] *Laws of the State of New York, 1870*, ch. 504.
[2] *Report of the Public Service Commission, First District of the State of New York*, 1913, vol. v, p. 1054.
[3] *Ibid.*, see chart ii, no. 19.

Third Avenue Railroad Company for a period of ten years,[1] which lease was renewed on November 1, 1880.[2] By a general act of the legislature passed June 12, 1879, any railroad corporation created by the laws of the state which was the lessee of any railroad might take a surrender or transfer of the capital stock of the lessor company.[3] Acting under this law, the Third Avenue Company took over the capital stock of the One Hundred and Twenty-fifth Street Railroad Company, the certificate of transfer being filed with the secretary of state on April 23, 1886.[4] The road thenceforth became a part of the Third Avenue system.

10. THE CENTRAL CROSSTOWN RAILROAD COMPANY OF NEW YORK

The legislature in 1873 granted franchises for the Central Crosstown, the Christopher and Tenth Street, and the Forty-second Street, Manhattanville and St. Nicholas Avenue Railroads.

The Central Crosstown Railroad Company was incorporated August 13, 1873, for nine hundred and ninety-nine years, with a capital stock of six hundred thousand dollars.[5] The original franchise was granted to John Sullivan, William Thompson, John C. Macauley and forty-four others,[6] for a railroad on Twenty-third street from the East river to Avenue A to Seventeenth street to Broadway to Fourteenth street to Seventh avenue to Hammond street

---

[1] *Report of the Public Service Commission, First District of the State of New York*, 1913, see chart ii, no. 19.

[2] *Ibid.*

[3] *Laws of the State of New York, 1879*, ch. 503.

[4] *Report of the Public Service Commission, First District of the State of New York*, 1913, vol. v, p. 1054; see chart ii, no. 19.

[5] *Ibid.*, vol. v, p. 265.

[6] *Laws of the State of New York, 1873*, ch. 160.

to Christopher street to the North river; returning from Christopher street to Greenwich street to Hammond street to Seventh avenue to Fourteenth street to Eighteenth street to Broadway.

The franchise for this route, like the other legislative grants, required that the road should be constructed on the most approved plan; that the fare should be limited to five

PLATE XVI

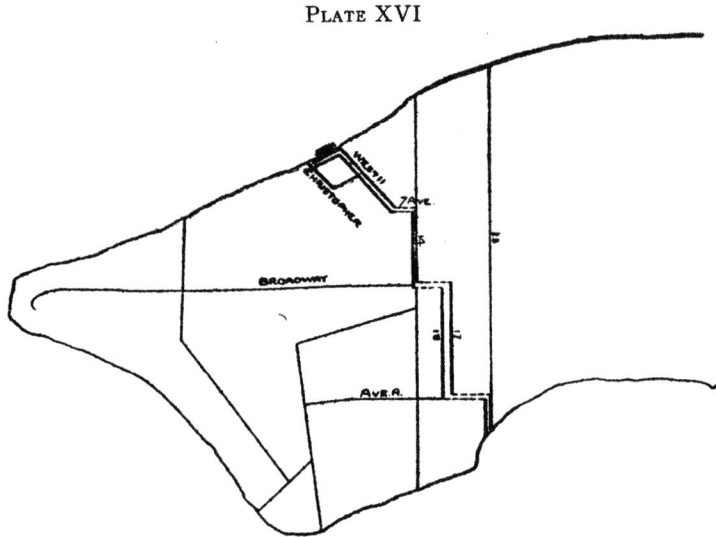

CENTRAL CROSSTOWN RAILROAD COMPANY OF NEW YORK
- - - - - trackage rights obtained on tracks of other companies
. . . . . franchise routes neither constructed nor used by this company

cents for each passenger, and that the city should receive three per cent of the gross receipts annually as compensation. This grant proved the exception, in that the grantees were specifically given the right of eminent domain in the streets in question.

The company has no franchise for its tracks from West street to the ferry at the foot of Christopher street. In 1874 the old ferry house at this point was destroyed by fire and the new house was built on a filled-in space one hundred and eighty feet to the west of the old site. The Christopher and Tenth Street Railroad Company, through its lessee, the Central Crosstown Company, extended its lines to the new ferry house. The Metropolitan Street Railway Company attempted to do likewise but was restrained by the Central Crosstown Company. After years of litigation the court ruled that the Christopher and Tenth Street Company had a right to maintain its tracks at this point inasmuch as it had prior franchise claims to West street.[1]

On February 8, 1904, the property and franchises of the company were leased to the Metropolitan Street Railway Company and the road is now operated by the New York Railways Company under a temporary arrangement.[2]

11. THE CHRISTOPHER AND TENTH STREET RAILROAD COMPANY

This company was chartered August 6, 1873, for one thousand years with a capital stock of six hundred and fifty thousand dollars.[3] On April 25, 1873, the legislature granted a special franchise to Lewis May, David James King, Jacob Sharp and thirty-four others for a road whose termini were to be the Christopher street ferry at the North river and the East Tenth street ferry at the East river.[4] The conditions laid down in the grant were the same as for the Central Crosstown road with the exception that no mention was made of eminent domain. The road was completed and in operation on June 8, 1874.

[1] *Central Crosstown Railroad Company v. Metropolitan Street Railway Company*, 16 N. Y. (App. Div.), 229.

[2] *Annual Report of the New York Railways Company for year ending June 30, 1918*, p. 27.

[3] *Report of the Public Service Commission, First District, State of New York*, 1913, vol. v, p. 286.

[4] *Laws of the State of New York*, 1873, ch. 286.

Since the opening of its line the Christopher and Tenth Street Company has made a number of trackage agreements with other railway companies.[1] In 1890 it leased its franchises and property for the remainder of its corporate existence to the Central Crosstown Railroad Company. The

PLATE XVII

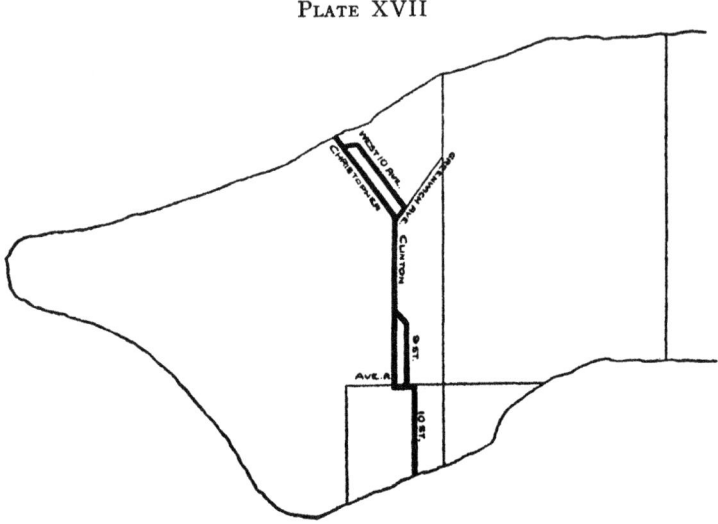

CHRISTOPHER AND TENTH STREET RAILROAD COMPANY

property of the latter company, together with its subsidiary holdings, was in turn leased to the Metropolitan Street Railway Company.[2] The route covered by the original franchise is at the present time owned, for the most part, by other companies; the tracks on East Tenth street alone remain the property of the Christopher and Tenth Street Company. The route covered by the franchise of 1873 is now operated by the New York Railways Company.[3]

[1] *Report of the Public Service Commission, First District of the State of New York*, 1913, vol. v, pp. 287-288.

[2] *Infra*, ch. viii.

[3] *Annual Report of the New York Railways Company for the year ending June 30, 1918*, p. 27.

12. THE SOUTH FERRY RAILWAY COMPANY

The South Ferry Railway Company was chartered by special act of the legislature [1] on May 20, 1874, for a period of one thousand years and with a capital stock of one hundred and fifty thousand dollars. The act authorized James Rogers, John Flanagan, Theodore P. Rutan and others to construct a street surface railway over a route of about two miles, commencing at the corner of Vesey street and Church street to Morris street to Greenwich street to Bat-

PLATE XVIII

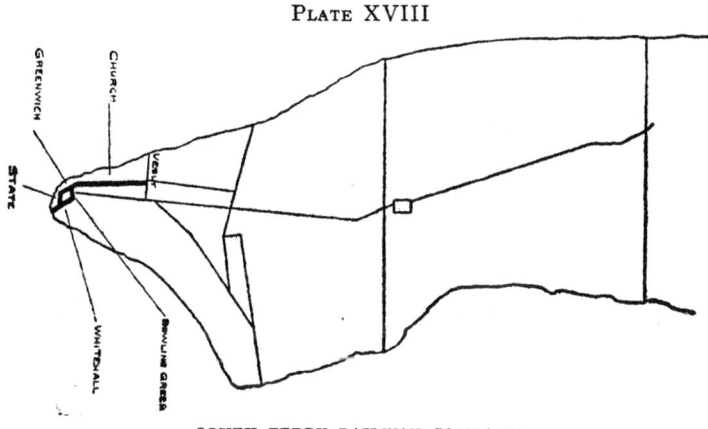

SOUTH FERRY RAILWAY COMPANY

tery Place to State street to Whitehall street to South ferry. This franchise differed from the usual legislative type only in that the company was to pay one per cent instead of three per cent of the gross receipts to the city. Charges of discrimination were made by other railway companies chartered during this period, and in the following year the rate was increased to two per cent of the gross receipts.[2]

[1] *Laws of the State of New York, 1874*, ch. 508.
[2] *Laws of the State of New York, 1875*, ch. 393.

On February 29, 1888, the franchise and property of the company were sold under foreclosure to George W. Vultee for two hundred and seventy thousand dollars. By deed executed December 27, 1888, Vultee transferred his rights to Henry Thompson who, on March 11, 1889, sold the property to the South Ferry Railroad Company.[1] The latter company was merely an ally of the Broadway and Seventh Avenue Railroad Company, of which Thompson was president. When Thompson deeded the property to the South Ferry Railroad Company he received of the company's capital stock shares of the par value of one hundred and forty-seven thousand dollars out of a total issue of one hundred and fifty thousand dollars; he received also the entire issue of three hundred and fifty thousand dollars' worth of first-mortgage five-per-cent bonds. A few years later further consolidation took place, this company being one of three which were merged to form the original Metropolitan Street Railway Company.[2]

[1] *Report of the Public Service Commission, First District of the State of New York*, 1913, vol. v, p. 1189.
[2] *Infra*, ch. viii.

CHAPTER V

HISTORY OF RAILWAYS INCORPORATED BETWEEN 1875 AND 1884

DURING the Civil War and for the decade following that struggle the population of New York city did not increase as rapidly as it did in the previous years of the nineteenth century. The average rate of increase by decades from 1800 to 1860 was fifty-four and two-thirds per cent, which fell off from 1860 to 1880 to an average of twenty-two per cent.[1] In spite of this very marked decline, the city expanded to the northward, the only direction in which it could expand owing to its peculiar configuration and topographical situation, and the population, which numbered a little over half a million in 1850, increased to one million, forty-one thousand, eight hundred and eighty-six in 1875.[2] Geographical expansion northward was a necessity, as lower New York was overflowing.[3] Several factors, both local and general, were responsible for this continued growth. The opening of the far West and the multiplication of railways stimulated to a remarkable degree the commercial and industrial activities of the city after the

---

[1] Davenport, John I., *Population of the City of New York*, p. 2.

[2] *United States Census Report*, 1910, vol. iii, p. 187.

[3] *Report of Industrial Commission*, vol. xv, pp. 452-459; Hourwich, I. A., *Immigration and Labor*, pp. 229-240. In 1870 the population of the city was 942,292, of which number 497,289 resided between the Battery and Fourteenth street; see Davenport, John I., *op. cit.*, p. 5.

Civil War. As previously noted, New York city enjoyed to a greater extent than any other Atlantic port the prosperity of the great central west.[1] Two local factors were of prime importance in the development of the city from 1865 to 1875. In the first place immigration, although it had fallen off considerably during the war, was soon renewed with increased vigor [2] and thousands of these immigrants went no farther than New York city.

The second local factor which had a marked influence upon these movements of the population to the northward was the extension and improvement of transit facilities. On the East Side as early as 1858 Second avenue cars were running up to One Hundred and Twenty-second street; the Third avenue road was in operation as far north as Eighty-sixth street; while the New York and Harlem Railroad Company had been running cars over its Fourth avenue line for a number of years prior to 1860.[3] The ever-increasing population followed these railways, and it was not long before their routes were lined with residences and

[1] *Supra*, ch. i.

[2] Bogart, E. L., *Economic History of the United States*, pp. 473-474.

[3] Mayor Charles G. Gunther in his inaugural message delivered January 4, 1864, urged that the surface railway companies extend their tracks. In dealing with the transportation problem, Mayor Gunther said: " The proper regulation of the city railroads is a matter of public interest in a city like New York, where a large portion of the population is compelled to use this means of conveyance to and from their places of daily avocation. These companies enjoying a valuable franchise and paying little for the use of the streets in comparison with the revenue derived therefrom, while they increase so materially the expense of cleaning and repairing, should be compelled at least to extend their tracks as far as the avenues they occupy are graded, and also to run cars as often as the local population reasonably demand; nor should they be permitted to use a rail endangering either life or property." *Proceedings of the Board of Aldermen*, vol. 93, p. 27.

stores.[1] By 1875 the East Side, up to Eighty-sixth street, had lost its suburban aspect and had become an integral part of the city proper.[2] Even on the West Side, which had lagged behind the more accessible part of the island, the Sixth avenue cars in 1868 were in operation up to Fifty-

[1] In 1872 the street surface railways carried 143,559,543 passengers.

Year	Population	Number of Railways making reports	Year	Reported Passenger Traffic
1859	515,547	2	1853	6,835,548
			1854	6,817,197
1855	629,810	4	*1855	18,488,459
			1856	23,153,050
			1857	22,190,431
			1858	27,900,388
			1859	32,888,794
1860	813,669	6	1860	36,455,242
			1861	26,274,360
			1862	35,878,044
			1863	40,412,357
			1864	60,900,200
1865	726,386	12	1865	82,054,516
			*1866	88,953,016
			1867	100,541,562
			1868	105,816,695
			1869	114,349,123
1870	942,292	12	1870	115,139,553
			1871	133,893,981
			1872	143,696,989
			1873	145,358,805
			1874	151,927,233
1875	1,045,223	12	1875	166,918,173

*One road not reported this year.

[1] Davenport, John I., *Population of the City of New York*, p. 18. These figures are substantiated by A. R. Robinson, engineer for the Manhattan Railway Company, in a statement made by that company to the New York State Constitutional Convention of 1867.

[2] Speech of Wright H. Olmstead on Rapid Transit, given at Lion Park, June 16, 1877.

ninth street, and the Eighth Avenue Railroad Company ran its cars to Sixtieth street.[1] Beyond these points there had been practically no development. As late as 1868 not more than a half-dozen modern houses had been built on the west side of Central Park.[2] The territory where today stand the magnificent residences of New York's wealthy citizens was at that time a wilderness of rocks, dotted here and there with dilapidated and weather-beaten shanties.[3] But these conditions did not long prevail, for a wave of speculation swept over the city which affected not only real estate but was instrumental in the creation of

[1] Shannon, Joseph, *Manual of the Corporation of the City of New York* (N. Y., 1868), p. 503; see also Map, frontispiece.

[2] *A History of Real Estate, Building and Architecture in New York* (N. Y., 1909), compiled by The Real Estate Record Association. A special New York State Senate Committee appointed in 1866 to "ascertain the best means for the transportation of passengers in the City of New York", reported that commercial, moral and hygienic considerations all demanded an immediate and large addition to the then existent means of travel. See *New York Senate Reports, 1866*, Doc. no. 28, p. 3.

[3] Van Dyke, John C., *The New New York*, p. 347; Ruggles, Samuel B., *Letters on Rapid Transit addressed to Mayor of the City of New York*, August, 1875, pp. 9, 11.

INCREASE IN POPULATION BELOW AND ABOVE FOURTEENTH STREET

	Whole Population	Below 14th Street	Above 14th Street
1830	202,589	191,781	11,808
1855	629,874	417,474	212,333
1860	814,254	469,502	245,412
1870	942,292	496,644	445,598
1875	988,618	477,597	511,021

	Total Value of Real Estate	South of 14th Street	North of 14th Street
1830	$125,238,508	$120,974,383	$4,264,135
1855	336,975,866	216,993,661	119,982,205
1865	427,360,884	254,020,144	172,340,710
1875	861,012,832	406,529,369	454,483,463

new companies, not the least of which was the street railway corporations. As a matter of fact, most of the street-railway franchises of New York city had been granted prior to the constitutional amendment of 1875. Grants for practically all the principal avenues of the city had been secured and franchises for many of the crosstown thoroughfares had been sanctioned.

This amendment to the constitution, which went into effect on January 1 of that year, did not repeal the act of 1860. This act, it is true, did prohibit special legislation granting exclusive franchises, and it required, as a condition precedent to construction of any street railway, the consent of the local authorities as well as of the owners of one-half the abutting property; or, in default of the latter, an order of the general term of the Supreme Court, based upon the report of three special commissioners, to the effect that the road should be built.[1] The consent of the local authorities, however, had to be made in each case pursuant to special authority from the legislature. In fact, when in 1882 all the laws relating to the city of New York were consolidated[2] the provisions of the Act of 1860 were incorporated.[3]

During the next ten years following this constitutional prohibition, few street-railway franchises were granted; in fact only one street surface railway of importance was incorporated during this period, that of the Forty-second Street, Manhattanville and St. Nicholas Avenue Railroad Company.

[1] *Supra*, ch. iii, p. 90.
[2] *Laws of the State of New York*, 1882, ch. 410.
[3] *Ibid.*, sec. 1943.

1. THE FORTY-SECOND STREET, MANHATTANVILLE AND ST. NICHOLAS AVENUE RAILWAY COMPANY

Although this company was not chartered until August 29, 1878,[1] the franchise for its road was granted by special act[2] of the legislature on June 24, 1878. This measure authorized Isaac M. Walton, Rufus K. McHarg, Richard L. Hill and fifty-four others to construct a railroad beginning at the western extremity of Manhattan street and extending eastward to St. Nicholas avenue to One Hundred and Tenth street to the East river, with branches from One Hundred and Tenth street and First avenue to One Hundred and Ninth street, thence to Avenue A and from Manhattan street along Tenth avenue to the Forty-second street ferry on the North river, thence along Twelfth avenue to Thirty-fourth street with a spur from Tenth avenue along Eighty-sixth street to the Hudson river. By the terms of this franchise the fare is fixed at five cents, and whenever "the track or tracks of said railway shall cross or intersect the track or tracks of any railway, by mutual agreement among the owners of said respective railways, transfer tickets may be issued to passengers at an additional rate of fare not exceeding three cents, said transfer tickets to be received in full for fare to any point on the line of the said connecting railways or either of them." Three per cent of the gross receipts were to be paid annually to the city.

By resolution of the board of aldermen, September 17, 1878, the company was permitted to extend its tracks in Forty-second street from Tenth avenue to the East river, the city to receive three per cent of the gross receipts and the company was required to keep the space between the

[1] *Report of the Public Service Commission, First District of the State of New York*, 1913, vol. v, p. 427.

[2] *Laws of the State of New York*, 1873, ch. 825.

tracks in good order. Mayor Ely vetoed this measure on the ground that it did not appear that the company had obtained the consent of the majority of the property-owners. He was also of the opinion that if the common council could by a two-thirds vote permit a company to extend its lines in Forty-second street, it could, in the same manner, empower any railroad corporation to lay tracks on Fifth avenue or Broadway.[1] The following month, October 14,

PLATE XIX

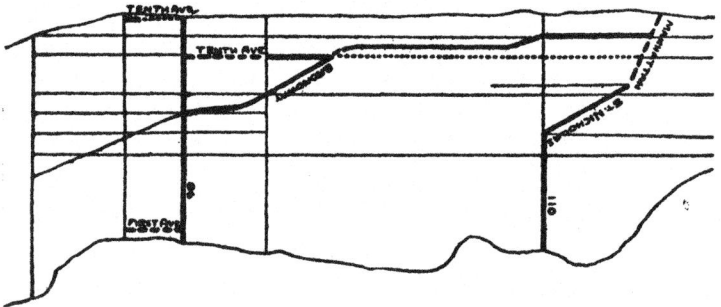

FORTY-SECOND STREET, MANHATTANVILLE AOD ST. NICHOLAS AVENUE RAILWAY COMPANY

- - - - - trackage rights obtained on tracks of other companies
. . . . . franchise routes neither constructed nor used by this company

1878, the Forty-second Street Crosstown Railroad Company applied for the Forty-second street franchise, offering to pay a bonus of fifty thousand dollars in addition to the annual three per cent of the gross receipts.[2] One alderman thought this franchise was worth one hundred thousand dollars, while another, John J. Morris, presented a remonstrance from the owners of seventeen million dollars' worth of property, protesting against making a free gift of the grant. Alderman Morris also offered a resolution that the

[1] *Proceedings of the Board of Aldermen*, vol. 152, pp. 83-84.
[2] *Ibid.*, p. 163.

franchise be sold at public auction, provided such action met the approval of the property-owners.[1] On December 3, 1878, the councilmanic committee on railroads reported in favor of awarding the grant to the Forty-second Street, Manhattanville and St. Nicholas Avenue Railroad Company.[2] The committee, after retrospectively considering the passenger transportation problem of the city for the past twenty-five years, stated that the country was just emerging from a monetary crisis and business depression, and that this particular railroad and similar enterprises which were so full of promise for the future should be encouraged; that three per cent of the gross receipts was " certainly a very liberal offer and should be at once accepted," that it would be to the interest of the city to construct it at public expense if it could not be built in any other way; that it would have been a paying investment had such a means of communication been built " twenty or more years ago ". Had such action been taken the West Side " would now be as thickly populated as the East Side and center of the city and the increased taxable value of the property thus benefited . . . would have yielded to the city the cost of the road and left a large margin besides." Finally, all franchises of this character should be sold at public auction to the highest bidder, but inasmuch as the Forty-second Street Company appeared to have a franchise from the state legislature the common council was powerless in this instance to dispose of the grant in this way. The report of the committee was adopted by a vote of fifteen to seven,[3] and on December 27, 1878, the resolution embodying the grant was passed over the mayor's veto.[4]

[1] *Proceedings of the Board of Aldermen*, vol. 152, pp. 163-165.
[2] *City Record*, vol. vi, pt. iv, pp. 1758-1759.   [3] *Ibid.*, p. 1759.
[4] *Proceedings of the Board of Aldermen*, vol. 152, pp. 771-773; *Ordinances, Resolutions, &c. passed by the Common Council and approved by the Mayor*, 1878, vol. xlvi, pp. 445-449.

This grant was delayed by litigation, and in 1884 the company petitioned for a franchise permitting a double-track line through Forty-second street to the East river and a similar line on First avenue from Forty-second to Thirty-fourth 'streets; also a line from Forty-second street through Seventh avenue to Broadway to Eighth avenue to the Boulevard to Manhattan street.[1] By resolution of the board of aldermen a franchise covering these extensions was granted on June 12, 1878.[2] The company was required to pay the city three per cent of the gross receipts annually during the first five years and five per cent thereafter. On December 8, 1892, the company obtained permission from the department of docks to lay tracks on the bulkhead at Avenue A, between One Hundred and Ninth and One Hundred and Tenth streets.[3] This permit is revocable and at present nets the city eight dollars and thirty-three cents per month.

While no additional franchises were granted during the nineties, a serious dispute arose during this time between the Forty-second Street, Manhattanville and St. Nicholas Avenue Railroad Company and the Ninth Avenue Railroad Company concerning trackage rights on Amsterdam avenue between Seventy-second and One Hundred and Twenty-fifth streets, both companies claiming franchise rights over this part of the avenue. The matter was finally settled when the legislature, on April 9, 1899, directed [4] that (1) no street surface railroad could operate between these two points by any motive power other than horse-power unless the tracks were twenty feet distant from either curb; (2)

[1] *Proceedings of the Board of Aldermen*, vol. 174, pp. 305-307.
[2] *Ibid.*, pp. 588-595.
[3] See *Report of Department of Docks, 1892.*
[4] *Laws of the State of New York, 1899*, ch. 371.

any street surface company having a valid right to operate a surface railroad between these two points by any power other than horse-power could lay its rails between the tracks of other companies already operating; and (3) all existing controversies were to be adjusted by the Supreme Court in an action to be brought by the party aggrieved. Right of appeal was given and the courts were to fix all damages. The act specifically stated that existing franchise privileges were in no way affected thereby.

The last franchise obtained by the company was for a loop extension at Fort Lee ferry; this grant was secured December 29, 1910, by contract with the board of estimate and apportionment.[1] The grant was made for a term of ten years, with the privilege of renewal upon revaluation for fifteen years; the company agreed to pay three per cent of its gross annual receipts for the first five years, and five per cent for the remainder of the term—in any event not less than three hundred and twenty-five dollars for the first five-year period, and five hundred and seventy-five dollars for the second five-year period of the original term. The company was required to keep in repair the pavement between the tracks and for a distance of two feet on either side thereof. At the expiration of the franchise the tracks were to revert to the city free of cost.

The company has made a number of trackage agreements.[2] In November, 1895, the Third Avenue Railroad Company obtained stock control of the company,[3] but the former corporation soon after transferred its holdings in the Forty-second Street, Manhattanville and St. Nicholas

---

[1] *Minutes of the Board of Estimate and Apportionment: Financial and Franchise Matters*, 1910, pp. 1197, 2110-2127, 3250.

[2] *Report of the Public Service Commission, First District State of New York*, 1913, vol. v, pp. 434-439.

[3] *Ibid.*, chart ii, no. 23.

Avenue Company to the Metropolitan Street Railway.[1] On February 1, 1908, after the collapse of the great railway monopoly of New York city, F. W. Whitridge, receiver of the Third Avenue Railroad Company, was appointed separate receiver for the Forty-second Street, Manhattanville and St. Nicholas Avenue Company. He turned the property back to the company on March 1, 1912. The road is now operated as a part of the Third Avenue Railway system.

[1] *Infra*, ch. viii.

CHAPTER VI

THE GENERAL LAW OF 1884 AND THE BROADWAY GRANT

FROM 1874 to 1884 no general street surface railway law was enacted by the legislature, although frequent attempts were made to put such a law on the statute books.[1] In 1883 a bill regulating the laying out and construction of railroads in cities of over five hundred thousand population, but excluding Broadway in New York city from its provisions, was passed by the legislature; it, however, did not receive the governor's approval.[2]

The following year a general act was passed on May 6th authorizing the incorporation of companies for the purpose of constructing and operating street surface railroads in cities, towns and villages.[3] By this act any number of persons exceeding thirteen might form a company for the purpose of constructing, maintaining and operating for compensation a street surface railway for public conveyance of persons and property in cars. This law required the incorporators in their articles of association to state the name of the company, the number of years it was to continue, the names of the cities, towns, villages and counties in which the road was to be built, and the names of the streets on which it was to operate, together with a statement of the approximate length of the road and the capital stock of the company. The articles of association were to be filed in

[1] See *Senate and Assembly Journals*, 1874-1883.
[2] *New York State Senate Journal*, 1883, 106th Session, p. 632.
[3] *Laws of the State of New York*, 1884, ch. 252.

the office of the Secretary of State when one thousand dollars of stock for every mile of railroad proposed to be constructed had been subscribed and ten per cent of it paid in. Any company organized under this law, or any existing street surface railway company should have the right to build and operate a street surface railway along any streets, avenues, roads and highways, and along or upon any private property acquired for this purpose on condition that the consent of the property owners was first obtained in accordance with the constitutional provision. The consent of the property owners was to be in the form of duly acknowledged deeds which were to be recorded. It was stipulated that the common council should act as the local authority for giving the consent of the city subject to such power as the mayor possessed to veto ordinances. In case, however, any other local authority had exclusive control of any particular street proposed to be used for a street railway, the consent of such other local authority or authorities was also required. In cities, all applications for franchises were to be in writing and grants were to be made only after publication for two weeks, and upon the express condition that the provisions of this law be complied with. Unless the company secured within one year the consent of the property owners or the authorization of the court, as provided for in the constitutional amendment of 1874, the consent of the local authorities would become void. The city's consent to the right of way through a street would also operate as consent for any property owned by the city abutting on such streets. Should consent of the required number of property owners not be obtained and the company, therefore, be obliged to apply to the court for authorization to construct its road, the company was then bound to serve upon every such property owner not consenting a notice of such application at least ten days prior thereto.

The seventh section of the act empowered the local authorities of any incorporated city to consent to the operation of a railway within their jurisdiction and, at their option, to provide for sale of the franchise at public auction. In cities having a population of two hundred and fifty thousand or more, every street surface railway company was required to pay annually to the city treasury three per cent of its gross receipts during the first five years after the commencement of its operation, and five per cent thereafter. All companies, including those organized under preceding acts, were to pay these percentages on extensions made thereafter. Each mile of extension was to be considered as earning the same proportion of the gross receipts as the average earning per mile of the company's entire system. Any corporation which failed to pay promptly at the stipulated time was required to pay, in addition to its regular percentage, five per cent per month on such percentage until the same was fully paid. On failure of any company to comply with this particular provision its corporate rights, privileges and franchises should be forfeited in a suit brought against it by the Attorney-General. The local authorities were to make such regulations as to speed, method of using tracks, removal of ice and snow, as the interest and convenience of the public might require. Any street railway corporation whose agents wilfully or negligently violated any such regulation would be liable to a penalty not to exceed five hundred dollars. Any company incorporated under, or seeking to extend its road in accordance with the provisions of this act, which failed to commence construction within one year after it had secured the necessary consents, or which failed to complete its road within three years after such consents had been acquired, would lose all its rights, privileges and franchises. Steam could not be used as a motive power but any other power was permissible with the consent of the local authorities and the property owners. Not more than a five cent rate of fare could be charged any passenger for one continuous ride from any point on the company's road or on any road or branch operated by it or under its control to any other point on such road or branch, or any connecting branch within the limits of any incorporated city. This provision, however, was not to apply to any street railway already built and then in operation, unless the existing companies applied for extensions; in such cases the fare on their roads, including the extensions, was to be no greater than the rates authorized prior to that time. Except for necessary crossings, no street surface railway could construct, extend or operate its road in that portion of any street in which another street surface railway was already constructed unless the consent of the company owning the other railway was first obtained. Provision was made, however, for the use of one company's tracks by another company for a distance not to exceed one thousand feet whenever the court, on application, was satisfied that such use was actually necessary to connect main portions of a line to be constructed as an independent railroad, and that public convenience required such use. It was made lawful for any company to lease or transfer its right to operate on the whole or any portion of the tracks to any other company or companies. Exception to this provision was made for cities of over three hundred thousand population in case the companies so concerned owned and operated parallel lines.

The Act of 1884, requiring all companies to pay certain percentages of their gross receipts to the city, made it thenceforth impossible for any franchise to be legally granted without providing for compensation to the city; in that respect the act was most commendatory. The law, as we have seen, did not, however, affect those street railways already constructed except in the event of extensions. In other words, the most important streets in the heart of the city continued to be occupied by lines of the already existing companies who returned no revenue to the city aside from the car-license fee; while suburban lines, developed by new companies, and extensions by existing companies, were required to pay a specific amount which was considerably in excess of the car-license fee. This arrangement was unfair as it not only discriminated against the new company but in the event that an old company desired to extend its lines provision was made for a tax on the earnings of the proposed extension reckoned on the theory that a mile of track in a sparsely settled section earned equally as much as a mile of track in the congested districts of the city. Any company, therefore, whether old or new, which constructed new lines was penalized by the Act of 1884. The effect of the law was two-fold: in the first place, if a company desired to extend its lines into the outlying districts it was tempted to do so by means of a dummy or subsidiary corporation whose gross receipts tax would be based upon the earnings of the extension itself rather than upon the average earnings of an equal mileage of the company's entire system. This is what actually happened in the case of the Ninth avenue extension, known as the Columbus and Ninth avenue railroad and the Houston, West street and Pavonia ferry railroad extension which worked through a dummy company known as the Lexington Avenue and Pavonia Ferry Railroad Company.[1] Secondly, the act discouraged the extension of transit facilities, and especially the extension of existing lines.

In spite of its many drawbacks, this act was the signal for a deluge of petitions to the councilmen for street surface railway franchise grants.[2] Interest centered mainly

[1] *Infra*, ch. vii.
[2] *Proceedings of the Board of Aldermen*, 1884; vol. 175, pp. 29, 108, 181, 226, 360, 392, 396, 471, 582; vol. 176, pp. 5, 180.

in the Broadway franchise. There were two principal competitors: The Broadway Surface Railway Company and The Broadway Railroad Company. The New York Cable Company was also an aspirant.[1] Jacob Sharp was the commanding spirit of the Broadway Surface Railway Company.[2] The men back of the Broadway Railroad Company

PLATE XX

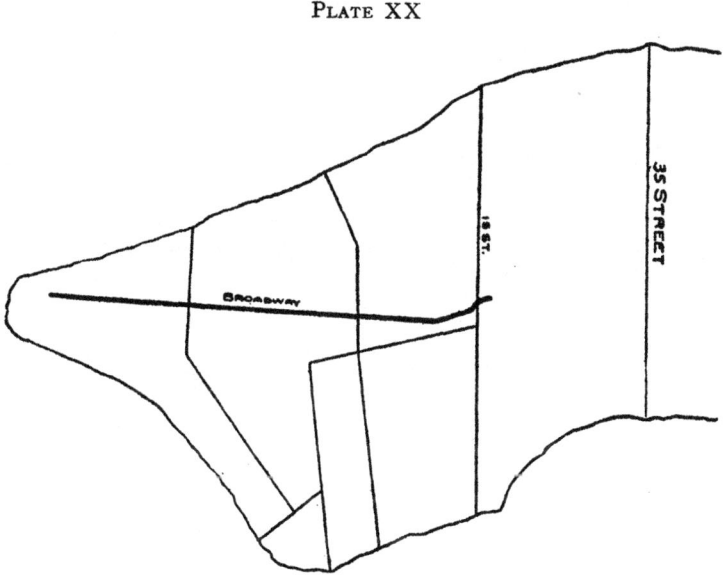

BROADWAY SURFACE RAILROAD COMPANY

were J. A. Roosevelt, Brayton Ives, George Henry Warren, George C. Haven, and William C. Whitney[3] On June 30, 1884, a petition of the Broadway Surface Railway Com-

[1] *Proceedings of the Board of Aldermen*, 1884, vol. 175, p. 553.

[2] See testimony of Sharp before Commissioners appointed by New York State Supreme Court in the matter of the Broadway Surface Railway Company, vol. ii, p. 788, *et seq.*

[3] *Proceedings of the Board of Aldermen*, 1884; vol. 175, p. 549.

pany was filed with the Board of Aldermen for permission to construct, operate and maintain a double-track surface railway on Broadway from the Battery to Fifteenth street.[1] The councilmen designated August 5th as the time for public consideration of the petition.[2] The day following the hearing, the aldermanic committee on railroads submitted a report in which they favored the granting of the Broadway franchise to the Broadway Surface Railway Company.[3] Alderman Hugh J. Grant at once offered an amendment providing for the sale of the franchise to the highest bidder. In his opinion this franchise was "the most valuable that had been at the disposal of the city for years." He said:

I am credibly informed that a number of years ago the city was offered one million dollars for the right to build a railroad on Broadway. If the franchise was worth that amount then, it is certainly worth it now. I believe it is worth a great deal more. If we should sell the franchise at auction no injustice would be done anybody, and the city would receive some benefit from it.[4]

This motion failed of adoption and a resolution embodying the recommendation of the committee was approved by a vote of twenty-one to one, Alderman Grant alone voting in the negative.[5] Later testimony before the courts proved that Sharp and his associates had as early as May, 1884, criminally paved the way for the subsequent action of the city fathers. At the trial of Alderman Arthur J. McQuade before Recorder Smythe on November 19, 1886, Alderman L. A. Fulgraff testified:

[1] *Proceedings of the Board of Aldermen*, 1884; vol. 174, p. 875.
[2] *Ibid.*, vol. 175, p. 71.
[3] *Ibid.*, pp. 235-239.
[4] *Ibid.*, p. 240; *New York Times*, August 7, 1884.
[5] *Ibid.*, p. 240.

A special meeting of the Board was held in my factory in Fulton street in the month of May, 1884. There were thirteen members present; they were DeLacy, Dempsey, McLoughlin, Sayles, McQuade, McCabe, Kenney, Jaehne, Cleary, Reilly, O'Neill, Duffy and myself. It was proposed that the thirteen should vote together on everything that came up except on political issues. It was determined to have a meeting at McLoughlin's house a week later. At this meeting the same thirteen were present. The first subject taken up was the Broadway franchise. It was stated that a cable railroad company had applied for the privilege. It was said that the company had offered $750,000, half cash and half bonds, and that the Broadway Company had offered $500,000 in cash. I think Jaehne said the acceptance of $750,000 from the cable road would be risky as the bonds could be traced. He thought the Broadway surface people would be safer.[1]

Fulgraff also testified that for this gift to the Broadway Surface Railway Company each alderman in the "deal" received $22,000.[2]

The Broadway Railroad Company, chagrined and outwitted but not yet defeated, had in the meantime addressed a letter to the editor of the *New York Sun*[3] in which William C. Whitney and J. A. Roosevelt on behalf of the company endeavored to win support by agreeing to offer one-half of the company's stock to the abutting property owners along the proposed line. On August 5th, the day before the grant was made, an editorial appeared in the *New York Sun* urging that the franchise be sold at auction to the highest bidder.[4] Just a week after the franchise resolution was

[1] *New York Tribune*, November 19, 1886; *New York Times*, November 19, 1886.
[2] *Ibid*.
[3] *New York Sun*, August 2, 1884; *Proceedings of the Board of Aldermen*, 1884, vol. 175, pp. 550-552.
[4] *New York Sun*, August 5, 1884.

passed the Broadway Railroad Company in a letter addressed to Mayor Franklin Edson, asking for an investigation of the proceedings of the councilmen relative to the franchise grant, stated that it was prepared "to bid at auction sale several hundred thousand dollars for the right to build and operate a railroad on Broadway."[1] The New York Cable Company on August 29th offered a million dollars for the franchise.[2]

On August 18th Mayor Edson vetoed the franchise resolution. After quoting freely from the law of 1884 he said:

I am convinced that this franchise can be sold for at least one million dollars, upon such terms and conditions as will protect the great thoroughfare from desecration, insure a proper construction and the use of rails which will produce the least possible obstruction in the streets, and at the same time guarantee efficient service. In such circumstances, to grant the consent asked for by "The Broadway Surface Railroad Company," without compensation, would, in my judgment, be equivalent to giving a private corporation for its unrestricted use, property of the city of the value of a million dollars.[3]

As there were many indications that the aldermen would pass the resolution over the mayor's veto, an injunction was procured on August 23 from Judge Donohue on the application of E. M. Knox, H. K. Thurber and others, taxpayers and business men,[4] restraining the board.[5] On August 29

[1] *Proceedings of the Board of Aldermen*, 1884; vol. 175, pp. 548-549.
[2] *Ibid.*, pp. 555-556.
[3] *Ibid.*, pp. 436-437.
[4] *Testimony before Commission appointed by New York State Supreme Court in the matter of the Broadway Surface Railroad Company*, vol. ii, pp. 969-997; *New York Times*, September 6, 1884.
[5] *Proceedings of Board of Aldermen*, 1884; vol. 175, pp. 452-453; *New York Tribune*, November 19, 1886.

it was alleged that Osborne Bright of the firm of Robinson, Scribner and Bright, with the aid of twelve thousand five hundred dollars bought off the opposing attorney, thus obtaining consent for the dissolution of the injunction [1] which was thereafter vacated by order of Justice Bartlett.[2] This legal obstacle removed, a meeting of the board of aldermen was hastily called for the next day at nine o'clock in the morning, and at this meeting the franchise resolution was passed over the executive's veto.[3] This action aroused bitter feeling. The leading men of the city issued a call for a mass meeting, which was held at Chickering Hall on the evening of September 4. The public was determined to force the aldermen to rescind their resolution of August 30.[4]

The next move was made on September 8 at which time the August 30 meeting of the board was declared illegal by Corporation Counsel E. H. Lacombe.[5] Sharp and his associates did not delay. Another petition was presented to the board of aldermen [6] by the Broadway Surface Railroad Company on October 5. The document stated that the petitioners had entered into an agreement with the Broadway and Seventh Avenue Railroad Company for the common use of tracks. Therefore, in case the desired franchise was granted, passengers would be carried from South ferry to Central Park without change of cars for a single five cent fare. October 29 was designated for the so-called pub-

[1] *Ibid.*, p. 500; *New York Tribune*, November 19, 1886; *New York State Senate Documents*, 1886; 109th Session, vol. iv, no. 52, p. 3.

[2] *Proceedings of the Board of Aldermen*, vol. 175, p. 499.

[3] *Ibid.*, pp. 503-504.

[4] *New York Times*, September 4 and 5, 1884.

[5] *Proceedings of the Board of Aldermen*, 1884, vol. 175, p. 601.

[6] *Ibid.*, vol. 176, pp. 5-181; *City Record*, October 7, 1884, vol. xii, pp. 2393-2394; *New York Tribune*, November 19, 1886.

lic hearing, the petition in the meantime being referred to the committee on railroads. The mayor on October 13 sent an elaborate message to the aldermen in which he vigorously objected to granting the franchise.[1] In discussing the question of financial return to the city, he showed by reference to the Bleecker street and Fulton ferry and the Twenty-third street railroad companies that the Broadway Surface Railroad Company and the Broadway and Seventh Avenue Railroad Company might have an agreement whereby the city would be defrauded out of the percentage funds provided by the law of 1884. He pointed out how the officers of the Bleecker street and Fulton Ferry Railroad Company and the Twenty-third street Railroad Company had always maintained

that it is impossible for them to separate the receipts of one road from the other. Its conductors collect the fares received from passengers indiscriminately over the whole route. . . . Should the application of the Broadway Surface Railroad Company be granted, there can, . . . be no doubt that the same method will be followed in order to defeat the claim of the city to the percentage intended to be secured to it by law.

After explaining how it was even possible that the two companies might have the same officers and that the estimated net annual income to the city from the company would be only about four hundred thousand dollars, he asked

Why should they [the Broadway Surface Railroad Company] of all the million and a half inhabitants of this city, have such an enormous fortune conferred on them at the expense of their fellow citizens? If a railroad is to be constructed on Broadway at all, consent to construct it should be conferred only upon those who will secure to the city the fullest equi-

---

[1] *Proceedings of the Board of Aldermen*, 1884, vol. 176, pp. 242-255.

valent, not only in the purchase money paid for the franchise, but also in the annual percentage of the gross receipts.

A shower of protests from various sources poured into the mayor's office and the aldermen likewise were petitioned.[1] These appeals, however, did not halt the city legislators. The mayor and the corporation counsel attempted to stay their hand through injunction proceedings.[2] The committee on railroads, after giving due consideration to the application,[3] made a report in favor of granting the franchise.[4] On November 12 Justice Barrett of the Supreme Court issued an order modifying the temporary injunction in such a manner as to make possible the awarding of the grant.[5] Two days later the franchise resolution was approved by a vote of twenty-two to two.[6] At the same time the board rescinded its action of August 30.[7]

In its provisions the new franchise was more favorable to the city. It provided for a horse-power road to be constructed according to the most improved plan; a five cent fare was to be charged and the usual provisions in regard to street repair and snow removal were incorporated. Further, the company during the first five years after the commencement of operations was to pay three per cent of its gross receipts into the city treasury annually; at the expiration of the five year period the rate was to be five per cent. A like annual payment was required from any other railroad company which might derive income from fares

[1] See daily papers, October 14-30, 1884.
[2] *Proceedings of the Board of Aldermen*, 1884; vol. 176, pp. 552-556.
[3] *City Record*, November 13, 1884; vol. xii, p. 2766.
[4] *Proceedings of the Board of Aldermen*, 1884; vol. 176, pp. 681-694.
[5] *Ibid.*, pp. 703-706.
[6] *Ibid.*, p. 718.
[7] *Ibid.*, p. 719.

collected from passengers riding in any of its cars which operated on Broadway below Fifteenth street. In addition, it was stipulated that an annual payment of forty thousand dollars, equivalent to the interest on a million dollars at four per cent, be paid into the city treasury annually.

Mayor Edson in vetoing this second grant stated that he did so for the same reasons as before. He further stated that if it should finally appear that public interests demanded that the city give up its principal thoroughfare to a private corporation " let it be so done as to leave no doubt in the mind of any citizen that the interests of the city have been guarded with the most jealous and conscientious fidelity by those to whom such interests are entrusted." [1] This communication was referred to the councilmanic committee on railroads.[2] In its report to the board the committee said that the mayor's action was " unwarrantable;" that his veto of the resolution of August 30 was in " bad faith and unbecoming " and " in defiance of all decency." [3] The public apparently thought otherwise.[4] On December 5 the franchise resolution was passed over the mayor's veto, Aldermen Grant and O'Connor voting in the negative.[5] Jacob Sharp, after more than thirty years of almost unrelenting effort, had secured control of Broadway.

The whole transaction aroused public ire and there were demands that the facts be made known. Even before the franchise was granted it was currently reported that the antimonopoly league had detectives at work compiling evidence

[1] *Proceedings of the Board of Aldermen*, 1884; vol. 176, pp. 777-784.
[2] *Ibid.*, p. 784.
[3] *Ibid.*, pp. 938-940.
[4] See editorial pages of *New York Tribune, New York Times* and *New York Sun* for October 14 and November 25, 1884.
[5] *Proceedings of the Board of Aldermen*, 1884; vol. 176, p. 937.

against several members of the board of aldermen.[1] Late in December, 1884, the Supreme Court named Sidney S. Harris, Samuel B. H. Vance and G. W. T. Lord as commissioners to examine into the Broadway surface matter and report upon the case.[2] On January 26, 1886, the state senate by resolution directed the railroad committee of the senate to investigate all matters relating to the Broadway Surface Railroad Company and to inquire into the proceedings of the board of aldermen which made the Broadway grant.[3] The committee employed as counsel Roscoe Conkling and Clarence A. Seward.[4] The leaders of the counsel for the railroad were James C. Carter and Elihu Root.

The testimony given before the committee unearthed the fact that the three commissioners appointed by the Supreme Court were not entirely free from suspicion. Jacob Sharp's son-in-law, Mr. Selmes, was employed as clerk and confidential bookkeeper by Vance; Harris was the Albany partner of Abraham Disbecker to whom Sharp gave seventy-five thousand dollars; while the third, Lord, was personally interested in a Broadway railroad.[5]

The committee after hearing all the testimony found that no legal authority had ever existed for the construction of the Broadway Surface railroad; that the company operating under this name was a mere sham and that the scheme had

[1] *New York Times*, September 4, 1884.
[2] New York State Supreme Court: *In the Matter of the Broadway Surface Railway Company*, vol. i, pp. 1-2.
[3] *New York State Senate Journal*, 1886; 109th Session, pp. 84-88.
[4] For their arguments before the Committee see *Senate Reports for 1886*, 109th Session, Doc. no. 79, pp. 1765-1820; or see separate document entitled *The Broadway Surface Railroad Company, Arguments of Clarence A. Seward and Roscoe Conkling before the Senate Committee on Railroads*.
[5] *New York State Senate Documents*, 1886; 109th Session, no. 52, p. 5; testimony No. 79, pp. 405-410.

been planned by certain officers and directors of the Broadway and Seventh Avenue Railroad Company; that wholesale bribery had been employed and the city defrauded. Finally the committee was of the opinion that the franchise should be immediately revoked.[1]

In the meantime the Supreme Court, after receiving the report of its commissioners, rendered a decision favorable to the railroad company.[2] Sharp lost no time in laying tracks, securing equipment, and buying up all the stage lines on lower Broadway.[3] But the storm of public indignation which had long been brewing now broke upon the heads of the " boodle " board of aldermen and the Broadway Surface Railroad Company. The charter of the company was annulled by the legislature,[4] but the validity of the act was questioned and in the notable case of The People v. O'Brien [5] the Court of Appeals held that the ill-gotten Broadway franchise of 1884 was perpetual and irrevocable. The court ruled that although the legislature had constitutional power to revoke the charter of the corporation, the grant itself was a contract protected by the federal constitution as interpreted in the Dartmouth College case; it therefore survived the corporation and as property was vested in the directors as trustees for the creditors and stockholders. The Court also went on to say that even though the right to amend, alter, or repeal any of its acts relative to corporations was specifically reserved, such a right could not be construed as authorizing it to repeal a franchise grant. This decision was certainly quite contrary to the common rule that stolen goods

[1] *New York State Senate Documents*, 1886; 109th Session, no. 52, pp. 1-6.
[2] Jenkins, Stephen, *The Greatest Street in the World*, p. 282.
[3] *Ibid.*
[4] *Laws of the State of New York*, 1886, ch. 268.
[5] 111 N. Y., 1.

may be recovered by the owner, and it undoubtedly gave extraordinary force to the old adage that "possession is nine points of the law."

Of the twenty-two aldermen all but two were found to be implicated; Aldermen Duffy, Fullgraff and Waite turned state's evidence.[1] Alderman Henry W. Jaehne, who was convicted by his own confession, was sentenced to state's prison for a term of nine years and ten months.[2] "Honest" John O'Neill, another member of the board, was sentenced to penal servitude for four and one-half years and to pay a fine of two thousand dollars.[3] Arthur J. McQuade was committed to state's prison for seven years and obliged to return five thousand dollars of the bribe money to the city;[4] two years later he was released from Sing Sing pending a new trial which was held at Ballston Spa, N Y.; here he was acquitted on July 20, 1889.[5] Of the other aldermen in the "deal" Keeney, DeLacy, Dempsey, Rothman, Sayles, and Moloney fled to Canada; two had died during the interval, and the remaining members were under indictment, but on May 19, 1891, the last of these indictments was dismissed.[6] Of the railroad officials, Sharp was sentenced to four years in prison and to pay a fine of five thousand dollars; his counsel, however, secured a new trial for him but Sharp died on April 5, 1888, before the retrial took place.[7] Of his

[1] *New York State Senate Committee on Cities*, 1890;, vol. iii, p. 2666.
[2] *New York Evening Post, New York Times, New York Sun, New York Tribune*, May 21, 1886.
[3] *New York Evening Post*, February 2, 1887; *New York Times*, February 2 and 3, 1887; *New York Tribune*, February 2 and 3, 1887.
[4] See New York papers, December 20 and 21, 1886.
[5] *Ibid.*, for July 20, 1889.
[6] *New York Times*, May 20, 1891; *New York Sun*, May 20, 1891.
[7] *New York Evening Post*, April 5, 1888. See also brief account of the fate of the "Boodle" Board of Aldermen in Myers, Gustavus, *The History of Tammany Hall*, pp. 316-317.

associates twelve were tried and acquitted, while James W. Forshay, the president of the Broadway and Seventh Avenue Company, died before trial. The reason assigned for so many acquittals of the indicted parties by Colonel John R. Fellows, the district attorney who prosecuted the cases, was due to the change in public sentiment. The tempest had subsided, the subject matter had grown old, the people had largely become tired of it and the public had come to appreciate the roads.[1] While this was true in part at least, there were persistent rumors at the time to the effect that political influence saved many of the dishonest group from prison terms.[2]

By 1889 most of the surface railroads in the city had made, or were contemplating a change in motive power from horse to cable. The Broadway and Seventh Avenue Company and the South Ferry Railroad Company, the successors to the Broadway Surface franchises, applied to the legislature for power to make the change. The legislature accordingly amended the general law of 1884 so as to take from the local authorities the right to determine what motive power should be used.[3] The local authorities, believing the law to be unconstitutional, disputed its validity.[4] Soon after the act of 1884 was amended, Mayor Hugh J. Grant received a communication from Elihu Root, counsel for the interested railroad companies, stating that Mr. Root's clients wished to obtain the consent and coöperation of the city authorities in making a change of motive power on their line from South Ferry to Central Park.[5] The mayor in

---

[1] *Testimony before New York State Senate Committee on Cities*, 1890 (Fassett Committee), vol. iii, pp. 2667-2668.

[2] See editorial pages of New York newspapers, May 20, 1891.

[3] *Laws of the State of New York*, 1889; ch. 531.

[4] *Proceedings of the Board of Aldermen*, vol. 194, pp. 369-370; vol. 196, p. 184.

[5] *Ibid.*, vol. 196, pp. 185-186.

transmitting this communication to the aldermen recommended that the board consent to the proposed change upon terms conducive to the best interests of the city. He deemed it advisable for the board of aldermen to exact from the petitioning company an annual rental of at least one hundred and fifty thousand dollars.[1]

On November 12, 1889 favorable action was taken by the board. It was stipulated that the company in making the change should install modern center bearing rails; should construction work require the changing of any conduit, such change should be made in agreement with the commissioner of public works; the usual pavement requirement was incorporated; cars were to be not less than twenty-four feet in length and to be lighted by the most approved method by either gas or electricity; lastly, the company was to pay the city an annual sum of one hundred and fifty thousand dollars in addition to the amount paid for licenses, fees and taxes. An amendment provided that cars should be operated during the night, and from two o'clock A. M. to five o'clock A. M., at least one car every twenty minutes.[2] The cable system was installed and the first cable cars were operated over the road in June 1893.

Walton Storm who became chairman of the councilmanic finance committee in 1889, testifying before the Fassett Committee in 1890, admitted that the yearly increase in the Broadway passenger traffic was such that within six years the company would have to pay one hundred and fifty thousand dollars annually under the five per cent gross receipts arrangement.[3] The testimony of Colonel Fellows before

[1] *Proceedings of the Board of Aldermen*, vol. 196, pp. 183-185.

[2] *Ibid.*, pp. 186-188.

[3] *Testimony before New York State Senate Committee on Cities*, 1890, vol. i, pp. 580-582.

the same committee was to the effect that the treasury of the city would have lost nothing if the franchise had never been granted.[1]

In conclusion it can be said that the franchise history of the Broadway surface railway is a story replete with bribery and corruption,—a story in which " boodle " aldermen, iniquitous legislators, complaisant courts and a swindled public were the leading characters.

[1] *Testimony before New York State Senate Committee on Cities*, 1890, vol. iii, p. 2668.

CHAPTER VII

HISTORY OF RAILWAYS INCORPORATED BETWEEN 1884 AND 1897

I. THE CHAMBERS STREET AND GRAND STREET FERRY RAILROAD COMPANY

SUBSEQUENT to the enactment of the General Street Surface Railway Law of 1884, several railroad companies were incorporated, and The Chambers Street and Grand Street Ferry Railroad Company was one of the first of these. It was chartered August 9, 1884, for one thousand years with a capital stock of eight hundred thousand dollars.[1] The company proposed to construct a crosstown surface railway over a two and a half mile route, commencing at the East river, at the foot of Roosevelt street, extending on South street to James Slip, thence to New Chambers street to the North river, with a branch on West street from Chambers street to Duane street, thence on Duane street from West street to Chatham street. A line was to be built on Madison street from New Chambers street to Grand street to the East river, and on Jackson street from Madison street to Cherry street to Grand street. The franchise for this route was obtained from the common council December 30, 1884.[2] This road, connecting Grand street ferry, Roose-

[1] *Report of the Public Service Commission of the State of New York, First District*, 1913, vol. v, p. 283.
[2] *Proceedings of the Board of Aldermen*, vol. 176, p. 1207.

velt street ferry and James Slip ferry on the East river with Pavonia avenue ferry on the North river would, in the opinion of the councilmanic railroad committee, afford

PLATE XXI

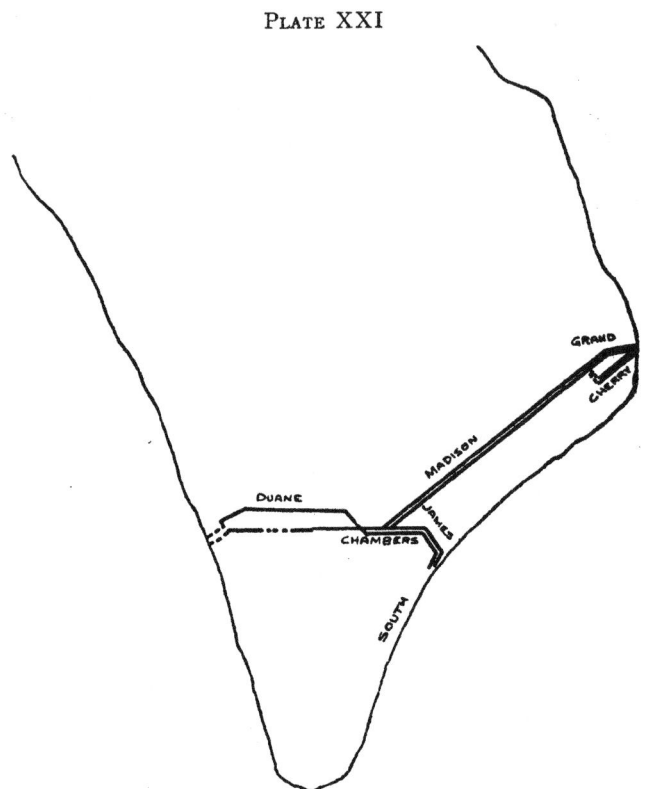

CHAMBERS STREET AND GRAND STREET FERRY RAILROAD COMPANY
- - - - - trackage rights obtained on tracks of other companies

a much-needed accommodation to the public, inasmuch as it would serve as a connecting link between Long Island and its railroad system and the Erie railroad. Further, the committee pointed out that it would be the only crosstown line south of Canal and Walker streets.¹ Mayor Edson in vetoing the grant, stated that while he was in favor of crosstown roads that would in any way promote the public convenience and facilitate the business interests of the city,² he was emphatically opposed to granting franchises from which the city would receive practically no compensation. In his opinion, the grant would benefit the Erie Railroad Company but would be a detriment to property owners along the proposed route. At best, if the privilege was to be granted at all, the mayor believed it should be sold at public auction to the highest bidder. The aldermen paid little attention to this advice and when it became evident that they intended to pass the measure, Theodore Roosevelt, Oscar F. Straus, Henry A. Oakley and George Haven Putnam obtained a temporary injunction, December 17, 1884, from Judge Miles Beach of the Court of Common Pleas, restraining the aldermen from further action in the matter.³ This restraining order was vacated on December 30 and the resolution was promptly passed over the mayor's veto by a vote of twenty-two to two.⁴

No further grants were made to this company with the exception of a permit by the department of docks, October 21, 1886, which enabled the company to lay its tracks and switches upon the newly made land in front of the Pavonia ferry; the permit, like similar privileges to other companies, might be revoked at any time.⁵

¹ *Proceedings of the Board of Aldermen*, vol. 176, p. 874. The franchise provided that all cars be propelled by horse-power; the company was to comply with all provisions of the general act of 1884.

² *Report of the Public Service Commission of the State of New York, First District*, 1913, vol. v, pp. 1016-1018.

³ See *Municipal Affairs*, 1900, vol. iv, p. 145.

⁴ *Proceedings of the Board of Aldermen*, vol. 176, p. 1207.

⁵ *City Record*, vol. xiv, pt. iv, p. 2662.

This company enjoyed a very brief career as an independent company, for in June 1886, its entire capital stock was acquired by the Metropolitan Traction Company.¹ Five years later it lost its identity when it became merged with the Houston, West Street and Pavonia Ferry Railroad Company which in time was absorbed by the Metropolitan Street Railway Company.²

2. THE THIRTY-FOURTH STREET RAILROAD COMPANY

The Thirty-fourth Street Railroad Company was incorporated December 27, 1884, with a capitalization of one

PLATE XXII

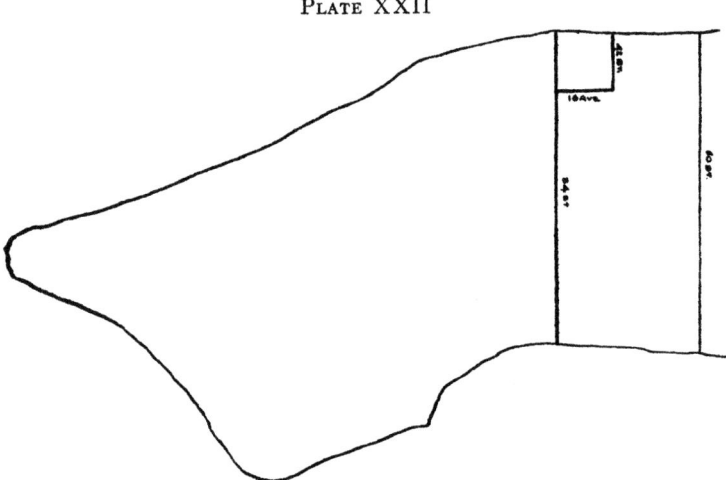

THIRTY-FOURTH STREET RAILROAD COMPANY

hundred thousand dollars, its duration to be two hundred years.³ The franchise granted by the common council of

¹ *Infra*, ch. viii.
² *Infra*, ch. viii.
³ *Report of the Public Service Commission of the State of New York, First District*, 1913, vol. v, p. 1320.

the city of New York and approved December 27, 1884, authorized the construction and operation of a surface road on Thirty-fourth street from the North river to the East river; on Tenth avenue from Thirty-fourth street to Forty-second street; and on Forty-second street from Tenth avenue to the North river.[1] Notwithstanding the fact that the road was not finally completed and in operation until January 10, 1895, it was leased on April 23, 1889, for a period of nine hundred and ninety-nine years, to the Thirty-fourth Street Ferry and Eleventh Avenue Railroad Company.[2]

3. THE THIRTY-FOURTH STREET FERRY AND ELEVENTH AVENUE RAILROAD COMPANY

This company, always closely associated with the Thirty-fourth Street Railroad Company, obtained a charter July 28, 1885, in which it was set forth that the company was capitalized at one million two hundred thousand dollars for the duration of one thousand years, and that its purpose was the construction of a surface railroad over a seven and a half mile route as follows:[3] Commencing at the Thirty-fourth street ferry on the East river, through Thirty-fourth street to Lexington avenue, to Thirty-second street to Fourth avenue; also from Lexington avenue and Thirty-third street through Thirty-third street to Fourth or Park avenue, to Thirty-second street, to Tenth avenue, to Thirty-fourth street, to Eleventh avenue, to One Hundred and Sixth street; also from Thirty-third street and Tenth avenue through

---

[1] *Proceedings of the Board of Aldermen*, vol. 179, pp. 1095-1097. The provisions for the franchise were the same as those for Chambers Street and Grand Street Ferry Railroad Company.

[2] *Report of the Public Service Commission of the State of New York, First District*, 1913, vol. v, p. 1321.

[3] *Ibid.*, vol. v, p. 1319.

Thirty-third street to Park avenue, to Thirty-second street; also from First avenue and Thirty-fourth street along First avenue to Thirty-third street, to Lexington avenue; also from First avenue and Thirty-third street through Thirty-third street to the East river; also from Thirty-fourth street and Eleventh avenue through Thirty-fourth street to the North river; also from Forty-second street and Eleventh avenue through Forty-second street to the North river; also from Sixty-fifth street and Eleventh avenue through Sixty-

PLATE XXIII

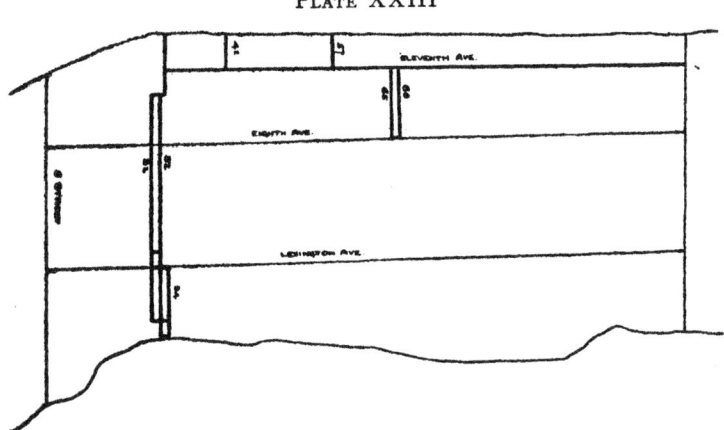

THIRTY-FOURTH STREET FERRY AND ELEVENTH AVENUE RAILROAD COMPANY

fifth street to Eighth avenue, to Sixty-sixth street and back to Eleventh avenue.[1]

The franchise for this route was sanctioned by a resolution of the board of aldermen on October 13, 1885, but Mayor William R. Grace vetoed it for the reason that the minimum amount of compensation to the city as fixed by law, three per cent of the gross earnings for the first five years and five per cent for all subsequent years, was less than

[1] *Proceedings of the Board of Aldermen*, vol. 180, pp. 107-109.

the real value of the proposed privileges;[1] and, furthermore, that the owners of three-fourths of the assessed valuation of the abutting property on Thirty-second and Thirty-third streets were opposed to the road. The mayor also objected to the franchise for the reason that it made possible the transportation of freight as well as passengers over the contemplated road.[2] In spite of these objections, the measure was passed on November 10, 1885, by a vote of twenty-three to one.[3]

Nothing further of importance in the franchise history of this company occurred until March, 1896, when it was united with the Thirty-fourth Street Railroad Company to form the Thirty-fourth Street Crosstown Railway Company,[4] which, in turn, soon became merged in the Metropolitan Street Surface Railway Company.[5]

4. THE CABLE PLAN

The period of New York city street railway consolidation was foreshadowed by an elaborate plan for installing the cable system of operating the railroads of the city. Although this plan failed to materialize, the franchise history of the period under consideration would be incomplete without a brief description of the New York Cable Railway Company.

In an effort to solve the transit problem of the city, which yearly became more difficult as the city grew in area and population, Mayor Edson, pursuant to a legislative act,[6]

[1] Practically the same conditions were stipulated as for the Chambers Street and Grand Street Ferry Railroad Company.
[2] *Proceedings of the Board of Aldermen*, vol. 180, pp. 433-436.
[3] *Ibid.*, p. 662.
[4] *Report of the Public Service Commission of the State of New York, First District*, 1913, vol. v, p. 1316.
[5] *Infra*, ch. viii.
[6] *Laws of the State of New York*, 1875, ch. 606.

appointed on November 30, 1883, a Rapid Transit Commission to inquire into and work out a plan for better passenger transportation facilities.[1] This commission, in reporting its proceedings to the mayor in April, 1884, requested that he transmit the same to the board of aldermen for their consideration and action. The mayor complied with this request.[2] At about the same time the cable company was incorporated for the purpose of " constructing a single or double track steam railway or railways over, under, through or across streets, avenues, places or lands in the City of New York."[3] This company, which had outlined twenty-nine different routes totaling between seventy and eighty miles, proposed a scheme of intramural transit involving a system of railways on the East and West side, extending from the Battery to the Harlem river, partly elevated and partly surface, with convenient crosstown lines connecting these longitudinal railways with all the important ferries on the North and East rivers. By means of a transfer system, a person would be enabled to travel over the entire route for five cents. Two and a half per cent of the gross earnings were to be paid to the city annually.[4] The plan in its entirety was identical with one submitted by the Rapid Transit Commission in its report to the mayor. An application for a franchise covering the proposed road was referred to the councilmanic committee on railroads, and

[1] The members of this Commission were Edwin R. Livermore, a prominent member of the New York Produce Exchange; Thomas E. Stewart, a former Congressman and Park Commissioner of the City; Edward L. Hedden, Collector of the Port of New York; Edmund D. Randolph, President of the Continental Bank; and Joseph M. De Veau, President of the Mt. Morris Bank.

[2] *Proceedings of the Board of Aldermen*, vol. 181, pp. 144-145.

[3] *Report of the Public Service Commission of the State of New York, First District*, 1913, vol. v, p. 867.

[4] *Proceedings of the Board of Aldermen*, vol. 180, pp. 1030-1034.

on December 8,, 1884, this committee submitted a favorable report,[1] which, however, was laid over for further consideration.[2] Before the next meeting of the common council took place, an owner of abutting property along one of the proposed routes secured a temporary injunction restraining the board from making the grant.[3] This injunction was dissolved, and immediately another owner obtained a similar writ, which continued in force until December 31, 1884. It was vacated too late to give the outgoing mayor opportunity to consider whether he should approve the consent of the board for the construction of the railway or railways in case the board adopted a resolution to that effect.[4] No sooner had the restraining writ been vacated than the matter came up for discussion; the board of aldermen, however, by the narrow vote of thirteen to twelve, decided to postpone consideration of the subject indefinitely.[5] The company, therefore, renewed its application for a franchise on January 19, 1886, which request went the way of the first petition.[6] The committee on railroads, in its report of March 2, 1886, urged that the franchise be granted,[7] and it is interesting to note that the committee practically apologized to the cable company for recommending compensation to the city.[8] This report was adopted and the franchise

[1] *Proceedings of the Board of Aldermen*, vol. 180, pp. 1030-1034.
[2] *Ibid.*, p. 1035.
[3] See *Documents of Public Service Commission*, 1913, vol. v, p. 880.
[4] *Proceedings of the Board of Aldermen*, vol. 181, p. 151.
[5] *Ibid.*, pp. 193-199.
[6] For petition in full see *City Record*, vol. xiv, pt. i, pp. 155-6.
[7] *Proceedings of the Board of Aldermen*, vol. 181, pp. 474-493.
[8] "Your committee has, however, in deference to the suggestion of Mayor Edson's Rapid Transit Commissioners reluctantly decided to acquiesce in the suggestion that the Cable Company pay as a consideration for its franchise two and one-half per cent of its annual net earnings into the city treasury." Report of Committee on Railroads; see *Proceedings of the Board of Aldermen*, vol. 181, pp. 474-493.

granted by a vote of nineteen to four.[1] On March 19, 1886, Mayor Grace returned the resolution with his veto, stating, among other things, that he did not consider two and one-half per cent of the net proceeds sufficient compensation.[2] He was not, however, opposed to the project as such, and even went so far as to suggest an alternative plan, as follows:

Let the city instead of being the grantor, become the lessor of street railway privileges; let the Commissioners of the Sinking Fund lease all franchises at public auction for a term of not less than ten or more than twenty years; let them appoint an auditor, who, with the officers of the road shall certify under oath the actual money value of the road and equipment at the time of construction, *i. e.*, real cost; let the comptroller prescribe the form in which the books of the company are to be kept, and let the sinking fund commissioners have an accountant continuously in the office of the company but shifting the accountants from week to week, as they are now shifted from day to day in the Money Order Bureau of the Post Office, to provide a check upon wrong doing or collusion on their part; let the person taking the franchise receive all profits on the operation of the road up to ten per cent on the actual investment for construction and equipment, all sums earned in excess of such ten per cent to be paid quarterly into the City Treasury. At the expiration of the lease, let the franchise be re-let as is now done with ferry franchises; and in case it is let to new parties, let the city pay the old lessee the estimated cost of replacing the plant, charging a like sum to the new lessee who shall be represented in the appraisement.

Such a system the mayor thought would result (1) in the city's reaping the benefit of the "unearned increment of value"; (2) it would furnish sufficient inducement to cap-

[1] *Proceedings of the Board of Aldermen*, vol. 181, p. 495.
[2] *Ibid.*, pp. 675-682.

ital; and (3) city franchises would, therefore, lighten the tax burden. This seems to have been the first comprehensive plan evolved for the solution of this difficult problem.

At this same meeting of the board of aldermen a resolution was introduced by Alderman Earle in which the statement was made that at the public hearing before the mayor on the New York cable-railways franchise application, certain individuals declared themselves ready and willing to pay into the city treasury ten million dollars " for the uses and benefits of the said franchise as granted." The resolution would authorize the president of the board of aldermen to appoint a committee of five to hold public meetings " to be devoted solely and exclusively to the residents and property owners along the line of the proposed cable roads." It was also provided that parties wishing to bid for this valuable franchise should be heard at the same time. The councilmen tabled this resolution.[1] The company made one further attempt, June 16, 1886, to secure the grant from the aldermen,[2] but its petition was never reported by the railroad committee of that body. Possibly the inner transactions of the board of aldermen relative to the Broadway surface railroad, the details of which were becoming public, were responsible, in part at least, for the nonpassage of this grant.

5. THE CANTOR ACT

Less than two years elapsed after the passage of the General Street Railway Act of 1884 before the people of the city of New York had conclusive proof of the wholesale bribery connected with the franchise grant for lower Broadway. To prevent a repetition of such a notorious scandal,

[1] *Proceedings of the Board of Aldermen*, vol. 181, pp. 688-689.
[2] *Ibid.*, vol. 182, pp. 650-651.

the legislature in 1886 passed a general law [1] requiring that all local franchises for street railways to be constructed " for the transportation of passengers, mails or freight," be sold at public auction to the bidder offering to pay the largest percentage of gross receipts into the city treasury, in addition to the minimum percentages already required under the act of 1884. In case of refusal to pay the percentages the purchasers would be liable to forfeiture of the grant by court decree after a proper hearing. In case of such forfeiture, the city had authority to re-sell the franchise. The act as amended [2] further provided that the purchasing company should complete the road and put it in operation within three years from the date of sale. This statute, known as the Cantor Act, so called in honor of the author, expressly reserved to the legislature the right to regulate the rate of fare, and the company was required to keep accurate account of all earnings and business transactions and its books were to be at all times subject to inspection by the local authorities. The act also expressly stated that all consents thereafter given by the local authorities should cease at the expiration of two years from their date, and that all consents which had already been obtained should terminate within two years from the date of the act, unless prior to the expiration of the prescribed time the company holding the consents should show a clear legal right to construct its road by acquiring the requisite consents of property-owners, or court approval, as provided for in the Act of 1884.

In the same year, 1886, the legislature further attempted to systematize and regulate the street railways by enacting a measure providing that whenever any street railway company had been dissolved, or its charter repealed by legisla-

---

[1] *Laws of the State of New York*, 1886, ch. 65.
[2] *Ibid.*, ch. 642.

tive act, the consent of the property-owners and of the local authorities for the construction of a road over a specified route, and the order of the court authorizing such construction, should not be deemed revoked, but that the legal right to the further enjoyment of such consents should be disposed of at public auction by the municipal authorities.[1] This railway legislation of 1886 subsequently was incorporated in the General Street Railway Law and its application restricted to New York city. The actual results of the Cantor Act were not altogether satisfactory, a fact amply illustrated by the franchise awards after 1886, attention to which will now be given.

6. THE TWENTY-EIGHTH AND TWENTY-NINTH STREET RAILROAD COMPANY

This company, one of the first to be incorporated under the Street Railway Law of 1884, was originally chartered as The Twenty-eighth and Thirtieth Street Railroad Company[2] on April 24, 1884. On September 25, 1885, the company received permission from the Supreme Court to change its corporate name to The Twenty-eighth and Twenty-ninth Street Railroad Company,[3] and on January 11, 1886, petitioned the common council for a franchise permitting a surface railway to commence at the West Forty-second street ferry, thence to Eleventh avenue, to West Thirty-fourth street, to Tenth avenue, to West Thirtieth street, to Ninth avenue, to West Twenty-ninth and West Twenty-eighth streets, to First avenue, to East Twenty-fourth street, to Avenue A, to East Twenty-third street to the East river, together with various branches and

[1] *Laws of the State of New York*, 1886, ch. 271.
[2] *Report of the Public Service Commission of the State of New York, First District*, 1913, vol. v, p. 493.
[3] *Ibid.*, p. 1324.

connections.[1] The petition was referred to the committee on railroads,[2] which reported favorably. It pointed out that the proposed line would greatly facilitate passenger transportation, inasmuch as the road would reach six important ferries as well as important business sections of the city.[3]

PLATE XXIV

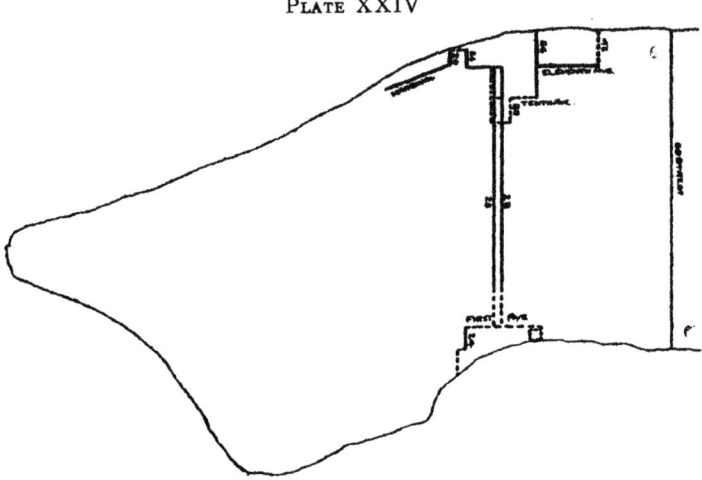

TWENTY-EIGHTH AND TWENTY-NINTH STREET RAILROAD COMPANY
- - - - - trackage rights obtained on tracks of other companies
. . . . . franchise routes neither constructed nor used by this company

The common council, by resolution of November 10, 1886, instructed the city comptroller to sell the franchise for this route "on the earliest practicable day."[4] Mayor Grace vetoed the ordinance on the ground that the Belt Line Railroad Corporation already held a franchise for a certain part of the proposed route and that its consent to operation by

[1] *Report of the Public Service Commission of the State of New York, First District*, 1913, vol. v, pp. 1328-1329.

[2] *Proceedings of the Board of Aldermen*, vol. 181, p. 282.

[3] *Ibid.*, vol. 184, p. 287.

[4] *Ibid.*, pp. 619-629.

another company, over this particular portion, was necessary before any franchise sale could take place.[1] The board of aldermen on November 6, 1886, passed the resolution over the mayor's veto [2] and the franchise was sold to the Twenty-eighth and Twenty-ninth Street Railroad Company for twenty-nine and two-tenths per cent of the gross receipts in addition to the minimum percentage payable under the General Street Surface Railroad Law of 1884, viz.: three per cent of the gross receipts for the first five years and five per cent thereafter.[3] The amount proved to be such a

[1] *Proceedings of the Board of Aldermen*, vol. 181, pp. 675-676.
[2] *Ibid.*, p. 836.
[3] The conditions stipulated were: (1) The franchise to be sold at public auction in accordance with the provisions of the Cantor Act; (2) equipment, materials, and work to be of the best quality and character; (3) side-bearing rails with outer edges flush with the pavement and with the inside drop not exceeding one inch in depth to be used; (4) cars to run for convenience of the public and no freight cars to be operated on the road; (5) the purchasing company should comply with all reasonable ordinances or regulations which the local authorities might make and was "absolutely and unqualifiedly bound" to keep in permanent repair the portion of the street surface between the tracks and for a space of two feet on either side; (6) all snow to be removed not merely from between the tracks, but from curb to curb "from that portion of the streets or avenues made use of for the construction and operation of the railroad so far as such snow may have fallen or ice may have formed" upon the tracks; such snow and ice was to be deposited at the nearest place used by the city authorities for the deposit of snow removed by the municipality; (7) cars were to be operated only by horse or animal power until authority to use some other motive power should be obtained pursuant to the General Street Railway Law; (8) the percentage payments were to be "computed upon a fare of five cents as having been received as part of the gross receipts from every passenger who should ride upon any part of the route and irrespective of the fact whether such passenger enters or leaves the car at any point upon the said route; (9) and finally, the purchaser was to file written statements under corporate seal of the company, properly attested by its president or treasurer and by virtue of a resolution of its board of directors accepting the grant on the terms and conditions set forth.

heavy financial burden that the company was unable to build the entire road, and on September 29, 1896, it was reduced by the Sinking Fund Commission to one-half of one per cent annually in addition to the statutory percentage. This so-called "compromise" was effected by legislative direction after the company had submitted figures to show that it was unable to pay its bid.[1]

The property and franchises of the company were sold under foreclosure on September 30, 1896, to Charles W. Truslow for twenty-five thousand dollars. The following day he transferred the property to the newly incorporated Twenty-eighth and Twenty-ninth Streets Crosstown Railroad Company.[2] The latter company, which was capitalized at one and one-half millions, obtained no special franchises except a revocable permit, dated May 1, 1909, from the Commissioner of Docks to extend its tracks for a distance of eighty-eight feet on Marginal street in the vicinity of West Twenty-fourth street.[3] For this privilege the company was required to make an annual payment to the city of fifty cents per linear foot of track. Many similar permits have been granted to other railway companies from time to time.

Just prior to its reorganization the company gave to the Metropolitan Street Railway Company the right to operate cars over its entire route during the corporate existence of both companies.[4] By this agreement the Metropolitan Com-

[1] *Laws of the State of New York*, 1893, ch. 434; West, Max, "The Franchises of Greater New York," *Yale Review*, 1898, vol. vi, p. 396; Wilcox, Delos F., *Municipal Franchises*, vol. ii, pp. 125-126.

[2] *Report of the Public Service Commission, First District, State of New York*, 1913, vol. v, p. 1331.

[3] *City Record*, vol. xxvii, pt. ii, p. 7884.

[4] *Report of the Public Service Commission, First District, State of New York*, 1913, vol. v, p. 1325.

pany agreed to pay the principal and interest on the company's first-mortgage five-per-cent bonds, totaling one million five hundred thousand dollars, and to keep the road in first-class condition. The Twenty-eighth and Twenty-ninth Streets Company retained the privilege of operating the road at any time it might feel so disposed.[1] This operating agreement was canceled on October 1, 1908, two days prior to the appointment of Joseph B. Mayer as receiver in an action brought in the Supreme Court by the Central Trust Company of New York to foreclose the first mortgage.[2] The line continued to be operated by the receiver until the date of its sale on January 4, 1912, to John W. Hamer, Horace A. Doan, A. Merritt Taylor, William C. Heppenheimer, and Charles F. Loxley, a committee of bondholders with authority to purchase.[3] This committee transferred the purchased franchises and property to a new company which they incorporated, the Mid-Crosstown Railway, Inc.[4] This company was simply a reorganization of the Twenty-eighth and Twenty-ninth Streets Crosstown Railroad Company; it is merely a subsidiary of the Third Avenue Railway Company and its lines are now operated as a part of that system.[5]

7. THE NORTH AND EAST RIVER RAILROAD COMPANY AND THE FULTON STREET RAILROAD COMPANY

The franchise grant to the North and East River Railroad Company, the predecessor of the Fulton Street Railroad Company, presents another striking instance of the

[1] *Report of the Public Service Commission, First District, State of New York*, 1913, vol. v, p. 1327.
[2] *Ibid.*, p. 1326.
[3] *Ibid.*, p. 1527.
[4] *Ibid.*, p. 709.
[5] *Ibid.*

sale of a grant under the Cantor Act at a high percentage rate.

The North and East River Railroad Company was incorporated for one thousand years with a capital stock of three hundred thousand dollars, for the purpose of building a street surface railway over a two-mile route commencing on Fulton street at Fulton ferry and running thence to Broadway, to West street, to the Cortlandt street ferry; also commencing on West street, at the southerly side of the street, and extending to Chambers street to the Pavonia ferry house; also a line from the Fulton ferry house through South street to Maiden Lane, to Broadway, to Cortlandt street, to West street to Fulton street; another branch road was to commence at the corner of South street and Maiden Lane and extend through Wall street, "together with switches and sidings running from the tracks of said railroad at the intersection of South street with Burling Slip into, over and along said Burling Slip to the southeasterly side of Front street." [1] In the franchise adopted by the Board of Aldermen [2] on December 30, 1886, part of the proposed line was eliminated. (See plate XXV.)

Many prominent individuals expressed themselves to the effect that the road should be built, inasmuch as there was at that time no means of conveyance, except by hacks and coaches, between Cortlandt street and Pavonia ferries and Fulton ferry and Burling Slip—the four great ferries in the lower part of the city. Acting upon this belief, the councilmanic committee on railroads, November 30, 1886, reported favorably on the franchise application of the North and East River Company.[3] Other companies already had legal

---

[1] *Report of the Public Service Commission of the State of New York, First District*, 1913, vol. v, p. 1032.
[2] *Proceedings of the Board of Aldermen*, vol. 184, p. 1217.
[3] *Ibid.*, pp. 846-858.

claims to certain streets covered by the proposed route,[1] and the common council, in order to prevent misunderstanding and possible litigation, referred the matter to Corpora-

PLATE XXV

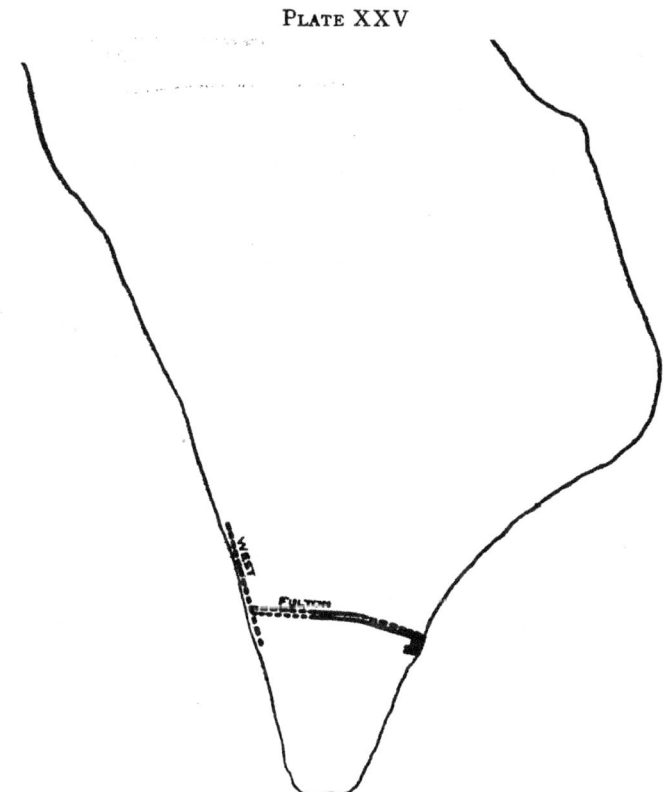

FULTON STREET RAILROAD COMPANY
- - - - - trackage rights obtained on tracks of other companies
. . . . . franchise routes neither constructed nor used by this company

tion Counsel E. H. Lacombe,[2] who concluded that no legal

[1] Notably between Fulton ferry and William street and on West street between Cortland street and Chambers street.

[2] *Proceedings of the Board of Aldermen*, vol. 184, pp. 898-899.

obstacle stood in the way of making the grant. He made it clear that the successful bidder would have to obtain the consent of a majority of the property-owners along the route as well as consent of companies owning existing railroad privileges in such streets as were covered by a portion of the route outlined in the proposed franchise.[1] Acting upon his advice, the common council, by resolution adopted December 7, 1886, gave its consent for the proposed road;[2] Mayor Grace interposed his veto, but the resolution was repassed.[3]

This franchise was acquired May 31, 1887, at a bid of thirty-five per cent of the company's gross receipts, to be computed after the road was in operation. It later developed that the company was unable to meet payment of this sum and, at the same time, maintain its solvency. After a lapse of six years figures were submitted to prove the company's financial condition and a reduction of the percentage was requested. Finally the sinking fund commissioners "compromised" the obligation by reducing the thirty-five per cent to one-eighth of one per cent of the gross receipts.[4]

After having entered into various intercorporate agreements, the company's franchises, rights, and privileges were sold under foreclosure proceedings to one John H. O'Rourke, who, on November 1, 1895, transferred the property to the Fulton Street Railroad Company, which had been or-

[1] *Proceedings of the Board of Aldermen*, vol. 184, pp. 929-931.

[2] *Ibid.*, p. 962.

[3] *Ibid.*, p. 1217. The conditions were very similar to those incorporated in the franchise for the Twenty-eighth and Twenty-ninth street railroad; a definite provision was made that cars be operated by electricity.

[4] *Report of the Public Service Commission of the State of New York, First District*, 1913, vol. v, p. 1033; Wilcox, Delos F., *Municipal Franchises*, vol. ii, p. 126; West, Max, "The Franchises of Greater New York," *Yale Review*, 1898, vol. vi, p. 397.

ganized for that purpose.[1] The corporate life of the new company was unlimited and its entire capital stock was fixed at half a million dollars;[2] it received no franchise privileges directly from the city, and soon after its incorporation its capital stock was acquired by the Metropolitan Street Railway Company.[3] Operation of this road was begun in the fall of 1895, and until June 1, 1908, was controlled by the Metropolitan Street Railway Company and its successors.[4] At that time, however, the road was abandoned and subsequently all the tracks owned by this company were removed from the streets by the city authorities.[5]

On October 20, 1913, the New York Railways Company made application to the Public Service Commission for authority to acquire the capital stock of the Fulton Street Railroad Company together with a controlling interest in other specified companies. The commission was agreeable to this but called attention to the fact that the Fulton Street Railroad Company's stock was no longer of any considerable value.[6]

Brief mention should here be made of another franchise sale under the Cantor law which was remarkable in many ways and clearly showed the weakness of the act. A franchise for the construction of an extensive system of routes in the Bronx was advertised to be sold at public auction. At first three companies competed, but finally one dropped out when it became known that the bids would exceed

[1] *Report of the Public Service Commission of the State of New York, First District*, 1913, vol. v, p. 446.
[2] *Ibid.*
[3] *Infra*, ch. viii.
[4] *Infra*, ch. viii.
[5] *Report of Public Service Commission &c., op. cit.*, p. 447.
[6] See Case No. 1749 for year 1913 for the First District, vol. i, p. 361.

three or four per cent of the gross receipts. The two remaining companies, The People's Traction Company and The New York Traction Company, between which there was intense rivalry, continued bidding; the percentages increased by fractional parts until forty per cent of the gross receipts had been offered for the franchise, when suddenly the representative of The People's Traction Company abandoned this cautious policy and jumped the bid to *ninety-seven per cent* of the gross receipts for the first five years and ninety-five per cent thereafter, which, with the percentages required by law, would cover the entire receipts of the proposed system. The New York Traction Company, not to be outdone by this procedure, raised this already extraordinary bid one-half of one per cent. Thereupon The People's Traction Company protested against the acceptance of any bid which covered more than the entire proceeds. The corporation counsel, to whom the question was referred, advised the comptroller to accept the highest bid made. Bidding was again resumed and from one hundred and one per cent there was a rash jump to one thousand per cent, followed in rapid succession by bids of one thousand and five per cent, two thousand per cent, two thousand and one per cent, two thousand five hundred per cent, two thousand five hundred and five per cent, two thousand six hundred per cent; again the fractional method was resumed, and at the time of adjournment the bidding had been in progress four hours and the last bid made was for *six thousand nine hundred seventy-five and one-sixteenth per cent*—or about seventy times the entire gross receipts. This farcical proceeding was interrupted by service of a restraining order. After more than a year of delay and litigation the grant was finally awarded to The People's Traction Company for ninety-seven per cent of the gross receipts for the first five years and ninety-five per cent for each year thereafter, together with the statutory requirements.¹ The People's Traction Company was not primarily interested in securing this franchise because it desired to operate over the routes covered thereby, but rather, as a commentator points out, for the purpose of excluding rival interests from the territory, and with the possible expectation that after the franchise had once been secured, the holders thereof might be able to effect a " compromise with the city authorities." ²

8. THE METROPOLITAN CROSSTOWN RAILWAY COMPANY

This company was incorporated March 22, 1889, for a thousand-year period and capitalized at three hundred thousand dollars. Its purpose was to construct a surface crosstown line from Grand street ferry on the East river to the foot of West Fourteenth street.³ The route extended along East street to Delancy street to the Bowery to Spring street to South Fifth avenue to Fourth street to McDougal street to Waverly Place to Bank street to Greenwich avenue to Thirteenth street to Horatio street to Eighth avenue to Thirteenth street to Thirteenth avenue to West Fourteenth street. The common council in granting a franchise for this route by resolution of December 24, 1889,⁴ decided that too many facilities for crosstown communication could not be had.⁵ The provisions contained in the franchise were practically the same as for the Twenty-eighth and Twenty-ninth Street Railroad Company. An effort was made to require the purchasing company to pay a percent-

¹ Wilcox, Delos F., *Municipal Franchises*, vol. ii, p. 106; West, Max, "The Franchises of Greater New York," *Yale Review*, 1898, vol. vi, p. 397.

² Wilcox, Delos F., *Municipal Franchises*, vol. ii, p. 127.

³ *Report of the Public Service Commission of the State of New York, First District*, 1913, vol. v, p. 675.

⁴ *City Record*, vol. xvii, pt. iv, pp. 4046-4047.

⁵ *Ibid.*, p. 3827.

age of two per cent for the first five years of operation and five per cent thereafter in addition to the statutory percentages named in the Act of 1884 and the percentage of gross receipts bid at the public sale of the franchise. In other words, under this arrangement, the city would receive five per cent of the gross receipts for the first five years and ten

PLATE XXVI

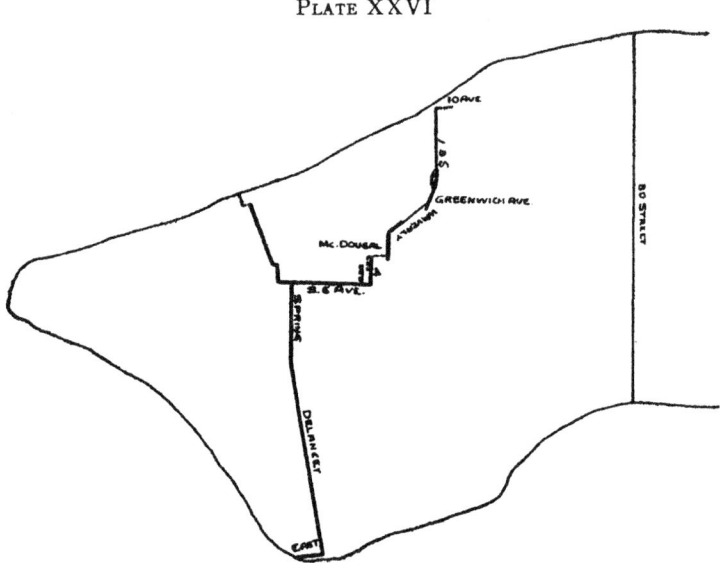

METROPOLITAN CROSSTOWN RAILWAY COMPANY
. . . . . franchise routes neither constructed nor used by this company

per cent thereafter, besides the purchasing percentage. This scheme, embodied in an amendatory resolution offered by Alderman Fitzgibbons, failed of adoption, and on February 24, 1890, the franchise was sold at public auction to the original petitioner, The Metropolitan Crosstown Railway Company, whose bid was six per cent of the gross receipts for the first five years and eight per cent thereafter.[1]

[1] *City Record*, vol. xvii, pt. iv, p. 4047.

With the exception of three short extensions, no new franchises were acquired by this company. The first extension was permitted in 1892, when on September 13 of that year the company petitioned the common council for authority to connect its road on South Fifth avenue with the line of the Houston, West Street and Pavonia Ferry Railroad Company on West street, this extension to extend through Broome street, to Sullivan street, to Watts street. In the same application the company sought to connect its line with the Desbrosses street ferry.[1] By resolution of the board of aldermen on September 29 a franchise covering the desired extensions was granted.[2] At the same time a similar grant was obtained jointly by The Metropolitan Crosstown Railway Company and the Broadway and Seventh Avenue Railroad Company for connection of their lines.[3] No new conditions were stipulated in either of these franchises, although an attempt was made to prevent the use of electricity for motive power. The petitioning companies did, however, agree to issue transfers over each other's lines or to arrange for a continuous passage for a single fare. A third extension franchise obtained from the councilmen at this time authorized the Metropolitan Crosstown Railway Company to connect its road with that of the Sixth Avenue Railroad Company over a route commencing at the intersection of South Fifth avenue and West Third street and extending along the latter to Sullivan street.[4]

The Metropolitan Crosstown Company soon became involved in the railway consolidation movement, and on Octo-

[1] *Proceedings of the Board of Aldermen*, vol. 207, pp. 245-246.
[2] *Ibid.*, pp. 382-383.
[3] *Ibid.* pp. 377-380.
[4] *Ibid.*, pp. 374-376. The Sixth Avenue Railroad Company also obtained a franchise by the same grant inasmuch as it was a joint petitioner with the Metropolitan Crosstown Company.

ber 14, 1892, it leased the Central Park, North and East River Railroad Company's property for the unexpired term of that company's charter at an annual rental of eight per cent on its outstanding capital stock of one million eight hundred thousand dollars for the first five years and nine per cent thereafter.[1] The following year the company leased the Forty-second and Grand Street Ferry railroad property for the unexpired term of the company's charter, agreeing to pay therefor eighteen per cent on the issued capital stock of seven hundred and forty-eight thousand dollars.[2] Two years later, May 28, 1894, the Metropolitan Company lost its identity by merging with other surface railway companies to form the Metropolitan Street Railway Company.[3]

9. LEXINGTON AVENUE AND PAVONIA FERRY RAILROAD COMPANY

Another company which obtained its franchise in accordance with the Cantor Law was the Lexington Avenue and Pavonia Ferry Railroad Company, a subsidiary of the Houston, West Street and Pavonia Ferry Company. Its charter was issued December 22, 1892, for one thousand years with a capital stock of five million dollars, its purpose being to acquire at public sale the franchise for the proposed extension of the Houston, West Street and Pavonia Ferry Company's line covering a seven-mile route, commencing at Forty-second street and Lexington avenue and extending thence northerly to the Harlem river, and from One Hundred and Sixteenth street and Lexington avenue to Morn-

[1] *Report of the Public Service Commission of the State of New York, First District*, 1913, vol. v, p. 677.
[2] *Annual Report of the New York Railways Company for year ending June 30, 1918*, p. 28.
[3] *Infra*, ch. viii.

ingside Park.¹ The Houston, West Street and Pavonia Ferry Railroad Company, the parent corporation, in petitioning for the proposed road, named the foot of East One Hundred and Sixteenth street as the eastern terminus of the One Hundred and Sixteenth street line.²

That there was some opposition to the proposed road on Lexington avenue, north of Forty-second street, was evi-

PLATE XXVII

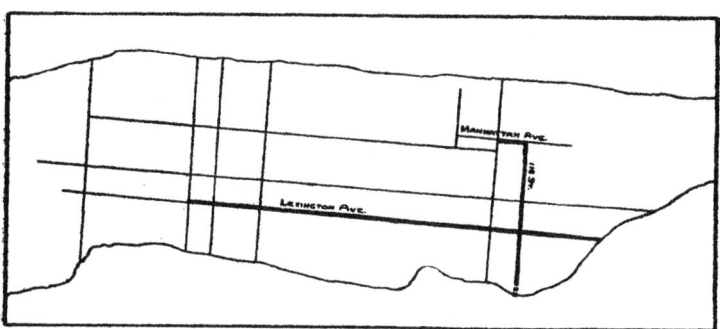

LEXINGTON AVENUE AND PAVONIA FERRY RAILROAD COMPANY
- - - - - trackage rights obtained on tracks of other companies

denced by protests of residents and property-owners along that avenue,³ notwithstanding the fact that Mayor Hugh J. Grant was favorable to the construction of this and other railroad extensions as an aid to transportation facilities of the city.⁴ In his judgment property interests in upper Manhattan were in a " languishing condition " due to the need of adequate means of transportation.⁵

¹ *Report of the Public Service Commission of the State of New York, First District*, 1913, vol. v, p. 575.
² *Proceedings of the Board of Aldermen*, vol. 207, p. 226.
³ *Ibid.*, pp. 347-348.
⁴ *Ibid.*, vol. 208, p. 73.
⁵ *Ibid.*

The common council in granting the franchise required in its provisions that the purchasers should construct a double-track cable railway, and as a guarantee that such road would be properly built and equipped the successful bidder was required to deposit one million dollars with the comptroller of the city; if at the expiration of two years from the date of sale the road had not been constructed, this sum would then revert to the city. In the event of failure to make such deposit the franchise was to be resold.[1] This provision tended, in a large degree, to remedy the chief defect of the Cantor Act; without some such guarantee irresponsible parties would be enabled to compete at public sales and to increase bids to unprecedented heights, as occurred in the case of the People's Traction Company and The New York Traction Company in the sale of the franchise for the Bronx system of roads. Again, such irresponsible parties were in a position to purchase franchises which oftentimes they never put into execution despite the fact that the particular section of the city mentioned in the franchise was in dire need of such railroad improvements.

The Lexington Avenue and Pavonia Ferry Railroad Company increased the value of its property when, on December 19, 1893, the board of aldermen granted its application for an extension from Livingston avenue and East Ninety-sixth street to Astoria ferry by way of East Ninety-third street and Avenue A.[2] The conditions were the same as in the original grant, with the exception that permission was given for the use of any motive power other than overhead trolley or steam locomotive.

After considerable litigation with the Third Avenue Railroad Company, due to intercorporate agreements, the

[1] *Proceedings of the Board of Aldermen*, vol. 207, pp. 372-377. The other conditions were those usually included.

[2] *Ibid.*, vol. 212, pp. 251-254.

Lexington Avenue and Pavonia Ferry Railroad Company consolidated on May 28, 1894, with certain other companies, to form the Metropolitan Street Railway Company,[1] and its lines are now operated by the New York Railways Company.[2]

10. COLUMBUS AND NINTH AVENUE RAILROAD COMPANY

This company, like the Lexington Avenue and Pavonia Ferry Railroad Company, was organized by Anthony N. Brady and others for the purpose of securing the valuable extension of the Ninth avenue railroad from Sixty-fourth street along Columbus avenue to One Hundred and Tenth street, with a short branch on One Hundred and Sixth street, totaling in all between three and four miles. This road by a series of extensions was subsequently lengthened to about seven and one-half miles.[3] The franchise was sold at public auction on December 30, 1892, for one-fourth of one per cent of the gross receipts, pursuant to a resolution of the common council adopted October 10, 1892.[4] The conditions of the franchise were identical with those of the grant to the Lexington Avenue and Pavonia Ferry Railroad Company.

Two years later the common council acted favorably upon the application of the company for leave to construct a double-track line on One Hundred and Ninth street from Columbus avenue to Manhattan avenue, and on Manhattan avenue from One Hundred and Ninth street to Cathedral Parkway, there to connect with the extension of the tracks

---

[1] *Infra*, ch. viii.

[2] *Annual Report of the New York Railways Company for the year ending June 30, 1918*, p. 4.

[3] *Report of the Public Service Commission of the State of New York, First District*, 1913, vol. v, p. 294.

[4] *Proceedings of the Board of Aldermen*, vol. 208, pp. 75-78.

of the Lexington Avenue and Pavonia ferry division of the Metropolitan Street Railway Company.[1] No new conditions were expressed in this grant. By the close of the year 1894 the road had been completed. The following year the company, with its parent organization, became a part of the

PLATE XXVIII

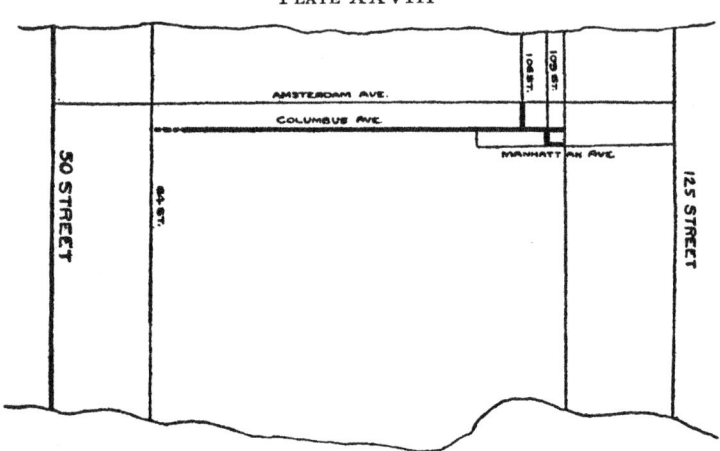

COLUMBUS AND NINTH AVENUE RAILROAD COMPANY
- - - - - trackage rights obtained on tracks of other companies

Metropolitan street railway system.[2] Today its lines are operated by the New York Railway Company.[3]

The provisions of the Cantor Act were, as we have seen, far from being sufficient; nevertheless they constituted a valuable supplement to the existing street railway law. The principle of selling the franchises at public auction instituted a much-needed reform in that it made bribery and collusion impossible and, at the same time, materially in-

[1] *Proceedings of the Board of Aldermen*, vol. 215, pp. 240-243.
[2] *Infra*, ch. viii.
[3] *Annual Report of the New York Railways Company for the year ending June 30, 1918*, p. 4.

creased the revenue of the city; the principal defect of the act was practically eliminated by the guarantee clause incorporated in the later railway grants. The law, however, made no provision for limited franchises, nor did it provide any means for the future acquisition by the city of either the franchise or the railroad property proposed to be constructed.

CHAPTER VIII

THE ERA OF CONSOLIDATION

A STUDY of the street surface railway franchise problem of New York city would be incomplete without indicating the manner in which the various independent railway companies holding franchises were consolidated and welded together until ultimately two giant railway corporations gained control, either through purchase, lease, or otherwise, of all franchise and property rights enjoyed by the former companies.

Until the beginning of the last decade of the nineteenth century each street-railway company, nominally at least, had been operated independently; although, as has been seen, many of them had practically the same officers and all had entered into intercorporate agreements involving stock transfers, route leases, or trackage privileges. By the nineties the movement toward industrial combination had affected almost every class of business, and practically everywhere manufacturing, trading and transportation enterprises were being reorganized. Business men saw that co-ordination and combination, rather than competition, would net larger financial returns on investments and would make possible improvement in both equipment and service.[1]

It is scarcely surprising perhaps that street surface railways, with a considerable natural tendency toward monop-

[1] Johnson, E. R., *American Railway Transportation* (N. Y., 1912), pp. 258-261.

PLATE XXIX

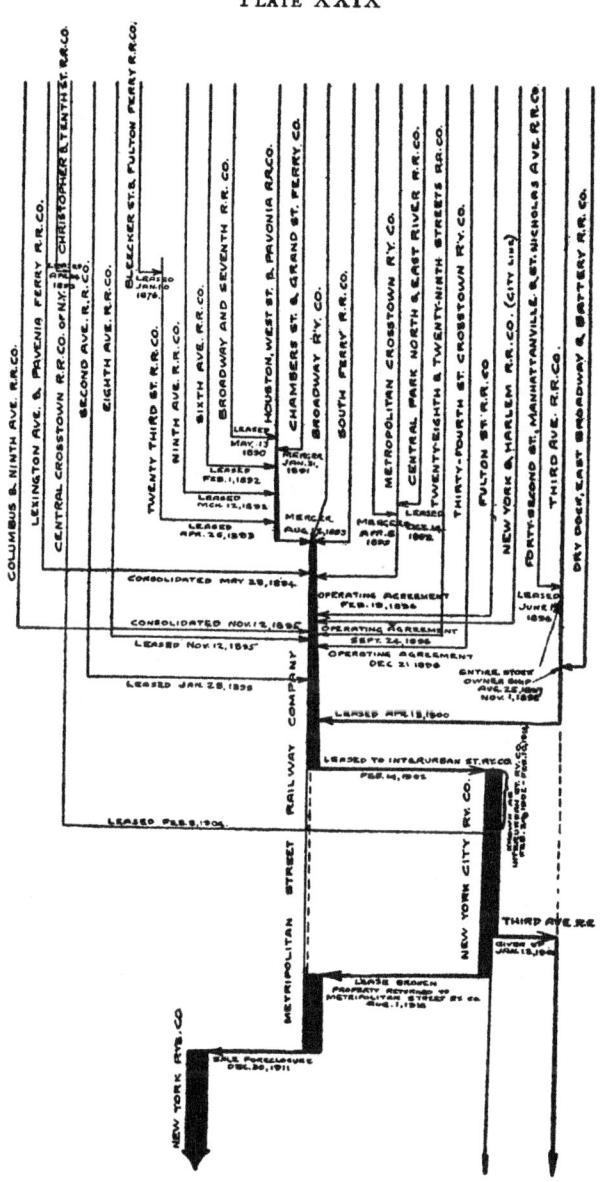

CONSOLIDATION OF INDEPENDENT SURFACE LINES

oly, were among the first enterprises to be organized on the basis of legal monopoly.[1] The railways of the American metropolis were no exception to this rule.

As early as February 19, 1886, The Metropolitan Traction Company, a holding company with an authorized capital stock of ten million dollars, had been incorporated in the state of New Jersey by a group of Philadelphia promoters headed by P. A. B. Widener, Thomas Dolan and W. L. Elkins.[2] This syndicate, after having gained control of the surface railways of Philadelphia and other cities, turned its attention to New York city. Two metropolitan financiers, William C. Whitney, ex-secretary of war under President Cleveland, and Thomas F. Ryan, who were already interested in the traction situation of Manhattan, became affiliated with The Metropolitan Traction Company of New Jersey. In June, 1886, this company secured control of the majority of the capital stock of two million one hundred thousand dollars of the Broadway and Seventh Avenue Railroad Company, which event marked the beginning of a series of financial manipulations and mergers leading finally to the incorporation of the Metropolitan Street Railway Company and to the consolidation of all the surface lines in Manhattan and the Bronx.[3]

Concurrent with the acquisition of the Broadway property the entire capital stock of two hundred and fifty thousand dollars of the Houston, West Street and Pavonia Ferry Railroad Company was taken over by the Metro-

[1] Bogart, E. L., *Economic History of the United States* (N. Y., 1916), p. 457.

[2] See testimony of Thomas F. Ryan in case of Wormser *v.* Metropolitan Street Railway Company, 184 N. Y., 83, introduced into the record in the investigation of the Interborough Metropolitan Company before the Public Service Commission, October 18, 1907, vol. iv, p. 1730.

[3] *Report of Public Service Commission, First District, State of New York*, 1913, vol. v, p. 49.

politan Traction Company.[1] The New Jersey corporation in June, 1886, also acquired the entire capital stock of the Chambers and Grand Street Ferry Railroad Company, amounting to eight hundred thousand dollars.[2] This holding company subsequently gained stock control of other Manhattan surface companies. On January 3, 1889, the entire capital stock of one hundred and fifty thousand dollars of the South Ferry Railroad Company passed into its hands;[3] and in March, 1890, the majority of the capital stock of six hundred thousand dollars of the Twenty-third Street Railway Company was acquired.[4] A few months later, October, 1890, all of the capital stock of the Broadway Company, amounting to one million dollars, was obtained by the Metropolitan Traction Company,[5] and in March, 1891, the total capital stock of three hundred thousand dollars of the Metropolitan Crosstown Railway Company passed to the New Jersey corporation.[6] In the meantime, the promoters of the holding company, using the Houston, West Street and Pavonia Ferry line as a nucleus, were consolidating the independent lines. On May 13, 1891, the franchises and property of the Broadway and Seventh Avenue Railroad Company were leased to the former company for the unexpired term of the latter company's charter at a rental of ten per cent on stock and fixed charges.[7] This

[1] *Report of Public Service Commission, First District, State of New York*, 1913, vol. v, p. 490.
[2] *Ibid.*, p. 284.
[3] *Ibid.*, chart i, Appendix.
[4] *Ibid.*
[5] *Ibid.*
[6] *Ibid.*, p. 674.
[7] *Ibid.*, pp. 50, 490, 691; see also Chart of Interborough Metropolitan system prepared for the New York State Public Service Commission, First District.

lease was followed by the absorption on January 31, 1891, of the Chambers Street and Grand Street Ferry Railroad Company.[1] In 1892 the franchises and property of two important north-and-south trunk lines were leased to the Houston, West Street and Pavonia Ferry Company; they were the Sixth Avenue Railroad Company, leased February 1, for a period of eight hundred years at an annual rental of one hundred and forty-five thousand dollars,[2] and on March 12 the Ninth Avenue Railroad Company for a ninety-nine year period at a rental of six per cent on the capital stock of eight hundred thousand dollars during the first five years and eight per cent thereafter.[3] The Pavonia Company on April 22, 1893, further acquired by lease the franchises and property of the Twenty-third Street Railroad Company for the unexpired term of the latter company's charter, which had been fixed at one thousand years, agreeing to pay therefor eighteen per cent on a capital stock of six hundred thousand dollars.[4] This lease included a ninety-nine-year sub-lease of the Bleecker Street and Fulton Ferry Railroad Company, which was capitalized at six hundred thousand dollars, and returned a rental of one and one-half per cent on stock together with fixed charges, including principal and interest, on seven hundred thousand dollars of first-mortgage bonds outstanding.[5] It should be noted that in every case, with the exception of the Sixth and Ninth avenue lines, the lease or merger was always preceded by entire stock ownership or control by the Metropolitan Trac-

[1] *Report of Public Service Commission, First District, State of New York*, 1913, vol. v, pp. 284, 490.
[2] *Ibid.*, 1913, vol. v, pp. 490, 691.
[3] *Ibid.*, pp. 490, 1031.
[4] *Ibid.*, pp. 490, 691, 1333.
[5] *Ibid.*, pp. 34, 490, 691.

tion Company of New Jersey, the tool of the promoters. Moreover, it was shown through subsequent investigations that with each transaction enormous profits were derived by the holding company.[1]

On August 4, 1892 the holdings of the Metropolitan Traction Company were transferred to the Metropolitan Traction Company of New York, a newly organized corporation,[2] differing from its predecessor only in name and capitalization, which was placed at eighteen million dollars. The " new " holding company continued to acquire either stock interest or entire stock control of additional surface companies. In August, 1892, it acquired a minority ownership of the stock of the Central Park, North and East River Railroad Company,[3] and in March, 1893, it secured ownership of a majority of the stock of the Forty-second Street and Grand Street Ferry Railroad Company, which was leased the following month to the Metropolitan Crosstown Railway Company.[4] Three other important stock transfers occurred prior to the organization of the first Metropolitan Street Railway corporation. In April, 1893, the entire capital stock of the Thirty fourth Street Ferry and Eleventh Avenue Railroad Company passed to the Metropolitan Traction Company of New York,[5] and in May of the same year the entire securities, stocks and bonds of the Columbus and Ninth Avenue Railroad Company and the Lexington Ave-

[1] See testimony of Thomas F. Ryan before Grand Jury investigating charges of criminal wrong-doing on the part of the management of the Metropolitan Street Railway, April, 1908.

[2] *Report of Public Service Commission, First District, State of New York*, 1913, vol. v, chart i; *Street Railway Review*, January, 1901, vol. xi, p. 17.

[3] *Report of Public Service Commission, First District, State of New York*, 1913, vol. v, chart i.

[4] *Ibid.*, pp. 426, 694.

[5] *Ibid.*, p. 1320; see also chart i.

nue and Pavonia Ferry Railroad Company were acquired by the holding company.[1] The acquisition of these two roads and their subsequent sale to the Metropolitan Street Railway Company was typical, as will be shown later, of the methods pursued by the promoters.

The first Metropolitan Street Railway company, incorporated December 12, 1893, was a consolidation [2] of the Broadway Railway Company, the South Ferry Railroad Company, and the Houston, West Street and Pavonia Ferry Railroad Company. Its corporate life was fixed at one thousand years and its capital stock of eight million two hundred thousand dollars was the equivalent of the capital stock of the three corporations merged to form the new company. Provision was made for the exchange of the stock of the new corporation for the capital stock of the consolidated corporations. No sooner had the new company been organized than its entire stock ownership passed to the Metropolitan Traction Company of New York.[3]

The next official step in the process of consolidation occurred on May 28, 1894, when Metropolitan Street Railway Company number two was incorporated for a term of one thousand years.[4] This company resulted from the merger of the first Metropolitan Street Railway Company, The Lexington Avenue and Pavonia Ferry Railroad Company,

[1] *Report of the Public Service Commission, First District, State of New York*, 1913, vol. v, pp. 295, 576; see also chart i.

[2] *Ibid.*, 1913, vol. v, p. 691; see also testimony of Thomas F. Ryan in case of Wormser *v.* Metropolitan Street Railway Company, 184 N. Y., 83, introduced into the record in the investigation of the Interborough Metropolitan Company before the Public Service Commission, October 18, 1907, vol. iv, p. 730; *Street Railway Review*, January 1901, vol. xi, p. 17.

[3] *Report of Public Service Commission, First District, State of New York*, 1913, vol. v, chart i, no. 19.

[4] *Ibid.*, p. 691.

and the Metropolitan Crosstown Railway Company. Its capital stock of thirteen million, five hundred thousand dollars was issued share for share in exchange for the capital stock of each of the consolidated corporations.[1]

This work having been successfully accomplished, the Metropolitan Traction Company proceeded in October, 1895, to secure the entire stock ownership of the North and East River Railway Company, whose line was still unconstructed.[2] Less than a year elapsed before plans were under way for further consolidation, and on November 12, 1895, the third Metropolitan Street Railway Company came into being through an amalgamation of the second Metropolitan Street Railway Company and the Columbus and Ninth Avenue Railroad Company.[3] The same method was followed in regard to capitalization as that used in the formation of the second Metropolitan Street Railway Company, the capital stock of sixteen million five hundred thousand dollars being issued share for share in exchange for the capital stock of each of the consolidated corporations. In the formation of both the second and third Metropolitan companies there was considerable stock-jobbing and stock-watering, the fact being frankly admitted in 1908 by Thomas F. Ryan, at that time the leading figure in the history of the Metropolitan Street Railway Company. Mr. Ryan's testimony in a Grand Jury proceeding disclosed the fact that when the Lexington Avenue Railroad Company was organized in 1893 it was authorized to issue five million dollars of stock and five million dollars of bonds. The Metro-

[1] *Report of Public Service Commission, First District, State of New York*, 1913, vol. v, p. 692.

[2] *Ibid.*, chart i.

[3] *Ibid.*, p. 694. For a brief account of the formation of the Metropolitan Street Railway Company see *New York Times*, November 20, 1898.

politan Traction Company contracted to build the road and to secure the right of way to the new company to operate its cars on Twenty-third street and Broadway in return for the stock and bond capital of the road. The ten million dollars' worth of stocks and bonds were turned over to the holding company, which sold the bonds at par and with the proceeds built the road. The stock, which for the time being remained in the treasury of the Traction Company, was subsequently transformed into the stock of the Metropolitan Street Railway Company. Identically the same procedure was followed with the Columbus and Ninth Avenue Company's six-million-dollars securities. " Hence," said Mr. Ryan, " there was no increase in capitalization to the public in any instance, all of the issued shares of subordinate companies being held in the treasury of the Metropolitan Company, or pledged under mortgage, and never offered for sale." [1] As a matter of fact, these stocks were " water "; they cost the holding company nothing in cash and became an added burden to the Metropolitan Street Surface Railway Company. Practically the same process was followed with other lines. The holding company having acquired the Thirty-fourth street road, worth about one hundred thou-

[1] Testimony of Mr. Ryan before the Grand Jury investigating charges of criminal wrong-doing on the part of the management of the Metropolitan Street Railway. For a clear and critical editorial on Mr. Ryan's testimony see *Outlook*, May 2, 1908, vol. lxxxix, pp. 1-4; a journalistic account of some of the incidents connected with the financial history of the Metropolitan Street Railway is that by Charles E. Russell, "Where did you get it, Gentlemen?" in *Everybody's Magazine*, January 1908, vol. xviii, pp. 118-127; another article written in popular style in which many statements are made regarding the early history of the Metropolitan Street Railway Company is that by Alfred H. Lewis, "Owners of America: Thomas F. Ryan," in *Cosmopolitan Magazine*, May, 1908, vol. xlv, pp. 141-152; it is inaccurate and unreliable. An excellent short account, written in popular style, is that by Burton J. Hendrick, "Great American Fortunes and Their Making," in *McClure's Magazine*, July, 1908, vol. xxx, pp. 33-48.

sand dollars, issued two million dollars of stocks and bonds on it and then compelled the Metropolitan Street Railway Company to purchase the securities at par. And again in the case of the Twenty-eighth and Twenty-ninth street lines, which were valued at two hundred and fifty thousand dollars, the syndicate issued three million dollars of securities, which were purchased by the Metropolitan at par.[1]

By 1897 the Metropolitan Traction Company of New York had acquired stock control of practically all the independent operating companies of Manhattan Island,[2] and having thus served the purpose for which it was created it was dissolved on September 16, 1897, its entire assets passing to the operating company, the Metropolitan Street Railway Company, which paid six million dollars therefor.[3]

The latter company, from the time of its incorporation in 1895 to 1900, was able further to consolidate the surface lines of the city. On November 23, 1895, it took a lease of the Eighth Avenue Railroad Company's property for a ninety-nine-year term at an annual rental of two hundred and fifteen thousand dollars, agreeing also to expend during the first two years of the lease one million dollars for equipment and change of power.[4] Another road was added to the system on June 11, 1896, by a lease for nine hundred and ninety-nine years of the city line of the New York and Harlem Railroad Company at an annual rental of three

[1] *New York Times*, September 6, 1907.

[2] *Report of Public Service Commission, First District, State of New York*, 1913, vol. v, p. 696; see also chart i; *Report of Investigation of Interborough-Metropolitan Company before Public Service Commission*, 1907, vol. iv, p. 1730.

[3] *Report of Public Service Commission, First District, State of New York*, 1913, vol. v, p. 698; chart i; *Street Railway Review*, January 1901, vol. xi, p. 17.

[4] *Report of Public Service Commission, First District, State of New York*, 1913, vol. v, p. 397.

hundred and fifty thousand dollars for the first five years and four hundred thousand dollars per year thereafter.[1] Shortly after making this lease the Metropolitan Company was authorized by the State Railroad Commission to increase its capital stock from sixteen million five hundred thousand dollars to thirty million dollars;[2] and on August 9, 1898, it was authorized further to increase its capital to forty-five million dollars.[3] No other additions were made to the system until January 28, 1898, when the Second Avenue Railroad Company leased its property for the unexpired term of its corporate life and " for any extension of such corporate life " for an eight per cent rental for the first three years and nine per cent thereafter on the company's capital stock of one million eight hundred and fifty-two thousand dollars.[4] On April 13, 1900, the final link was added, when the Third Avenue Railroad Company, with its allied interests, was leased for nine hundred and ninety-nine years,[5] the Metropolitan Company agreeing to pay as rental for the first four years " a sum equal to the net earnings from the operation of the leased road and its subsidiary companies, less a proportion applicable to the shares of stock not owned by the company." At the end of the four-year period the Metropolitan Company was to pay " annual dividends of five per cent on the outstanding cap-

[1] *Report of Public Service Commission, First District, State of New York*, 1913, vol. v, p. 774.
[2] *Report of New York State Railroad Commission*, 1896, vol. i, pp. 65-66.
[3] *Ibid.*, p. 188.
[4] *Report of Public Service Commission, First District, State of New York*, 1913, vol. v, p. 1150. This lease was terminated November 12, 1908.
[5] *Street Railway Review*, January 1901, vol. xi, p. 17. The Third Avenue Company was at this time in the hands of Hugh J. Grant as receiver.

ital stock of the company for two years, six per cent for the next four years, and seven per cent during the remainder of the term of the lease." Both rentals and dividends were based upon the outstanding stock of the Third Avenue Company, totaling at that time sixteen million dollars. The Metropolitan Company further agreed to pay interest and principal on the fifty million dollars of the company's bonds held by the Morton Trust Company.[1] This lease carried with it stock control of the various units of the Third Avenue system.[2] On August 2, 1900, the capitalization of the Metropolitan Street Railway Company was increased from forty-five million dollars to fifty-two million dollars[3] largely on the strength of the statement that with the addition of each independent line to the Metropolitan system its value was greatly enhanced, or, as stated by Mr. Whitney, " each separate franchise was made a great deal more valuable by being combined together so as to make the joint business a great deal larger."[4]

Although the Metropolitan Street Railway in 1900 was in control of all the surface lines of the city, it was nevertheless financially embarrassed; greatly overcapitalized and water-logged, its supporters began to cast about for relief, with the result that on February 14, 1902, all the stocks held by the company passed to the Interurban Street Railway Company, which at this time leased the franchises,

[1] Thomas F. Ryan was president of this company; see *Testimony before Public Service Commission in investigation of Interborough-Metropolitan Company*, 1907, vol. iv, p. 1749.

[2] *Report of Public Service Commission, First District, State of New York*, 1913, vol. v, pp. 1298-1299.

[3] *Report of New York State Railroad Commission*, 1896, vol. i, p. 165.

[4] Testimony of William C. Whitney in case of Wormser *v.* Metropolitan Street Railway Company, 184 N. Y., 83, introduced into the record in the *Investigation of the Interborough-Metropolitan Company before the Public Service Commission*, October 18, 1907, vol. iv, p. 1752.

property, rights and privileges of the Metropolitan system for a nine hundred and ninety-nine year period.[1] According to the terms of this lease, the Interurban Company, which had been organized in 1901 for the purpose of taking over the property of the defunct North Mount Vernon Railway, a Westchester County line, agreed to furnish the Metropolitan Company with twenty-three million dollars with which to pay the latter company's debt and, in addition, to pay an annual rental of seven per cent on the fifty-two million dollars of capital stock of the lessor company. In return for the payment of the twenty-three million dollars, eleven millions of which was to be used to take up the debt incurred in the purchase of the control of the Third Avenue railway system and to refund other floating indebtedness, and the balance to be used in the reconstruction of the Metropolitan lines, the Metropolitan company transferred to the Interurban Company all its capital stock holdings in the Third Avenue Railway Company, the Central Park, North and East River Railroad Company, the Forty-second Street and Grand Street Ferry Railroad Company, the Central Crosstown Railroad Company, and the Forty-second Street, Manhattanville and St. Nicholas Avenue Railway Company, together with stocks and bonds of other corporations which it owned, totaling altogether twenty-four million dollars.

It is of interest to note that this lease was consummated through the banking house of Kuhn, Loeb & Company, which, after months of negotiation with the promoters of the Metropolitan system — Messrs. Ryan, Whitney, Dolan, Widener, Elkins, Vreeland and others—agreed to "supply"

[1] *Report of Public Service Commission, First District, State of New York*, 1913, vol. v, pp. 538, 699, chart i; see also *Report of Public Service Commission in investigation of Interborough-Metropolitan Company*, 1907, vol. i, pp. 9, 43.

a corporation with legal powers and "equipped" with twenty-three million dollars which would take a lease of the Metropolitan system.[1] It was also arranged as part of the general plan that a holding company, the Metropolitan Securities Company, be organized with a capital stock of thirty million dollars for the purpose of financing the Interurban Company and thus enabling it to advance the twenty-three million dollars to the Metropolitan Street Railway Company. In consideration of this financial backing the Interurban Company agreed to deliver to the Metropolitan Securities Company its entire capital stock.[2] In other words, the Interurban Street Railway Company operated the Metropolitan system and a holding company, the Metropolitan Securities Company, financed it. The twenty-three million dollars, however, was really "new cash" put into the enterprise by the Metropolitan Street Railway stockholders through their subscriptions to the stock of the Metropolitan Securities Company.[3]

[1] Testimony of Thomas F. Ryan in case of Wormser v. Metropolitan Street Railway Company, 184 N. Y., 83, introduced into the record in the *Investigation of the Interborough-Metropolitan Company before the Public Service Commission*, October 18, 1907, vol. iv, p. 1733.

[2] *Ibid.*, p. 1739; *New York Times*, September 6, 1907.

[3] Certain transactions of the Metropolitan Securities Company in its acquisition of the capital stock of the Fulton, Wall Street and Cortlandt Street Railway Company, were severely criticized when in 1907 it became known that the franchise for this road had been sold in 1898 to Joseph B. Donald in the interest of Anthony N. Brady who was influential at that time in the affairs of the Brooklyn Rapid Transit Company. Mr. Brady's testimony before the Public Service Commission in 1907 indicated that the road cost him $250,000, but he sold it to the Metropolitan Securities Company for $965,607.19, and of this amount $111,652.78 was paid to each of the following: William C. Whitney, Thomas F. Ryan, Thomas Dolan, P. A. B. Widener and W. L. Elkins. It was further shown that this money came out of the treasury of the Metropolitan Street Railway system which in return received a road "whose only assets were a charter and an injunction forbidding that

On February 10, 1904, the name of the Interurban Company was changed to New York City Railway Company, and until August 1, 1908, this company continued to operate the lines of the Metropolitan system. During this period the task of further consolidating the surface lines of the city progressed. On February 8, 1904, the New York City Railway Company took a lease of the Central Crosstown Railway Company's property for nine hundred and ninety-nine years; this lease was modified May 1, 1908, and the rental was placed at fifteen per cent on the capital stock together with the payment of all fixed charges.[1] Other minor companies operating in the northern part of the city were also brought into the system.[2]

In the investigation of the transportation facilities of the city conducted by the Public Service Commission in 1907, it was shown that practically the same individuals were interested in the Metropolitan Street Railway Company, the Metropolitan Securities Company and the New York City Railway Company. In this connection attention is called to the directorates of the three companies.[3]

charter to be used." Rumor had it that the money was used by Mr. Whitney for political purposes but this fact has never been proved. See testimony of Mr. Brady before Public Service Commission in *Investigation of Interborough-Metropolitan Company*, 1907, vol. iv, pp. 1601-1618; *Commercial and Financial Chronicle*, August 27, 1898, vol. lxvii, p. 428; *Outlook*, May 2, 1908, vol. lxxxix, pp. 2-3.

[1] *Report of Public Service Commission, First District, State of New York*, 1913, vol. v, p. 267.

[2] *Ibid.*, chart i.

[3] See Exhibits 11, 12 and 13 of the *Investigation of the Interborough-Metropolitan Company by the Public Service Commission*, 1907, vol. iv, pp. 58-60.

THE ERA OF CONSOLIDATION

Metropolitan Street Railway Company December 2, 1901	Metropolitan Securities Company April 3, 1903	New York City Railway Company November 1, 1903
H. H. Vreeland	H. H. Vreeland	H. H. Vreeland
D. B. Hasbrouck	W. H. Baldwin, Jr.	W. H. Baldwin, Jr.
D. C. Moorehead	Edward J. Berwind	Edward J. Berwind
Charles E. Warren	Paul D. Cravath	Paul D. Cravath
Aren Root, Jr.	Thomas P. Fowler	Thomas P. Fowler
P. A. B. Widener	P. A. B. Widener	P. A. B. Widener
Thomas Dolan	Thomas Dolan	Thomas Dolan
W. L. Elkins	Thomas F. Ryan	Thomas F. Ryan
H. A. Robinson	George G. Haven	Charles E. Warren
	James H. Hyde	John D. Crimmins
	Augustus D. Juillard	
	Edward W. Sayre	

It should be further noted that while Thomas F. Ryan and his associates were securing stock control of and were consolidating the street surface lines of the city, August Belmont and his business associates, controlling the management and business policy of the Interborough Rapid Transit Company, were engaged in financing and operating the elevated lines and the first subways.[1] After a period of keen rivalry these two groups amalgamated their interests in January, 1906, through the organization of the Interborough-Metropolitan Company, which thus came into financial control of all the transportation lines of Manhattan and the Bronx.

The New York City Railway Company went into a receiver's hands on September 24, 1907, and on August 1, 1908, the Metropolitan street railway property was turned back to receivers who had been appointed for that company on July 16, 1908.[2] Operation was continued by the receivers until December, 1911, when the Metropolitan Company

[1] For excellent statement of facts see case of Burrows v. Interborough-Metropolitan Company, 156 Fed. Rep., 389.

[2] *Report of Public Service Commission, First District, State of New York*, 1913, vol. v, chart i.

was reorganized as the New York Railways Company, the present operator of the system.[1]

The financial difficulties which the operating companies are experiencing are in part attributable to over-capitalization and high rentals, for most of the leases made during the period of consolidation are still in force.[2] Recently the operating companies have applied for permission to increase their rate of fare. It would seem, however, that any adjustment in fares should be accompanied by an equitable reduction of the high rentals to subsidiary companies. This opinion has recently been expressed by the corporation counsel of the city, who points out, among other things, that rentals as high as eighteen per cent are not justified.[3]

From the very brief survey which has been made it can be said that the consolidation movement is a story featured with extravagant leases, rash expenditures, watered securities, and financial knavery,[4] all of which have reacted detrimentally to public interest.[5]

[1] *Report of Public Service Commission, First District, State of New York*, 1913, vol. v, p. 987. Operation of the Third avenue railway system was given up January 12, 1908; it still operates as an independent system.

[2] *Report of the New York Railways Company for year ending June 30, 1918.*

[3] See statement of Corporation Counsel, William P. Burr, *New York Times*, March 2, 1919.

[4] William M. Ivins, Counsel for the Public Service Commission in 1907, said that the surface lines had been ruined both physically and financially by the division among certain stockholders of enormous capital in interest and dividends of money that was not earned; that dividends and rentals were paid from funds that should have gone for the maintenance of the physical plant. In his opinion the financial history of the Metropolitan Street Railway " presents no sadder ruin and no more hopeless problem." *New York Tribune*, March 17, 1908.

[5] The New York Railways Company, successor to the Metropolitan Street Railway Company, recently passed into the hands of a receiver. The officials of the company deny that excessive capitalization is a cause for the present financial condition of the company, maintaining that abnormal conditions due to the war are responsible for the company's serious financial situation. See *Your Street Car Service—A Statement of the Facts about the Situation of the New York Railways Company* (1919), pamphlet issued by New York Railways Company.

CHAPTER IX

FRANCHISE GRANTS UNDER THE CHARTER OF GREATER NEW YORK

DURING the period of street-railway consolidation a movement was inaugurated to revise the city charter, which resulted in the drafting of a charter for Greater New York. This went into effect in part on May 4, 1897,[1] and differed from the usual type of municipal charters in that it gave considerable attention to municipal functions as well as to the mere framework of government. An attempt was made to have the structure fit the particular functions which after all are of chief importance in the charter or constitution of any efficient democratic government. In no part of the charter of the greater city is this fact more apparent than in the provisions governing the granting of public franchises. It has been noted that, for the most part, prior to 1897 special franchise privileges in the streets of New York city were usually given away with little or no return to the city, but a more serious error was committed by the authorities granting these privileges who either failed to retain or utterly neglected to exercise adequate powers of regulation or control over these valuable grants.

The charter of 1897 incorporated a new franchise policy, which prescribed a single set of regulations for all kinds of street franchises for all the territory included within the boundaries of the greater city. The chapter on franchises opens with the significant preamble:

[1] *Laws of the State of New York*, 1897, ch. 378.

The rights of the city in and to its water-front, ferries, wharf property, land under water, public landings, wharves, docks, streets, avenues, parks, and all other public places are hereby declared to be inalienable.[1]

The charter of 1901, amended as to the franchise article in 1905,[2] proceeds to limit the duration of all street franchises and prescribes the procedure necessary for granting them. No franchise or right to use the streets of the city should be granted for a longer period than twenty-five years, provision being made, however, for renewals at fair revaluations of the franchises and no renewals to aggregate more than twenty-five years. In other words, franchise grants in perpetuity are no longer possible, and instead of this policy, which had prevailed up to that time, a period of fifty years, with a revaluation in the middle of the period, was fixed as the maximum life for all future franchise grants. At the termination of every franchise the plant and property in the streets belonging to the grantee became the property of the city, with or without compensation according to the terms of the original contract. In case compensation is provided for, there is to be a fair valuation of the property, excluding any value derived from the franchise itself. After the city had acquired ownership of the property it might either operate the plant and property on its own account or lease the property and franchise for a limited period, similar to the manner in which it leased ferries and docks. On the other hand, if the property was taken without compensation, the city had a choice between municipal operation or leasing the property and right of way for a period not to exceed twenty years. It was further stipulated that every franchise grant should make adequate

[1] Ch. iii, Section 71.
[2] *Laws of the State of New York*, 1905, ch. 629; Wilcox, Delos F., *Great Cities of America*, pp. 98-101.

provision by way of forfeiture or otherwise to secure efficient service at reasonable rates and the maintenance of the property in good condition throughout the full term of the grant. All grants or contracts were to specify the mode of determining the valuation and revaluation of the railway franchises.

By section 74 of the charter as amended [1] in 1914, all franchises, including extensions and renewals, were to be granted by the board of estimate and apportionment only after due publication of all the terms and conditions, including fares and other charges. This was to be accomplished by publishing the application of the petitioner for at least ten days in the *City Record*, the official daily paper of the city, and in two daily newspapers published in the city to be designated by the mayor. This section also requires that no franchise be granted until after the board of estimate and apportionment have made inquiry as to the money value of the franchise with reference to the adequacy of the proposed compensation to be paid for it. In this respect a definite responsibility is placed upon the individual members of the board of estimate and apportionment.

The original charter sought to protect the city further in franchise matters by having a bicameral board pass upon all proposed grants and making necessary a three-fourths vote of all members elected to each branch of the municipal assembly for the enactment of any ordinance granting a franchise, or a five-sixths vote in case of veto by the mayor. In the charter revision of 1901 the bicameral board was abolished and the present board of aldermen substituted for it. This body, to which was transferred the power of passing upon franchises, used its power in an obstructive way, especially in the case of the Pennsylvania Railroad Com-

[1] *Laws of the State of New York*, 1914, ch. 467.

pany which desired to construct a connecting link between its Long Island lines and the New York, New Haven and Hartford railroad. The grant for this connection was held up by the aldermen for reasons known only to an inner circle of that body;[1] in consequence, the power of passing upon franchise grants was taken from the aldermen by the legislature in 1905 and lodged in the board of estimate and apportionment,[2] where it still remains. At the present time every contract or resolution containing a franchise grant requires for its passage three-fourths of the total number of votes to which the members of the board of estimate and apportionment are entitled. Furthermore, every contract or resolution to be valid must have the separate and additional approval of the mayor.[3]

Since the creation of Greater New York the city has evolved a standard form of franchise, based primarily upon the charter requirements, which for the past ten years has been applied fairly consistently to all franchise grants. It is therefore unnecessary to examine in detail each of the street railway grants made since the consolidation of the Metropolis. Of the few important grants that have been made, the grant to the South Shore Traction Company admirably illustrates the present street-railway policy of the city.[4]

This company was incorporated March 2, 1903, for nine hundred and ninety-nine years with a capital stock of two

[1] Wright, H. C., "Development of Transit Control in New York City" in *Annals of the American Academy of Political and Social Science*, 1908, vol. xxxi, p. 28; Walker, J. B., *Fifty Years of Rapid Transit* (N. Y., 1918), p. 204.

[2] Wright, H. C., *op. cit.*, p. 28.

[3] As amended by Laws of the State of New York, 1914, ch. 647.

[4] An excellent account of the early history of this company is to be found in *Municipal Franchises*, by D. F. Wilcox, vol. ii, pp. 129-138.

million dollars,[1] for the purpose of constructing a system of street surface railroads connecting all the important towns and villages on the south shore of Long Island. The line was to extend from the Manhattan end of the Queensboro bridge directly through the Borough of Queens over practically the only available route [2] to the eastern boundary of the city, a distance of about fourteen miles, thence easterly to Brook Haven, Suffolk County, a distance of approximately fifty-one miles.[3] On May 20, 1909, the company, through a contract with the city, obtained authority for the construction of that part of the road within the city limits.[4] Owing to the sparseness of population along part of the route, the city decided to issue the grant for the maximum period of twenty-five years with the privilege of a twenty-five-year renewal. As compensation for this grant the company agreed to pay twenty thousand dollars in cash together with minimum annual sums totaling during the twenty-five-year period two hundred and sixty-seven thousand dollars. These minimum payments were estimated on the basis of three per cent of the company's gross receipts for the first five years; five per cent for the next ten years; and six per cent for the remaining years of the franchise. In the event that the minimum payments stipulated were less than the amount accruing under these percentages, the company was to pay on the percentage basis. The company was further required to pay a toll of five cents per round

[1] *Report of the Public Service Commission, First District of the State of New York*, 1913, vol. v, p. 1192.

[2] Due to the character of the street layout in Queens and the location of the Sunnyside railroad yard at the eastern terminal of the Queensboro bridge.

[3] *Report of the Public Service Commission, First District of the State of New York*, 1909, vol. ii, pp. 104-105.

[4] See *Documents Public Service Commission*, 1913, vol. v, p. 1195.

trip for every car crossing the Queensboro bridge, the tracks thereon being owned by the city; also four per cent on the cost of the terminal facilities at either end of the bridge furnished by the city, and a graduated rental aggregating sixty-two thousand five hundred dollars for the use of the viaduct over the railroad yards at the eastern approach to the bridge. The company was further required to contract away the right which it enjoyed under the franchise-tax law to subtract these payments, made to the city, from the amount of its franchise taxes. The inclusion of this requirement was not peculiar to this contract. When the special franchise-tax law was enacted by the state legislature in 1899 provision was made that any percentages of gross earnings or other income or license fee of any amount paid to the city in the nature of a tax might be deducted from the franchise taxes collected,[1] with the idea of equalizing the tax burden. It, therefore, in effect permitted those companies which were required by the law of 1884 to pay a gross earnings tax to deduct it from the sum of the special franchise tax, thus removing the discrimination that had existed in favor of the earlier established companies who paid no gross-receipts tax as against the new, undeveloped and less profitable roads. The city was very much opposed to this legislative policy and, to a certain degree, defeated the purpose of the law by insisting that all applicants for street railway grants should renounce their rights under the law and accept a disadvantageous position as compared with the companies which had preceded them.[2] This arrangement was perfectly legal and it became the policy of the city to include it in every new grant.

The South Shore Traction Company's contract of 1909

---

[1] *Laws of the State of New York*, 1899, ch. 712.
[2] Wilcox, Delos F., *Municipal Franchises*, vol. ii, pp. 128-129.

stipulates that in case the company decides to renew the contract, revaluation of the franchise is to be arrived at either by agreement at least one year prior to the expiration of the original period, or, failing in this, then by appraisal. The renewal percentage rates are to be reasonable but not less than the rate in force during the last year of the original term. The appraisers are to be chosen one by the board of estimate and apportionment, one by the railroad company, and the third by the two thus chosen.[1] In their work the appraisers are to have access to the books of the company and are privileged to examine the company's officers under oath. All expenses incident to the revaluation by appraisal are to be shared equally by the city and the company.

At the termination of the contract for either the original or renewal period or upon termination of the franchise for any other cause, or upon dissolution of the company, it is stipulated that the tracks and equipment constructed in accordance with the terms of the franchise shall automatically revert to the city to be used or disposed of as the city shall see fit. In the event that the city does not care to take over the property, the board of estimate and apportionment may, by resolution, compel the company, on thirty days' notice, to remove its tracks and equipment from the streets and restore the latter to their original condition. The contract, in this respect, is weak, as a contemporary authority [2] points out, in that it fails to make any provision for the acquirement by the city, either by reversion or by purchase, of the rolling stock, power-houses, or other portions of the company's operating plant which were not classed as street fixtures.

---

[1] No provision was made for the appointment of the third member in case of a deadlock between the first two chosen.

[2] Wilcox, Delos F., *Municipal Franchises*, vol. ii, p. 131.

The franchise requires the company to permit the joint use of its tracks by other companies who might be properly authorized to do so. This provision, it was thought, would prevent litigation with other companies claiming street-railway rights in this particular territory. Any company desiring to use the tracks jointly with the grantee must make compensation by means of (1) an initial payment to be determined in practically the same manner as valuation is to be determined in renewals, and (2) an annual payment which is to equal the legal interest on the cost of the road, its equipment, upkeep and additions, and in proportion to the number of cars operated. This rate may be increased beyond the legal rate by petitioning the board of estimate and apportionment if in the opinion of the board such action is justified.[1]

[1] The clauses are as follows: "(a) An initial payment to be mutually agreed upon by said corporation or individual and the company, and in case of failure on the part of such individual or corporation and the Company to agree upon the amount of such initial payment, such amount shall be determined by three disinterested freeholders selected in the following manner: One disinterested freeholder shall be chosen by the company, one disinterested freeholder shall be chosen by the individual or corporation; these two shall choose a third disinterested freeholder, and the three so chosen shall act as appraisers and shall determine the amount of such payment. Such appraisers, in fixing such amount, shall consider compensation to the Company for: First, the sinking fund which may have been or should have been set aside for the retirement of the total investment represented by such property of the Company as is used by said individual or corporation, from the date of the granting of this franchise to the date upon which said individual or corporation begins the use of such property of the company; second, the moneys expended by the Company in its organization and promotion; third, the increased value of the territory as a district suitable for railway operation, which increase may have resulted from the operation of the Company; fourth, the loss of business to the Company which may result from direct competition on its own lines; fifth, any other purpose or purposes which the appraisers may deem as justly due to said Company by such individual or corporation for the use of such property.

The original agreement stipulates that at any time after ten years from the date of the contract the city may, on twelve months' notice, compel the company to substitute underground electric current for its overhead trolley system from Queensboro bridge to Jamaica. Construction was to commence within six months after securing the required consents of the property-owners, or from the date of authorization by the Appellate Division of the Supreme Court in lieu of such consents. The franchise was to become void and all money paid by the company to the city, including the twenty thousand dollars cash payment and the twenty thousand dollars penalty fund, was to be forfeited unless the road was completed and in full operation within two years from the date of such authorization. All grade crossings over other railroads are to be eliminated by the company's constructing its lines either over or below the grade. If the

The compensation and expenses of the said appraisers shall be borne by such individual or corporation.

"(b) An annual payment which shall equal the legal interest on such proportion of the actual cost of the construction of such railway and structures, and additions and betterments thereto, as the number of cars operated by such individuals or corporations shall bear to the number of cars operated by the companies then using the same; and also such proportion of the cost of keeping the tracks and electrical equipment in repair, and the cost of additions and betterments thereto, such proportion of laying and repairing of pavement and removal of snow and ice and all other duties imposed upon the Company by the terms of this contract in connection with the maintenance or the operation of said railway so used, as the number of cars operated by such individual or corporation shall bear to the number of cars operated by the companies then using the same, together with the actual cost of the power necessary for the operation of the cars thereon of such individual or corporation. Provided, however, that if, in the opinion of the Company, the legal rate of interest upon the cost of such railway shall be an insufficient sum to be paid for the use of such tracks, it may appeal to the Board, and the Board may fix a percentage upon the cost to be paid to the company, at a sum in excess of the legal rate of interest, if, in its opinion, such action is justified."

city changes the grade of any street over which the company operates, the company is required to lay its tracks in conformity with the new grade at its own expense. Should the city authorities be of opinion that any particular street is too narrow to accommodate both a roadway and a railroad, the company is compelled to widen such street at its own expense, in order to allow space for vehicular traffic. Several other obligations are imposed upon the company,[1] which are similar in character to those stipulated in the earlier franchises.

It is explicitly stated that all annual charges or payments agreed upon shall continue throughout the whole term of the franchise notwithstanding any clause in any statute or

[1] The company is to repair the surface of the streets between its rails and for two feet on either side; the city reserves the right to change the material or the character of the paving on any street, and in such event the company is to replace the pavement in and about its tracks as directed by the city authorities without cost to the city; to water the streets three times in every twenty-four hours to a width of sixty feet whenever the temperature is above thirty-five degrees fahrenheit without cost to the city; with the approval of the proper city authorities oil may be used instead of water, and in this contingency the oiling is to be done twice during each summer season and in such a manner as to prevent the raising of dust; the company is further required to remove ice and snow from the space in and about its tracks, free of charge to the city, unless at the option of the borough president it enters into a contract with the city to clean an equivalent amount of street surface from curb to curb. The franchise is not to interfere with the progress of any municipal work in the streets and in case it does the company is required at its own expense to protect or remove its tracks or appurtenances until the improvement is completed. The rate of fare is limited to five cents, but over the Queensboro bridge a charge of not more than three cents or two tickets for five cents may be made. Policemen and firemen in full uniform are to enjoy free transportation. Operation of freight cars over the road is prohibited, and rates for carrying express matter are to be subject to regulation by the board of estimate and apportionment. The usual provisions in regard to light, fenders, wheel-guards and heat during cold weather are included.

in the charter of any company providing for franchise payments at a different rate. The franchise is not transferable nor can it be leased or sublet unless the assignee or lessee shall covenant to exercise it subject to all the conditions of the franchise contract. Further, the city reserves the right to require the company to improve or increase its equipment whenever directed to do so by the board of estimate and apportionment. A detailed annual report of the company's yearly financial transactions must be submitted to the board of estimate and apportionment, and the books of the company must be open to inspection by the comptroller for verification of the company's financial statements. The contract contains a detailed penalty system for failure of the company to give efficient service at the rates fixed in the ordinance or for failure to keep the railroad property in good condition throughout the term of the grant. This system is well summed up by Mr. Delos F. Wilcox as follows:

> The sum of $250 a day was stipulated as fixed or liquidated damages for every default of the company in any of these particulars, in case such default should remain unremedied for an unreasonable time after notice from the board of estimate and apportionment. The company was required to deposit with the comptroller a fund of $20,000 in money or approved securities upon which the city could draw for penalties inflicted upon the company, or for any necessary expenses in performing work neglected by the company. The penalty for failure to observe the provisions of the franchise relating to headway, the heating and lighting of cars, fenders, wheel guards and the watering of pavements, was fixed at the sum of $50 a day for each day of violation, plus the further sum of $10 a day for each car not properly heated, lighted or fendered in case the complaint related to these matters. The procedure to be followed for the imposition and collection of penalties was set forth in detail. When complaint was made the board of estimate and apportionment was to give the company notice to

appear on a certain day, not less than ten days after the serving of the notice, to show cause why it should not be penalized in accordance with the provisions of the franchise. If the company failed to appear, or after a hearing was judged in default by the court, then the prescribed penalty was to be imposed forthwith, or in cases not covered by the specific penalties set forth in the franchise the board was to fix the amount and, without legal procedure, direct the city comptroller to withdraw the amount of the penalty from the security fund deposited with him. Whenever any drafts had been made upon this fund, the company was required upon ten days' notice to restore it to the original amount of $20,000, or in default of doing so, to be subject to the annulment of the franchise at the option of the board of estimate and apportionment.[1]

This franchise was condemned by the public service commission for the first district mainly on the ground that it gives the company a virtual monopoly for fifty years of the only available street-railway route between Manhattan and Jamaica by way of the Queensboro bridge, for, in the opinion of the commission, the terms as to the joint use of the tracks are practically prohibitive.[2] The commission refused to approve the exercise of the franchise and the company appealed to the courts, and obtained a reversal of the commission's decision.[3] The commission then took the matter to the Court of Appeals, where the judgment of the Appellate Division was affirmed October 26, 1909.[4] After the company had secured confirmation of its rights the original

[1] Wilcox, Delos F., *Municipal Franchises*, vol. ii, pp. 136-137.
[2] *Report of the Public Service Commission, First District, State of New York*, 1909, vol. ii, p. 104.
[3] People *ex rel* South Shore Traction Co. *v.* Willcox, 133 App. Div., 556.
[4] *Ibid.*, 196 N. Y., 212. In this case the court did not pass upon the merits of the franchise but made its decision on questions of jurisdiction.

franchise through an agreement was considerably modified, so that the financial obligations to the city were reduced; subsequently the validity of this grant again became a subject of litigation,[1] which ultimately resulted in its abrogation. A new contract, dated October 29, 1912, differed from the agreement of 1909 in two important particulars.[2] In the first place, other companies might obtain franchises for the same streets covered by the South Shore Traction Company's contract; and, secondly, the financial return to the city was modified, the company agreeing to pay to the city for the first five years three per cent of its annual receipts, with a minimum of three thousand five hundred dollars per year; for the next five years, five per cent of its annual receipts with a minimum of seven thousand dollars; for the third five years, five per cent with a minimum of twelve thousand dollars; and for the next ten years, five per cent with a minimum of fourteen thousand seven hundred dollars. The car fee for the use of the Queensboro bridge was not changed and remained at five cents for each round trip. For the use of the tracks across the bridge the company was to pay four per cent per annum upon a valuation of thirty thousand dollars per mile of single track used, while the same rate was prescribed upon the cost of construction for the use of the terminal loops. The other provisions remained practically unchanged. This franchise, which was approved by the Public Service Commission on August 9, 1912,[3] is typical of the standard form of street railway franchises now granted by the city of New York.

Among the criticisms which have been made regarding the charter may be mentioned, in the first place, the repeal

[1] Wilcox, Delos F., *Municipal Franchises.*, vol. ii, pp. 135-136.
[2] *Report of Public Service Commission, First District State of New York*, 1913, vol. v, pp. 1197-1198.
[3] *Ibid.*, 1912, vol. i, pp. 369-370.

of the Cantor Act. At the time the charter was drafted a brief section was incorporated which in effect nullified that portion of the General Railroad Law requiring street railway franchises to be sold at auction.[1] The supporters of the auction-sale principle asserted that the haste with which the charter was rushed through the legislature prevented a thorough public discussion of the document, and the point was, therefore, overlooked.[2] The advocates of competitive sales, while they realized that the provisions of the Cantor Act were far from perfect, vigorously defended the basic principle of the act on the theory that without competition the board of estimate and apportionment would be at a loss to determine the actual value of a new franchise. In the opinion of the supporters of the sales principle, no one is in a better position to know the value of a new franchise than those who apply for it, and it is only when competitors are bidding against one another that any real disclosure is given as to the actual value of the proposed grant.[3] Whatever may have been the merit of the Cantor Law, it certainly did not always record the true measure of the monetary worth of the franchise under consideration, as has already been noted in the application of the auction principle to Bronx franchises.

Again, no provision was made in the charter for the reservation to the city of the right to purchase those portions of the railway plant, such as power-houses, car-barns, and their equipment. In the event of municipal ownership it is conceivable that the tracks might be of very little value without these accessories.

[1] Section 77, of ch. iii.
[2] West, Max, "The Franchises of Greater New York," in *Yale Review*, 1898, vol. vi, p. 395.
[3] *Ibid.*, p. 400.

CHAPTER X

GENERAL CONCLUSIONS

FROM the study that has been made certain reasonable conclusions may be deduced:

1. It can scarcely be said that New York city has ever had a scientific franchise policy; rather it has been blindly groping to evolve such a policy. Until the creation of the Greater City, the franchise-granting body, whether common council or state legislature, awarded franchises to those individuals or corporations offering the greatest monetary inducement or exercising the greatest political influence.

2. In making franchise grants, the public was utterly disregarded. Ordinances were rushed through with practically no opportunity for publicity or careful consideration.

3. The executives, both state and municipal, by their veto power made a greater effort to protect the interests of the public than did the legislative bodies.

4. The majority of the grants were given in perpetuity, were exclusive or monopolistic in character, and invariably brought little revenue to the city.

5. The franchise grants or contracts were loosely drawn and the conditions embodied therein were trivial in character; no provision was made for financial regulation.

6. Consolidation of the independent lines was accompanied by over-capitalization, high rentals, and stock-jobbing.

These observations force us to conclude that today, with the awakened interest in public affairs, the city should formulate a definite and comprehensive program with respect not only to its street-railway franchises but also to other public utilities.[1] The time has come when the city can no longer

[1] In this connection it is interesting to note the recommendations made by the Committee on Franchises of the National Municipal League at its Detroit meeting, November 22, 1917:

" 1. That every state remove the handicaps from municipal ownership by clearing away legal and financial obstacles, so far as they are now embedded in constitutional and statutory law.

" 2. That every state provide expert administrative agencies for the regulation and control of public utilities. These agencies should have full jurisdiction over interurban services and over local services where the local authorities are unwilling or unable to exercise local control. They should have limited jurisdiction wherever the local authorities are in a position to exercise the full normal functions of municipal government, and should even have jurisdiction with respect to accounting and reports in the case of utilities owned and operated by municipalities.

" 3. That every city where public utilities are operated primarily as local services definitely recognize these services as public functions and set in motion at once the financial machinery necessary to bring about the municipalization of public utility investments at the earliest practicable moment.

" 4. That every such city, pending the municipalization of its utilities, recognize the necessity of giving security to public utility investments and to a fair rate of return thereon, and to that end assume as a municipal burden the ultimate financial risks of public utility enterprises and insist upon receiving the benefits naturally accruing from this policy in the form of a lowered cost of capital.

" 5. That every city definitely adopt the policy of securing public utility service to the consumers either at cost, or at fixed rates not in excess of cost with subsidies from taxation whenever needed for the maintenance of the service at the rates fixed.

" 6. That every large city provide itself with expert administrative agencies for the continuous study of local public utility problems; for the adjustment of complaints as to service; for the preparation and criticism of public utility contracts and ordinances; for the formulation of standards of public utility service; and for adequate representation of itself and its citizens in proceedings before the state commission or other tribunals affecting the capital stock and bond issues, the intercompany agreements, the accounting methods, the reports, the valuations, the rates, and the practices of public service corporations operating in whole or in part within the city's limits." See Wilcox, Delos F., " Recent Developments in the Public Utility Field Affecting Franchise Policies and Municipal Ownership," *National Municipal Review*, March 1918, vol. vii, pp. 157-158.

afford to pursue a policy the outstanding characteristics of which are looseness and inefficiency. It should take a courageous attitude and map out a policy which will insure to the people of today and tomorrow adequate and efficient transit service, which is one of the mainsprings of our industrial system. In the adoption of such a policy there are certain important problems which should be considered. One of these, the solution of which is of vital importance to the city, is the matter of street-railway extensions. Private utility corporations usually are reluctant to extend their lines unless the additional construction promises to net a substantial profit.[1] In the past, threatened or real competition furnished a motive for building certain extensions;[2] but the street-railway business of New York city is no longer competitive, and is not likely to be so in the future.[3] Further-

[1] A recent case, New York and Queens Gas Company *v.* McCall, 245 U. S., 345, is typical. In this case the Public Service Commission ordered the Gas Company to extend its mains to meet the reasonable needs of a growing community about a mile and half distant from the end of the company's mains, but within the limits of New York city. The company maintained that in proportion to the expenditure required a sufficient financial return would not be obtained. The company appealed from the order of the Commission and the case finally went to the United States Supreme Court on the ground that the order of the Commission was illegal and void in that it deprived the company of property without due process of law and denied equal protection of the laws in violation of the Fourteenth Amendment. The order of the Public Service Commission was upheld. For comments on this case see 2 *Cornell Law Review*, 126; 31 *Harvard Law Review*, 644; 27 *Yale Law Journal*, 705.

[2] For instance, the keen rivalry between the Metropolitan Street Railway Company and the Third Avenue Railroad Company for possession of the Kingsbridge extension.

[3] In a sense, however, the automobile and the jitney may be looked upon as competitors. As to the importance of this competition see Delos F. Wilcox, "Problem of Reconstruction with Respect to Urban Transportation," in *National Municipal Review*, January, 1919, vol. viii, p. 38.

more, extensions have been built which, at the time, were not vitally important to the community; they were constructed to aid the real-estate speculations of the officials or stockholders of the company, or were built by reason of subsidies received by the company from persons interested in real-estate development.[1] Fortunately the city may be protected against both of these eventualities by the State Public Service Commission, which has power to order extensions or refuse to approve the exercise of any grant.[2] Despite this the extension problem as it now stands is, in so far as it affects the future franchise policy of the city, a complicated one. The charter of the city provides for limited grants with the reversion to the city of the tracks and other street fixtures of the railroad at the end of the franchise period or its renewal. In some instances the property reverts without any money payment on the part of the city. As a well-informed contemporary[3] points out, this is possibly a short step in the direction of securing ultimate control of the street franchises of the city; but the question has well been asked whether a company, knowing that at the end of a stated period it must surrender certain parts of its road to the city, will maintain its physical property in good condition unless it has some guarantee of being properly compensated for the property it is called upon to surrender.

In this same connection mention should be made of perpetual franchises. Neither the state legislature nor the city has taken definite action to secure control of those most val-

---

[1] Many of the franchise extensions of the Union Railway Company are typical. Recently many unprofitable extensions have been abandoned. See *Reports of Public Service Commission for 1910-1918*.

[2] *Laws of the State of New York*, 1907, ch. 429; article iii, sections 50 and 53.

[3] Wilcox, Delos F., *Municipal Franchises*, vol. ii, p. 138.

uable franchises which were bartered away in perpetuity and without which the tip-end twigs or branches of the street-railway-franchise tree will be of little value to the municipality.[1] Of course there is a possibility that with the constant growth of the city the companies holding franchises in perpetuity will desire to extend their lines and, being reluctant to surrender the use of those parts already in control of the city, they will be ready to accept limited franchises in return for their present perpetual grants. This, however, is only a remote possibility; and experience has demonstrated that the companies intrenched behind irrevocable and perpetual franchises tenaciously resist every effort to dislodge them.[2]

As a result of war prices and labor costs there is some hope that the city can secure control of the perpetual grants through their voluntary surrender by the railway companies in return for authorization to impose higher fares. Overcapitalization and high interest rates, together with increased costs of operation, have reduced the street railway companies to dire financial distress.[3] In 1918 the Third Avenue Railroad Company,[4] and more recently the New York Railways Company,[5] applied to the Public Service Commission of the First District for an increase in transportation rates, although practically all the franchise con-

[1] Certain associations of the city have, however, advocated municipal control. See *Report of the Transit Conference of New York City*, January 25, 1906.

[2] See "Report of the Committee on Franchises of National Municipal League," November, 1913, printed in *National Municipal Review*, January, 1914, vol. iii, p. 25.

[3] Wilcox, Delos F., "Problem of Reconstruction with Respect to Urban Transportation," in *National Municipal Review*, January, 1919, vol. viii, pp. 34-36.

[4] See *Public Service Commission Reports*, 1918, vol. ix.

[5] *New York Times*, February, 1918.

tracts of the several companies embraced in the street surface railway systems of New York city specifically stipulate that not more than a five-cent fare shall be charged. To date (March, 1919) the desired increases have not been granted. The Public Service Commission undoubtedly realizes the necessity for adequate revenue, without which, if present conditions continue, it may be impossible for the operating companies to give satisfactory service. The commissions of this state insist that they are powerless to change rates so long as the present franchise contracts, containing fixed rates,[1] are in force, and in this contention they are supported by the New York Court of Appeals. In the Rochester rate case,[2] decided April 5, 1918, the whole question of the effect of rate and fare limitations stipulated in franchise contracts was passed upon. The court held that the public service commissions of the state have no authority to increase railway fares fixed by municipal franchise contract without the consent of the municipal authorities. The decision of the court seems to have been based upon both constitutional and statutory grounds. At least as to franchises granted pursuant to the Constitution,[3] the court made this significant statement:

Our Constitution, by requiring the consent of the local authorities, recognizes that our municipalities are *pro tanto* independent of legislative control, exercising some fragment of power, otherwise legislative in character, which has been thus

[1] See *Opinion Public Service Commission, First District, June 6, 1918, re Application of Third Avenue Railroad Company et al.*, vol. ix.

[2] In the Matter of Quinby et al, 223 N. Y., 244. For an excellent discussion of this case see Ransom, William L., "The Agitation for Higher Rates," *The Survey*, July 20, 1918, vol. xl, pp. 443-446. State *ex rel.* Tacoma Ry. and Power Co. *v.* Public Service Commission, 101 Wash., 601, is in accord with Quinby case.

[3] Article iii, Section 18 (Street Railway Franchises).

irrevocably transferred by the fundamental law from the legislature to the locality. The grant by the municipality of authority to use the streets is not a mere privilege or gratuity. Once accepted, it becomes a contract which neither the state nor its agencies can impair. (People *v.* O'Brien, 111 N. Y., 1.)

The court did not rule that a rate limited by a franchise contract could not be increased when changed conditions and increased costs of operation make an advance in fare advisable. It simply held that the fare provided for in the contract cannot be changed unless both parties consent. In other words, if a company wishes to change the contract, it must first ask for a modification at the hands of the franchise-granting authority. The same opinion was expressed by the Public Service Commission in its consideration of the application of the Third Avenue Railroad Company:

That many or all of these petitioning companies, and the " system " which they make up, need additional revenue or diminished expenditure, during the abnormal period of operating costs, we have no disposition to deny. It is a duty resting upon the proper public authorities, of which one instrumentality is this commission, to secure to these companies an adequate fare for the service rendered—a rate which if the volume of traffic be adequate, will yield a sum sufficient to maintain the service, preserve the property from deterioration and reward the investors with a fair return upon their outlay. But it may be pointed out that the difficulties of these companies are largely of their own creation. We do not refer now to the era of pyramid financing, gross over-capitalization, wasteful expenditures and the payment of dividends at the expense of the upkeep of the property. All of these incidents of earlier management are still having their effects, although such offenses against safe investment and good service have now been ended by the enactment of the Public Service Commission law. The difficulties of these companies as to franchise terms are of their own seeking. It is a matter of public recollection and record that the franchises were not forced upon reluctant and unwilling companies by rapacious municipalities which overpowered their capacity for resistance. The companies, at the instance of their boards of directors and high officials, *sought* these and similar franchises, fare—limitations and all; they plotted for them, schemed for them, dickered for them, gave concessions and gained advantages, got something which they thought they wanted, something which they could capitalize and over-capitalize, long term rights to use and occupy pivotal streets and avenues of the world's richest city. They gained favorable terms and for the sake of them accepted some terms which have now proved unfavorable, at least temporarily. But by the same legal concept (People *v.* O'Brien, 111 N. Y., 1) which has long denied the right of the municipality to impair or modify that franchise without the consent of the company, the company now finds itself unable to obtain the modification of a vital franchise term without the municipality's consent. The rule thus fairly works both ways, and the company has no right to expect that a commission created for the purpose of determining the reasonableness of rates should serve to relieve the company from temporarily " unprofitable terms " to which it perhaps " ill-advisedly " agreed in order to obtain street rights which it deemed of priceless value. The commission may well determine, under proper circumstances, what a company's rate or fare ought to be, but for release from a contract term, the company can hardly complain if it is required to repair to the municipality with which it made the contract. It was the company's solemn contract, not the commission, which gave the municipality an essential part in the mechanism and procedure for any readjustment of the company's rates.

By the companies' own choice, the local municipality has both a power and a responsibility, and no resort to a fragmentary plan of charging for transfers should avail to enable these companies now to avoid dealing with the municipality as to the terms and conditions on which a modification as to fares will be permitted. The city may be unqualifiedly willing that an increased fare on all surface and rapid transit lines shall be temporarily charged; it may be willing to consent to such an increase in return for terms and concessions of present or future public advantage; or it may not be willing to release the companies from their contract obligation at all. The matter of terms rests with the municipality, because the companies wanted the franchises so much that they bargained on the subject of fares and agreed to be ever bound by a five cent limitation, at the city's option when the franchise limitations no longer stand in the way the companies may come to the commission for the fixation of a reasonable and adequate rate, notwithstanding statutory barriers.

The Quinby case stands at variance with the general trend of decisions in the courts of other states. The courts of Wisconsin,[1] Colorado,[2] Oregon,[3] Missouri,[4] and Massachusetts[5] have held that the authority of public utilities commissions is paramount with respect to rates. It may be of interest to note that a bill is now (March, 1919) pending before the New York State legislature which attempts to give to the public service commissions authority to modify franchise contracts.[6] In the event of its passage the whole matter will again probably go to the Court of Appeals for a

[1] Milwaukee E. R. and L. Co. v. Railroad Commission, 238 U. S., 174, affirming 153 Wisconsin, 592; Duluth Street Ry. v. R. R. Commission, 161 Wis., 245.

[2] Denver & South Platte Ry. Co. v. City of Englewood, 62 Col., 229.

[3] City of Woodburn v. Public Service Commission of Oregon, 161 Pac. Rep., 391. This case was decided on basis of police power of state.

[4] State ex rel. Missouri S. R. R. Co. v. Public Service Commission, 168 S. W. Rep., 1156.

[5] Arlington Board of Survey v. Bay State Railway Co., 224 Mass., 463.

[6] Carson-Martin bill. For a detailed discussion of this bill from the standpoint of the street railway interests, see explanation of the bill by George W. Morgan, the legislative agent of the Interborough traction interests in *The Evening Post*, March 11, 1919.

final determination as to whether such a law is valid under the constitutional provision requiring local consent, upon which so much stress was laid in the Rochester rate case. If, however, the present ruling of the Court of Appeals stands, it would seem that the city is in an advantageous position to procure just and desirable changes in franchise terms which would open the way for the adoption of a policy suitable to the needs of the present and the immediate future. If the companies must have increased revenue, the city could demand that the old franchises, granted in utter disregard of public rights as to duration and terms, be surrendered; and it is difficult to see how the companies could fail to recognize the propriety of any reasonable demand for franchise changes which the municipality might wish to make in the interest of the public.

There is, of course, the possibility that the city may not have this opportunity of bargaining with the companies. Yet it cannot, it would seem, continue indefinitely its present policy of indeterminate and perpetual franchises. Ultimately it must obtain control of the perpetual grants, the existence of which, as the Committee on Franchises of the National Municipal League has pointed out, is " wholly contrary to sound public policy and inimical to the future welfare of cities."[1] The whole matter is well stated as follows:

The attempt to mix perpetual franchises with short-term or indeterminate franchises in the same city is a good deal like the attempt to mix oil and water. As a rule, where important perpetual franchises exist they are the old franchises, on the central streets, representing the most profitable field of operation. No city can ever adequately control the development of its transit system, for example, unless it can control the

[1] See Report of this Committee in *National Municipal Review*, January, 1914, vol. iii, p. 25.

portion of the transit system that operates in the business district. It seems to us largely futile, therefore, for charter commissions to write into new charters elaborate provisions governing the granting of new franchises, which, if they apply at all, will apply only to outlying areas, to relatively unimportant extensions, or to competing lines in the back streets. A charter full of franchise safeguards that apply only to future grants, while the entire profitable area of the city is already occupied by utilities operating under perpetual rights, is a delusion in law-making.[1]

It is of interest to note that in 1915, just before the assembling of the seventh New York State Constitutional Convention, the suggestion was made that certain provisions be incorporated in the proposed constitution which would give the cities of the state more adequate control over the franchises of municipal public-utility corporations.[2] The following recommendations were made:

1. A provision specifically conferring upon all cities the right to acquire, own and operate public utilities within or without their corporate limits, the exercise of such right outside of the corporate limits being subject to supervision by a state commission.

2. A provision authorizing cities to issue bonds outside the general debt limit upon the security of the property and revenues of utilities owned by the city.

3. A provision conferring upon cities the franchise-granting power and making the action of the cities final except as to franchises to be used merely for through service. In the case of the latter, the refusal of the municipality to grant the franchise, or the conditions upon which the franchise is granted, should be subject to review by a state board.

[1] See Report of this Committee in *National Municipal Review*, January, 1914, vol. iii, p. 26.
[2] Wilcox, Delos F., "The Constitution and Public Franchises," in *Proceedings of the American Academy of Political Science*, April, 1915, vol. v, pp. 451-462.

4. A provision prohibiting the grant of perpetual franchises, and requiring that all franchises be granted subject to the right of the city or of the state to take over the physical property of the utility upon making proper compensation for such property.

5. A provision forbidding the grant of additional franchises, powers or privileges to corporations or individuals claiming perpetual or very long-term franchises, except on condition that such claims be surrendered and that new franchises, in accordance with the spirit and the letter of the new constitution, be accepted in their place.

6. A provision prohibiting the opening or acceptance of a public street subject to public utility easements previously granted by the owners of the land.

7. A provision prohibiting the recognition of perpetual franchise rights except on clear proof that such rights were granted by a formal recorded act of the proper authorities and in strict compliance with the law, and that such rights have not been forfeited by non-use, misuse or failure to comply with the terms and conditions of the grant.

These recommendations, while not adopted by the constitution-makers, indicated the trend of thought of those who have given serious consideration to the evolution of a franchise policy suitable to the needs not only of New York city but also of the other cities of the state.

Any constructive street-railway policy which the city may adopt should provide for labor adjustments. There has never been, nor is there at present, any permanent and effective machinery, either state or municipal, for the adjustment of labor difficulties. In the past, wages and conditions of labor have been determined largely, as in all industry, by the employing companies or by a process of " bargaining " between the employers and unionized employees. Strikes have not been unknown,[1] the employees have had recourse

[1] For instance, in 1916. See Andrews, J. B., "Labor and Labor Legislation," in *American Year Book*, 1916.

to this weapon as a means of securing their demands. It is not within the scope of this study to discuss the merits of the strike, but the day has arrived when the city of New York can no longer afford to risk the danger of tying-up its transportation system with a resulting paralysis of industry and business and a possibility of civic disorder. In this connection a leading authority on franchise problems has ventured the opinion that the power to fix wages and working conditions will have to be conferred upon the same public bodies that have power to fix rates.[1] The proposal seems feasible provided our public utilities commissions function as municipal agencies and not merely as state organizations which may become the tools of our public utility corporations. As long as private ownership and operation of our street railway continues, a board of three members, one chosen by the railway workers, one by the railway corporations, and one appointed by the mayor of the city would be eminently more satisfactory; for with this arrangement both of the important economic groups as well as the public would be represented. Whatever may be the merits or defects of either of these plans, the city should not delay in evolving some arrangement whereby the danger of a tie-up of the transportation systems of the city through strikes will be minimized or entirely eliminated.

Lastly, mention should be made of another matter which should be taken into consideration in dealing with the surface railway franchise problem. It has been shown that the street surface railways of New York city are over-capitalized. While this thesis is not primarily concerned with the financial history of the street surface railways of the city, nevertheless any discussion involving franchise control,

[1] Wilcox, Delos F., "Problem of Reconstruction with Respect to Urban Transportation," in *National Municipal Review*, January, 1919, vol. viii, p. 44.

either by negotiation or condemnation, must necessarily take into account the question of the value of the several franchises to be acquired. There seems to be little likelihood that the companies will surrender their perpetual franchises in exchange for limited grants unless forced to do so under stress of financial conditions. The city, therefore, if it desires control, must have recourse to either purchase or condemnation. In either case it would be contrary to a wise public policy and wholly unethical for the city to pay the alleged values which have attached to these perpetual grants. Watered stock and values which do not exist except on paper should be eliminated. The city should pay what the franchise is actually worth, but it would not be justified in assuming an additional financial burden by compensating for bulging, inflated franchise values unless it proposed to take into consideration the innocent purchaser of bonds representing such values.[1]

Over-capitalization and perpetual franchises must disappear before there can be any fundamental and lasting solution of the street surface railway problem. The perpetual franchise must be superseded by limited grants and false profits must be wiped out. Then, and only then, will the city be in a position to act intelligently in regard to the future of the street surface railway.

[1] For a brief discussion of this question see Delos F. Wilcox, "Problem of Reconstruction with Respect to Urban Transportation," in *National Municipal Review*, January, 1919, vol. viii, pp. 42-43. See also a recent opinion by William P. Burr, Corporation Counsel of the city of New York in *New York Times*, March 2, 1919.

BIBLIOGRAPHICAL NOTE

IN the preparation of this monograph the writer has found it necessary to depend very largely upon source material. Especially valuable has been the magnificent collection of documents relative to the incorporation, franchise rights and intercorporate relations of the transportation companies operating within the boundaries of the present city of New York which have been filed with the Public Service Commission of the First District and compiled by the Commission under the title *Documentary History of Railroad Companies* (1913); also The *Proceedings of the Councilmen and Aldermen of New York City*; The *State Senate and Assembly Journals* of New York State; The *Laws of the State of New York*; and the excellent *Compilation of the Existing Ferry Leases and Railroad Grants Made by the City of New York and the Legislature of the State for the Use of the Streets of New York City* (1866), compiled by David T. Valentine.

In addition to these, valuable material was found in court reports, newspapers, pamphlets, magazines, and, to a small degree, in secondary works.

I. BIBLIOGRAPHIES

Appleton's *Cyclopedia of American Biography*.
King, C. L., *The Regulation of Municipal Utilities*, New York, 1912.
Lamb's *Biographical Dictionary*.
McLaughlin, A. C., and Hart, H. B., *Cyclopedia of American Government*, 3 vols., New York, 1914.
New York Public Library, *Bibliography of City of New York*, New York, 1906.
Readers' Guide to Periodical Literature, New York, 1900.
Stevens, D. L., *A Bibliography of Municipal Utility Regulation and Municipal Ownership*, Boston, 1918.

II. CASES

Arlington Board of Survey *v.* Bay State Railway Co., 224 Mass., 463.
Beekman *v.* The Third Avenue Railroad Company, 153 N. Y., 144.
Burrows *v.* Interborough-Metropolitan Company, 156 Fed. Rep., 389.
Central Crosstown Railroad Company *v.* Metropolitan Street Railway Company, 16 N. Y. (App. Div.), 229.

City of Woodburn *v.* Public Service Commission of Oregon, 161 Pac. Rep., 391.
Davies *v.* The Mayor &c. of New York City. (Duer's Reports.)
Denver & South Platte Railway Company *v.* City of Englewood, 62 Colo., 229.
Duluth Street Railway Company *v.* Railroad Commission, 161 Wis., 245.
Gilchrist *v.* Forty-second Street, Manhattanville & St. Nicholas Avenue Railroad Company, 23 N. Y. (App. Div.), 625.
Mayor, Aldermen and Commonalty of the City of New York *v.* Dry Dock, East Broadway and Battery Railroad Company, 112 N. Y., 137.
Mayor, Aldermen and Commonalty of the City of New York *v.* The Eighth Avenue Railroad Company, 118 N. Y., 389.
Mayor, Aldermen and Commonalty of New York City *v.* The Second Avenue Railroad Company, 32 N. Y., 261.
Mayor, Aldermen and Commonalty of the City of New York *v.* The Twenty-Third Street Railway Company, 113 N. Y., 311.
Milhau *v.* Sharp, 27 N. Y., 611.
Milwaukee, E. R. & L. Co. *v.* Railroad Commission, 238 U. S., 174.
New York Central and Hudson River Railroad Co. *v.* The City of New York, 202 N. Y., 212.
New York and Queens Gas Co. *v.* McCall, 245 U. S., 345.
People *v.* Compton *et al.* (Duer's Reports.)
People *ex rel* Bleecker Street and Fulton Ferry Railroad Company *v.* Commissioner of Taxes &c of New York City, 60 N. Y., 638.
People *v.* O'Brien, 111 N. Y., 1.
People *ex rel* South Shore Traction Co. *v.* Willcox, 133 App. Div., 556.
People *ex rel* South Shore Traction Co. *v.* Willcox, 196 N. Y., 212.
People *v.* Third Avenue Railroad Company, 45 Barb., 63.
Potter *v.* Collis, 156 N. Y., 16.
In the Matter of Quinby *et al.*, 223 N. Y., 244.
State *ex rel* Missouri S. R. R. Co. *v.* Public Service Commission, 168 S. W. Rep., 1156.
State *ex rel* Tacoma Ry. & Power Co. *v.* Public Service Commission, 101 Wash., 601.
Stuyvesant *v.* Pearsall *et al.*, 15 N. Y., 244.
In re Third Avenue Railroad Co., 121 N. Y., 536.
Wetmore *v.* Story, 22 Barb., 414.
Wormser *v.* Metropolitan Street Railway Co., 184 N. Y., 83.

III. LAWS—NEW YORK STATE

For the following years: 1807, '31, '32, '46, '50, '54, '55, '57, '59, '60, '66, '67, '69, '70, '71, '72, '73, '74, '75, '79, '82, '84, '86, '88, '90, '92, '93, '97, '99, 1905, '06, '07, '14, '17.

IV. DOCUMENTS

Annual Report of New York Railways Company for year ending June 30, 1918.

Burr, David H., *Map of the City and County of New York with Adjacent Country in 1832.*

City Record, 1884 to 1918.

Lincoln, Charles Z., *Messages from the Governors of the State of New York,* Albany, 1909.

Minutes of the Board of Estimate and Apportionment of the City of New York, 1909, 1910, 1912.

New York State Assembly Documents, 1860.

New York State Assembly Journals, 1857-1880.

New York State Senate Documents, 1886.

New York State Senate Journals, 1859-1880.

Ordinances, Resolutions, &c Adopted by the Common Council and Approved by the Mayor, New York, 1878.

Proceedings of the Board of Aldermen, New York, 1831-1897, 1913.

Proceedings of the Board of Councilmen, New York, 1854.

Report of Commission to Investigate the Surface Railroad Situation in the City of New York on the West Side, 1918.

Reports of City Executive Officials, New York, 1831-1897.

Reports of the Public Service Commission, First District, State of New York, 1907, 1909, 1913, 1914.

Report of the New York State Railroad Commission, 1896.

Reports of State Legislative Committees and Commissions, especially New York State Senate Committee on Cities, 1890. (Fassett Committee.)

United States Census, 1910.

Valentine, David T., *Compilation of the Existing Ferry Leases and Railroad Grants made by the City of New York and the Legislature of the State for the Use of the Streets of New York City,* New York, 1866.

Valentine, David T., *Ordinances of the Mayor, Aldermen and Commonalty of the City of New York,* New York, 1859.

V. NEWSPAPERS

New York *Commercial and Financial Chronicle.*
Morning Courier and New York *Enquirer.*
New York *Evening Mail.*
New York *Evening Post.*
New York *Herald.*
New York *Sun.*

New York *Times.*
New York *Tribune.*
New York *World.*

VI. MAGAZINES

Annals of American Academy of Political and Social Science, 1908.
Atlantic Monthly, 1901.
2 *Cornell Law Review,* 126.
Cosmopolitan Magazine, 1908.
Everybody's Magazine, 1908.
31 *Harvard Law Review,* 644.
McClure's Magazine, 1908.
Municipal Affairs, 1900.
National Municipal Review, 1914, 1918, 1919.
Outlook, 1908.
Proceedings of American Academy of Political Science, 1915.
Street Railway Review, 1901.
The Survey, 1918.
World Almanac, 1918.
27 *Yale Law Journal,* 705.
Yale Review, 1898.

VII. PAMPHLETS

Butler, W. A., *New York City, Its Growth, Misgovernment and Needs,* New York, 1852.
The City and the Eighth Avenue Railroad, New York, 1897.
Davenport, John I., *Population of the City of New York,* New York, 1875.
New York Railways Company, *Your Street Car Service—A Statement of the Facts About the Situation of the New York Railways Company,* New York, 1919.
Prince, L. B., *The Proposed Amendments to the Constitution of the State of New York,* New York, 1874.
Roth, Louis, *History of Rapid Transit Development in the City of New York.* (Unpublished.)
Ruggles, Samuel B., *Letters on Rapid Transit Addressed to Mayor of The City of New York,* New York, 1875.
Willson, H. B., *Communications to the Constitutional Convention on Special Railway Legislation,* New York, 1867.

VIII. SECONDARY WORKS

Alexander, D. S., *A Political History of the State of New York,* 3 vols., New York, 1906-1909.
American Year Book, 1916.

Bayles, W. H., *Old Taverns of New York*, New York, 1915.
Belden, E. P., *New York, Past, Present and Future*, New York, 1849.
Bogart, E. L., *Economic History of the United States*, New York, 1916.
Byrne, Stephen, *Irish Immigration to the United States*, New York, 1873.
Comstock, Sarah, *Old Roads From the Heart of New York*, New York, 1915.
Fox, D. R., *Decline of Aristocracy in the Politics of New York*, New York, 1919.
Francis, C. S., *A Stranger's Handbook of New York City*, New York, 1857.
Goodnow, F. J., *Municipal Problems*, New York, 1907.
Haswell, C. H., *Reminiscences of an Octogenarian, 1816-1860*, New York, 1896.
Hemstreet, Charles, *When Old New York was Young*, New York, 1902.
Holley, O. L., *A Description of New York in 1847*, New York, 1847.
Hourwich, I. A., *Immigration and Labor*, New York, 1912.
Janvier, Thomas A., *In Old New York*, New York, 1894.
Jenkins, Stephen, *The Greatest Street in the World, The Story of Broadway, Old and New*, New York, 1911.
Johnson, E. R., *American Railway Transportation*, New York, 1912.
King, Moses, *Handbook of New York City*, Boston, 1832.
King, Charles, *Progress of New York City During the Last Fifty Years*, New York, 1852.
Lamb, Martha J., *History of the City of New York: Its Origin, Rise and Progress*, New York, 1877-1896.
Leonard, J. W., *History of the City of New York, 1609-1909*, New York, 1909.
Myers, Gustavus, *History of Tammany Hall*, New York, 1907.
Pratt, E. E., *Industrial Causes of Congestion of Population in New York City*, New York, 1911.
Real Estate Record Association, *A History of Real Estate, Building and Architecture in New York*, New York, 1909.
Richmond, J. F., *New York and Its Institution, 1609-1871*, New York, 1871.
Roosevelt, Theodore, *New York*, New York, 1895.
Ruggles, Edward, *A Picture of New York in 1846*, New York, 1846.
Scisco, Louis D., *Political Nativism in New York State*, New York, 1901.
Shannon, Joseph, *Manual of the Corporation of the City of New York*, New York, 1868.
Van Dyke, John C., *The New New York*, New York, 1909.
Walker, J. B., *Fifty Years of Rapid Transit*, New York, 1918.
Watson, J. F., *Annals and Occurrences of New York City and State in the Olden Time*, Philadelphia, 1846.
Wilcox, Delos F., *Municipal Franchises*, 2 vols., New York, 1911.

Wilcox, Delos F., *Great Cities in America, Their Problems and Their Government*, New York, 1913.
Williams, Edwin, *New York As It is in 1833*, New York, 1833.
Wilson, J. G., *Memorial History of the City of New York*, New York, 1893.
Wilson, R. R., *New York, Old and New*, Philadelphia, 1909.

INDEX

Anti-Monopolist party, 24
Appleton, William H., 106
Avenue C. Railroad Company, trackage agreements, 118; incorporated, 132-133

Barrett, Justice, 165
Bartlett, Justice, 163
Beach, Judge Miles, 175
Beadleston, Ebenezer, 133
Belmont, August, 106, 219
Belt Line Railway Corporation, 112, 186
Bleecker Street and Fulton Ferry Railroad Company, 119; extension, 119; incorporated, 121; lease of, 124, 125, 129, 208; directorate, 128
Bloomingdale, 14
"Boodle" Board, 168, 172
Boston Post Road, 14
Brady, Anthony N., 201
Bribery, 46-49, 66-67, 97
Bright, Osborne, 163
Broadway, 14; fight for, 78-107; railroad on, 78; opposition to, 78-80, 82; resolution for, 79; injunction against, 79-80; offers to construct railroad on, 78-79, 85, 102; first attempt to acquire franchise for, 80-81; second attempt to acquire franchise for, 84; Senate bill (1860), 86; protest against, 87; third attempt to acquire franchise for, 94-99; fourth attempt to acquire franchise for, 99-100; fifth attempt to acquire franchise for, 100-103; municipal road proposed, 104; proposals for, 104-106; perpetuity of, 107
Broadway Railway Company, 134
Broadway Railroad Company, 159, 161, 162

Broadway and Seventh Avenue Railroad Company, trackage agreements, 118, 163; incorporated, 119; lease of, 121, 207; extensions, 126; allied with, 142; motive power, 170
Broadway Surface Railway Company, 159, 160, 161, 163, 167, 168
Bromner, Henry, 71
Bronx system, 193, 200
Brown, William, 97
Butler, John, Jr., 109

Cable plan, 179
Cantor Act, 183, 184, 190, 193, 200, 202, 234
Carter, James C., 167
Central Crosstown Railroad Company, 129, 137, 140, 218
Central Park, 40, 146
Central Park, North and East River Railroad Company, 108; extension, 111; trackage agreements, 111, 118; lease of, 111-112, 198, 209; receivership, 112; mortgage foreclosure and sale, 112; reorganization, 112; operating agreement, 112
Chambers Street and Grand Street Ferry Railroad Company, 173, 207, 208
Christopher and Tenth Street Railroad Company, 118, 129
Citizens Union, 66
City Reform party, 48, 49
Civil War, 143, 144
Clark, Myron S., 109
Clinton, Mayor Dewitt, 11
Columbus and Ninth Avenue Railroad Company, 158, 201, 211, 212
Commerce, 15
Commissioners, 11
Conkling, Roscoe, 167

Conover, John T., 112, 127
Consolidation, era of, 204
Constitutional Commission of 1874, 103
Cornell, Edward, 112
Coulter, James E., testimony of, 46
Curtis, Charles, 114

Dartmouth College Case, 168
Devlin, John E., 114
Dewey, Horace M., 47
Directorates, 128, 219
Doan, Horace A., 189
Dolan, Thomas, 206, 216
Donohue, Judge, 162
Dry Dock, East Broadway and Battery Railroad Company, 114; extension, 116; court decision, 117; trackage agreements, 118
Durant, Charles W., 109

East Side, 144, 145, 150
Edson, Mayor Franklin, 126, 128, 162, 166, 175, 179
Eighth Avenue Railroad Company, 41, 44; profitable line, 46; lease of 53, 213; attempt to acquire Broadway, 95, 98-99
Elkins, W. L., 206, 216
Ely, Mayor, 149
Erie Canal, 16
Erie Railroad Company, 175

Fassett Committee, 171
Flagg, A. C., 45
Flynn, James W., testimony of, 47
Foreword, 9
Forshay, James W., 170
Forty-second Street Crosstown Railroad Company, 149
Forty-second Street and Grand Street Ferry Railroad Company, 112, 114; trackage agreements, 118; lease of, 198, 209
Forty-second Street, Manhattanville and St. Nicholas Avenue Railroad Company, 118, 147, 148; extension, 148, 151, 152; trackage agreements, 152
Franchises, auction sale of, 89; power of legislature to grant, 57, 89-93, 108; general, 147, 165
Franchises, grants to:
  Avenue C Railroad Company, 132, 133

Franchises, grants to:
  Bleecker Street and Fulton Ferry Railroad Company, 121, 122, 123, 125, 126, 129
  Broadway, 159, 160
  Broadway and Seventh Avenue Railroad Company, 119, 197
  Central Crosstown Railroad Company, 138, 139
  Central Park, North and East River Railroad Company, 109-111, 113
  Chambers Street and Grand Street Ferry Railroad Company, 173
  Columbus Avenue and Ninth Avenue Railroad Company, 201
  Dry Dock, East Broadway and Battery Railroad Company, 114, 115, 116, 117, 118
  Eighth Avenue Railroad Company, 41, 44; violation of, 45; validity of, 46, 50-52
  Forty-second Street and Grand Street Ferry Railroad Company, 112, 113, 115
  Forty-second Street, Manhattanville and St. Nicholas Avenue Railroad Company, 147, 148, 150, 152
  Fulton Street Railroad Company, 192-193
  Houston, West Street and Pavonia Ferry Railroad Company, 134, 198
  Hudson River Railroad Company, 33-35, 36-38; perpetuity of, 38
  Lexington Avenue and Pavonia Ferry Railroad Company, 198
  Metropolitan Crosstown Railway Company, 195
  New York Cable Railway Company, 183
  New York and Harlem Railroad Company (1831), 17-19; (1832), 19, 21-23, 24, 25, 27-32
  Ninth Avenue Railroad Company, 72; validity of, 73-74, 75-77
  North and East River Railroad Company and the Fulton Ferry Railroad Company, 189, 196

Franchises, grants to:
  One Hundred and Twenty-fifth Street Railroad Company, 135-136
  Second Avenue Railway Company, 54-55; validity of, 56
  Seventh Avenue Railroad Company, 93
  Sixth Avenue Railroad Company, 41-43, 44, 53, 54; validity of, 46, 50-52
  South Ferry Railway Company, 141, 142
  Third Avenue Railroad Company, 59-61; legality of, 64-66; Kingsbridge extension, 63-69
  Thirty-fourth Street Crosstown Railway Company, 179
  Thirty-fourth Street Ferry and Eleventh Avenue Railroad Company, 177, 178
  Thirty-fourth Street Railroad Company, 176-177, 179
  Twenty-eighth and Twenty-ninth Street Railroad Company, 185, 186, 187, 195
  Twenty-third Street Railway Company, 130, 131
Fulgraff, L. A., 160, 161, 169
Fulton Street Railroad Company, 189, 192, 193

General Railroad Law (1850), 112; (1884), 154, 173, 183, 184, 185, 187, 196
Grace, Mayor William R., 178, 182, 186, 192
Grant, Hugh J., 160, 170, 199
Greater New York, 117, 221, 224, 235
Greenwich Village, 14
Gridiron bill, 89; opposition to, 89

Hamer, John W., 189
Harlem, 14
Harris, Sidney S., 167
Haughton, Nicholas, 105
Haven, George C., 159
Heppenheimer, William C., 189
Hill, Richard L., 148
Hoffman, Mayor, 30, 100
Horse cars, 23
Houston, West Street and Pavonia Ferry Railroad Company, trackage agreements, 118; lease of, 121, 129; incorporators, 133; extension, 158; mergers, 176; connections, 197, 199; sale of, 206
Hudson River Railroad Company, chartered, 33; extension, 35; consolidation, 35-36; opposition to, 36; commission to investigate, 36; condemnation, 36-38

Immigration, 15, 16, 17, 39
Interborough Rapid Transit Company, 219
Interurban Street Railway Company, 121, 215, 217, 218
Iselin, Adrian, 71
Ives, Brayton, 159

Jaehne, Henry W., 169

Kelley, John, 119
Kerr, John, 114, 119
King, David J., 128, 139
Kingsbridge extension, 63-69
Kingsland, Mayor, 45, 79
Kip, Lawrence, 107
Kipp, Solomon, 47
Knox, W. M., 162

Lacombe, E. H., 163, 191
Law, George, 74
Lexington Avenue and Pavonia Ferry Railroad Company, 114, 158, 198, 201, 210; extension, 200; consolidation, 201
Lord, G. W. T., 167
Lorillard, Pierre A., 106, 107
Loxley, Charles F., 189

Macauley, John C., 137
Madison Square, 13
Martine, Theodore, testimony of, 47
May, Lewis, 139
Mayer, Joseph B., 189
McHarg, R. K., 148
McQuade, A. J., 160, 169
Mechanics party, 24
Metropolitan Crosstown Railway Company, 111-114, 119, 195-198, 207, 209, 211
Metropolitan Securities Company, 217, 218

Metropolitan Street Railway Company, 112, 114, 118, 120, 121, 129, 134, 139, 140, 142, 176, 179, 188, 193, 198, 201, 202, 206, 210, 215, 218
Metropolitan Traction Company, 114, 176, 206, 209, 211
Mid-Crosstown Railway, Inc., 189
Morgan, Governor Edwin D., 85-86, 90, 110, 112
Morningside Heights, 14
Morris, John J., 149
Municipal reform, 27, 85.

New York Cable Railway Company, 159, 162, 179, 180
New York City, growth of, 15, 39-40, 133; population (1830), 11; (1850), 39; (Civil War period), 43
New York City Railway Company, 218, 219
New York and Harlem Railroad Company, 17-19; extension, 21-25, 27-32; operation, 22, 134; first car, 22; steampower, 25, 27; city line, 28, 213; opposition to extension, 30-31; lease of, 32; financial return from, 32; attempt to acquire Broadway, 95, 98
New York Passenger and Baggage Line Company, 88-89
New York Railways Company, 112, 114, 118, 121, 129, 132, 140, 193, 201, 202
New York Traction Company, 194, 200
New York and Yonkers Railroad Company, 82-83
Ninth Avenue Railroad Company, 72; extension, 74, 76; sale of, 74; trackage rights, 76, 77, 151; lease of, 77, 208
North and East River Railroad Company and the Fulton Ferry Railroad Company, 189, 190, 211

Oakley, Henry A., 25, 175
Omnibus, 29, 30
One Hundred and Twenty-fifth Street Railroad Company, 135.
O'Neil, "Honest" John, 169
Opdyke, Mayor George, 95
O'Rourke, John H., 192

Parker, Charles A., 66
Party, Anti-Monopolist, 24; Mechanics, 24; City Reform, 48, 49; Republican, 66
People's Traction Company, 194, 195, 200
Pettigrew, John, 47
Putnam, George Haven, 175

Rapid Transit Commission, 180
Real estate, 23
Republican party, 66
Reynolds, James B., 66
Road houses, 14
Roberts, William R., 104
Roe, Stephen R., 121
Rogers, James, 141
Roosevelt, J. A. 159, 161
Roosevelt, Theodore, 175
Root, Elihu, 52, 167, 170
Ruggles, Samuel, 23
Rutan, Theodore P., 141
Ryan, Thomas F., 206, 211, 216, 219

Sauer, William, 104
Searles, Gideon, 97
Second Avenue Railway Company, 54, 55; route changed, 56; extension, 57, 59; trackage agreements, 59, 118; lease of, 59, 214
Senate bill (1860), 86; protest against, 87
Seventh Avenue Railway Company, 93
Seward, Clarence A., 167
Seymour, Governor Horatio, 97, 98
Sharp, Jacob, 119, 126, 127, 128, 139, 159, 160, 163, 166, 168, 169
Sixth Avenue Railroad Company, 41; limited grant, 43; route changed, 43; extension, 44, 53; lease of, 54, 208
Sloane, John, 106, 107
Smith, Hugh, 121
Smythe, Recorder, 160
South Ferry Railway Company, 134, 141; motive power, 170; sale of, 207
South Shore Traction Company, 224, 226
Southworth, Alvan S., 126, 127
Squires, Robert, 135, 136

Stages, 14, 24, 40
Stephenson, John, 23
Stevens, Albert Gallatin, 107
Storm, Walter, 171
Straus, Oscar F., 175
Street Railway Act (1854), 49, 50; (1860), 57, 89, 93, 108
Strong, Mayor, 111
Sullivan, John, 137
Sweeney, Peter B., 119, 121

Tammany Hall, 27, 66
Taxes, 48
Taylor, A. Merritt, 189
Telegraph Stage Company, 116
Third Avenue Railroad Company, extensions, 61-66, 69-70, 153; Kingsbridge extension, 63-69; motive power, 70-71; trackage agreements, 71, 118, 152, 200; lease of, 71, 137, 214; reorganized, 71, 189; application to increase rates, 239, 241
Thompson, Henry, 142
Thompson, James R., testimony of, 97
Thompson, William, 137
Thurber, H. K., 162
Thirty-fourth Street Ferry and Eleventh Avenue Railroad Company, 177, 209
Thirty-fourth Street Railroad Company, 176, 177

Tiemann, Mayor Daniel F., 28, 84, 89
Tilden, Samuel J., 27
Tomlinson, Theodore E., 104
Truslow, Charles W., 188
Tweed ring, 85, 103
Twenty-eighth and Thirtieth Street Railroad Company, 185
Twenty-eighth and Twenty-ninth Streets Crosstown Railroad Company, 88, 188, 189
Twenty-eighth and Twenty-ninth Street Railway Company, 118, 185, 188, 189
Twenty-third Street Railway Company, 118, 124, 125, 127, 128, 130, 207, 208

Vance, S. B. H., 128, 167
Vultee, George W., 142

Wallace, James W., 71
Walton, Isaac M., 148
Washington Square, 13
West Side, 145, 150
Whitney, William C., 52, 159, 161, 206, 216
Whitridge, F. W., 71, 153
Widener, P. A. B., 206, 216
Wilcox, Delos F., 52, 231
Wood, Fernando, 27-28, 94

VITA

The author was born in Greenfield, New York, January 22, 1884. He prepared for college in the public schools of Saratoga County, graduating from the Corinth High School in 1903. From 1903 to 1905 he taught in a rural school. In 1905 he entered Syracuse University and was graduated from this institution in 1909 with the degree of Bachelor of Philosophy. From 1909 to 1913 he was principal of the Rhinebeck High School, Rhinebeck, New York. In 1913-1914 he was a graduate student in Syracuse University, from which institution he received the degree of Master of Arts in 1914. During the years 1914-1917 he held the position of instructor in History and Political Science in Syracuse University. During the summer of 1915 he was a graduate student at Columbia University, attending lectures of Professors James T. Shotwell, C. J. H. Hayes, and Mr. H. F. Munro. In 1917-1918 he again took courses in the School of Political Science at Columbia University, chiefly under Professors McBain, J. B. Moore, Powell, Beard, and Sait, together with a seminar with Professors Beard and McBain. In 1918 he was appointed instructor in History in Columbia University, and in 1919 to a professorship in History and Politics in Syracuse University.

UNIV. OF MICH.

JUL 2 2 1924

BOUND

HE
4491
N55
C287s

Carman
The street
surface railway
franchises of
New York City